WINNING
AT
MATH

Your Guide to Learning Mathematics Through Successful Study Skills

FIFTH EDITION

Paul D. Nolting, Ph.D.
Learning Specialist

Academic Success Press, Inc.
F L O R I D A

This book is dedicated to my son, Eric, and to my wife, Kim. It is also dedicated to the thousands of students who are having difficulty learning mathematics and the instructors who are teaching them.

Winning at Math:
Your Guide to Learning Mathematics
Through Successful Study Skills
(Fifth Edition)
by Paul D. Nolting, Ph.D.

New, Expanded and Revised Fifth Edition, 2008

Copyright © 2008 by Paul D. Nolting, Ph.D.

ISBN-10: 0-940287-39-0
ISBN-13: 978-0-940287-39-6

C3S ISBN-10: 0-940287-40-4 (includes C3S CD-ROM)
C3S ISBN-13: 978-0-940287-40-2 (includes C3S CD-ROM)

Published by Academic Success Press, Inc.
Produced by Rainbow Books, Inc.

Editor: Daniel Crown
Assistant Editor: Kimberly Nolting

Photo Credits: Unless otherwise noted, all photos and clipart are reproduced with the permission of Comstock (www.comstock.com) and ClipArt.com.

Academic Success Press
6023 - 26th St., W.
PMB 132
Bradenton, FL 34207

www.AcademicSuccess.com

Printed in the United States of America.

Contents

Contents

Preface

Math Is Important

Math is one of the most difficult subjects in college. Every student must pass math to graduate. In fact, some colleges and universities require students to take and pass up to four math classes to graduate. Too many students are intimidated by math because they have a poor high school math background or are starting college after many years away from school.

What kind of assistance do most students want? Students want tips and procedures they can easily use to help improve their math grades. The math study suggestions, however, have to be based on educational research, and they must be statistically proven to increase students' learning and grades. *Winning at Math* is the only math study skills book that offers statistical evidence demonstrating an improvement in students' ability to learn math and to make better grades.

A book based on research

The study of math study skills, anxiety reduction, and test-taking procedures provided in *Winning at Math* are based on Learning Specialist Dr. Paul D. Nolting's 25 years of research. This research has concentrated on students who had difficulty learning math at colleges and universities throughout the United States. The *Winning at Math* techniques are effective with both students who are taking math for the first time and those who have previously failed math. In fact, the evidence also suggests grade improvement in other non-math courses. These techniques can definitely work for you!

Reaching out to new students

The fifth edition of *Winning at Math* is of special interest to a new group of students taking math courses. These new students may have a different type of learning style, may have a disability, or may have to take a distance learning course. These students face additional challenges to be successful in math and to graduate. This text provides research-based, practical suggestions to this new group of students. The text also has a special website that contains additional information to improve student success. These suggestions will also improve the success of all students in the area of mathematics learning and their grades.

Acknowledgments

Several mathematics instructors and educators gave their time and suggestions to help revise and improve this text. Each person listed is a national expert. Several of these national experts were part of the Houghton Mifflin Faculty Development team. They reviewed the old version of *Winning at Math* and made constructive suggestions and/or helped develop new sections.

Michael Hamm, Ph.D., who was a member of the Houghton Mifflin Mathematics Faculty Development team, has been teaching developmental mathematics and college-level mathematics for over 15 years. Dr. Hamm's expertise is in collaborative learning and graphing calculators. He taught collaborative learning in the Interdisciplinary Studies Program at Brookhaven College in several disciplines. He is also a consultant for Texas Instruments. He conducts regional and national workshops on collaborative learning, math study skills, real-world applications, and the graphing calculator. His contributions to this revised text are the 10 steps for using the graphing calculator and information on collaborative learning.

William Thomas, Jr., who was also part of the Houghton Mifflin Faculty Development team, has a Master's degree in mathematics and education from the University of Toledo. He currently teaches at the University of Toledo's Community and Technical College, Toledo, Ohio, for which he has served as Director of Developmental Education. He currently is the Developmental Mathematics Specialist. Mr. Thomas' expertise is in mathematics reform and multicultural learning. He was the Vice-Chair of the Developmental Mathematics Committee of American Mathematical Association of Two-Year Colleges. He was on the writing team that formulated and wrote *Crossroads in Mathematics: Standards for Introductory College Mathematics before Calculus* (AMATYC). He was chair of the AMATYC developmental math committee. His contribution to this revised text is in suggesting how teaching student learning strategies integrates with mathematics reform.

Thomas Hamersma, M.S., is an Assistant Professor of Mathematics at Manatee Community College in Bradenton, Florida. Tom has been teaching developmental students for over 10 years. Tom was also the Math lab Director at Manatee Community College. Tom's Master's project was developing an independent study math study skills component for his developmental math classes. Students who came to the math lab were assessed for test anxiety and math study skills, and they were given the math study skills they needed, based on the assessments. He had over a 90 percent pass rate with the students who he helped with math study skills. I would like to thank Tom for reviewing *Winning at Math* and for his contribution to improve this text. He made suggestions on the sections concerning reading, homework, test anxiety, and he gave insight on how to improve the figures.

Dr. Paige Hamersma is a Professor of Mathematics at Manatee Community College in Bradenton, Florida. She recently graduated from the University of South Florida with a Doctorate in Mathematics Education. Her dissertation was on teaching students to use visual, computer-based techniques to learn complex numbers in trigonometry. She has been teaching developmental students for the last 15 years and has a reputation of helping some of the most challenging students. I would like to thank Paige for her proofing of this text, and her suggestions on learning styles, how math is different, test taking, and some of the figures.

Irene Doo works as a training consultant for Pearson Education. In addition, she teaches developmental and college level mathematics courses online through Austin Community College. Prior to this, Irene was a full-time instructor at Austin Community College, and while there, piloted a study skills component to developmental courses. Irene is currently serving as Secretary on the Executive Board of AMATYC, and has also served on the board of TexMATYC. Her additions were suggestions on distance learning study skills, The Ten Steps for Doing Online Homework, and editing the text.

Ellen Soash is an Instructor of Mathematics at Pasco-Hernando Community College. She has a B.S. degree in Mathematics and a M.Ed. in Curriculum and Instruction, Math Education from the University of South Florida. Ellen has been teaching at Pasco-Hernando for 2 years as an adjunct and was recently hired as the newest member of the mathematics faculty. Learning math study skills using *Winning at Math* is required for all students taking any developmental math course at PHCC.

Gail Freed is the Mathematics Laboratory Coordinator at Pasco-Hernando Community College. She has been at PHCC for the last two years after being an adjunct at Hillsborough Community College for a year. She has a B.S. degree in Mathematics from Florida State University. Gail both teaches developmental mathematics classes and tutors developmental students. She requires students in her classes read *Winning at Math* and recommends it to students that come to the Math Lab.

Mrs. Pamela Watkins is a mathematics instructor at Georgia Southern University. She has a B.S. degree in Computer Science and an M.S.T. in Mathematics. She has taught mathematics, including remedial mathematics and computer science, at the college level for 20 years. She has implemented a study-skills course for students with math deficiencies. She has also led numerous workshops on topics ranging from "Using Writing to Teach Mathematics" to "Graphing Calculators: Applications and Lessons." This new edition includes her specific suggestions on math study skills and how to take notes and use a calculator at the same time. This text also includes her suggestions on developing a problem log and notebook organization.

Mrs. Julie Francavilla is an Assistant Professor in the math department at Manatee Community College in Bradenton, Florida. Julie taught a special elementary algebra section of students who were repeating the course or had disabilities. Julie, with the help of Dr. Paul Nolting, taught math study skills in her class and her class made recommendation to improve and develop new math study skills.

Additional thanks to **Daniel Crown**, editor, and a final thanks to my wife **Kimberly Nolting**, A.B.D., who is an expert in study skills and an excellent editor. Her experience with teaching developmental education students in the class and in learning assistance services along with her Masters in teachinng and her training at the Kellog Institute for Developmental Education made her input as editor invaluable. She included valuable information, proofread the entire text, and made editing suggestions.

Introduction

Studying and learning math is different from most other courses. For this reason, many students make "A's" and "B's" in all other courses but have difficulty passing math. By using the suggested study procedures in *Winning at Math*, you will be able to improve your math comprehension and make better grades.

The format of the fifth edition of *Winning at Math* has been revised to make it easier to read and contains more proven math study skills techniques. The chapters have been expanded and rearranged to present the most important information first. The chapter on test anxiety has been expanded since more and more students have problems with test taking. A special section of this chapter has been dedicated to students with math anxiety, not just test anxiety. The math anxiety section focuses on how students developed math anxiety and how to decrease the anxiety. The chapter also has a Test Attitude Inventory that students can take to measure their level of anxiety. The new Learning Modality Inventory for Math Students will improve student learning. The chapter on taking control of math has been expanded to help students to become more motivated to learn math. Other chapters also include new information. Some of the new topics include:

- Math is like a puzzle, sport, and musical subject
- Math is the only socially acceptable course to fail
- Learning math will pay ($) off
- Obstacles to your math success
- New Web based math study skills evaluation
- Test Attitude Inventory
- Locus of Control survey
- Math Learning Profile Sheet
- How to Reduce Test Anxiety CD
- Learning Modality Inventory for Math Students
- Study Skills Plus/C3S (some texts)
- General Learning Profile Sheet
- *Winning at Math* Student Resource Web site
- Types of negative self-talk
- Math autobiography

- Causes for breakdown in the Stages of Memory
- Website for math mnemonic devices, acronyms and virtual flash cards
- How to read the syllabus
- How to do online homework
- Watch out for shortcuts
- Why instructors return tests
- Understand self-efficacy
- Using the SMART goal setting system
- Improving positive self talk
- How to communicate with your math instructor
- Web site for students with disabilities
- Improving positive self talk

Other chapters in the fifth edition go into more explanation of important topics. These topics include:

- More interactive student assignments to be turned in
- Having a bad math attitude
- Student learning styles
- Math study skills assessment
- Assessing your math anxiety
- Assessing your math test anxiety
- Math relaxation techniques
- Using your learning style to improve memory
- Seven steps to math note-taking
- Math glossary and flash cards
- Why instructors assign homework
- How to read the text book
- Ten steps to better test-taking
- How to develop internal locus of control
- How students can motivate themselves
- Reasons disabilities cause math learning problems
- Accommodations for students with disabilities
- Study strategies for students with disabilities

You can win with *Winning at Math* by studying it on your own, using it as part of a traditional course or as an independent study program through a math or learning resource center. Combined with the CD, *How to Reduce Test Anxiety*, *Winning at Math* becomes even more effective. Also by going to www.academicsuccess.com and clicking on Winning at Math Student Resources using wam as the user name and student as password you can assess the Math Study Skills Evaluation and other resources.

How Learning Math Is Different and Why It Pays Off

1

In Chapter 1
you will learn these concepts:

- Learning math is different than learning other subjects, and it requires a different study system.
  - ✓ Math is a sequential subject that requires students to think how concepts apply to problems and connect with each other.
  - ✓ Math is also like a foreign language, and it requires students to learn vocabulary and practice consistently.
  - ✓ Finally, students are required to learn and demonstrate math at a quick pace.
- Even though math is an unpopular subject to study, and many students have bad math attitudes, students can still learn math.
- There are differences between high school and college math, so it is important that you select the best type of scheduling and the math instructor who will be best for you.
- It is important to get a good start to make sure you earn a good grade on the first math test.
- Learning more math means a better career and more money.

Introduction

Math courses are not like other college courses. Because they are different, they require different study procedures. Learning general study skills can help you pass most of your college courses — except math. Passing most of your other classes mainly requires that you read, understand and recall the subject material. To pass math, however, an extra step is required; you must use the information you have learned to correctly solve math problems.

Special math study skills are needed to help you learn more and get better grades in math. Many students sit in their first math class, nervous, wondering what is going to take place. Taking charge and learning a set of math study skills to help you succeed will reduce nervousness typically experienced by math students. The reward of learning more math is a better job or making more money. The first step is to explore what learning math is all about.

Learning Math Is Different

In a math course, you must be able to do four things:

1. *Understand* the material,
2. *Process* the material,

3. Apply what you have learned to correctly solve a problem, and

4. Remember everything you have already learned to learn new material.

Of these four tasks, applying what you have learned to correctly solve a problem is the hardest. These four tasks work together to help you master the math you must learn. If you do not complete one of the tasks, the others will not be completed either.

> **Examples:** Political science courses require that you learn about politics and public service, but your instructor will not make you run for governor to pass the course. Psychology courses require you to understand the concepts of different psychology theories, but you will not have to help a patient overcome depression to pass the course. In math, however, you must be able to correctly solve problems to pass the course. For example, you learn about factoring techniques, but then you must solve problems involving factoring to pass the course.

Math as Sequential Learning

Regular study every day cements each building block together

Learning math is different from learning many other subjects because it follows a sequential learning pattern. "Sequential learning pattern" simply means that the material learned on one day is used the next day and the next day, and so forth. You can compare learning math to building a house. Like a house, which must be built foundation first, walls second and roof last, math must be learned in a specific order. Just as you cannot build a roof first, you cannot learn complex problems without first learning simple ones. Unlike other subjects, you cannot forget the material after a math test. Each chapter is a foundation block for the next chapter. This building-block approach to learning math is the reason why it is difficult to catch up when you get behind. *All* building blocks must be included to be successful in learning math. You can't skip information in one chapter to hurry up and get caught up in the next chapter.

Math knowledge is built brick by brick.

> **Example:** In a history class, if you study for chapters 1 and 2, and do not understand chapter 3, and end up studying for and having a test on chapter 4, you *could* pass. Understanding chapter 4 in history is not totally based on comprehending chapters 1, 2 or 3. To succeed in math, however, each previous chapter has to be completely understood before continuing to the next chapter.

Sequential learning affects studying for *tests* in math, as well. If you understand chapter one and two but do not understand chapter three, you will also have problems understanding chapter four. When test time approaches, you end up trying to teach yourself too many concepts while studying for the test when you should be just reviewing and practicing. And, of course, the test results won't be the best you can do.

Because of the sequential nature of learning math, the math knowledge you have at the beginning of your course determines how smooth or bumpy your learning experience might be. Students who forgot or never acquired the necessary skills from their previous math courses will have difficulty with their current math courses. They will have to relearn the math concepts from the previous course as well as the new material for the current course. In most other courses, like the humanities, previous class knowledge is not required. However, in math you must remember what you learned in the previous course to be prepared for the current one. Measuring previous math knowledge will be explained in Chapter 2, "Assessing and Using Your Math Learning Strengths."

Take time to make sure you are placed in the correct course.   Math placement test scores are determined by how well you learned previous math and whether you took the courses in a sequence where you could build a strong foundation. Then, the way these scores are used to place you into a math course can set you up for success or a hard time of it. If you barely scored high enough to be placed into a math course, then you will have gaps in the math that you must know to do well in that particular class. Learning problems will occur when new math material is based on one of your learning gaps.

In addition to considering how well you placed into a course, the age of the placement test score must also be considered. Placement test scores are designed to measure your *current* math knowledge and are to be used immediately. If you wait a year after taking the placement test to take your first math course, and your placement is based on these scores, you really have forgotten more math during that year and may have difficulty in the class.

Remember: Sequential learning is interrupted if math courses are taken irregularly. By taking math courses each session, without session breaks in between, you are less likely to forget the concepts required for the next course. The "building blocks" still support your new learning.

Now that you understand the "building block" nature of math, think about your math history.

What is your experience in learning math?
- What are your previous math grades?
- How well did you do on the math placement test at your college?
- How long has it been since you took a math course?
- When you look at your math history, are there times when you did not take math?

These questions are important because if there was too much time in between your different math courses, you may have forgotten important math concepts that you need in your current class. To use the building block analogy, the blocks may not be as strong any more.

Now that you understand how learning math is a building experience, what should you do? *First,* don't get anxious. Stay calm. *Second,* if your college has a diagnostic math inventory in the tutoring center or math lab, take it to see what math concepts you have forgotten. Then ask your instructor where you can go to relearn these math concepts. *Third,* take the time to follow through. Many students just give up too easily, or they think they will catch up a little at a time. Don't think that and don't give up. The energy put into your class at the beginning of the session will be more productive than energy put into class at the end of the session when you try to learn everything during the last week before the final exam. *Fourth,* study and really learn the math; don't practice mimicking it. *Finally,* when it is time to register for the next session, register immediately so you will be able to get into the math class you need. Why do all this? Because math is sequential!

Do not skip a session or quarter of math.

Math as a Sequential Course

Another reason math courses are different from other subjects, is that you need to be continuously enrolled in the courses until your last math requirement is met. Information learned in your current course proves just as vital in your next one, so it must remain fresh in your mind. For example, while a student could in theory maintain success by taking U.S. History I and then waiting a year to take U.S. History II, taking Beginning Algebra and then taking Intermediate Algebra a year later could decrease their success rate by 20%, according to Miami Dade College research. Other research has indicated that even skipping *one* session can decrease your math course success rate.

The same problem has also been documented at Rutgers University where students were allowed to take their developmental courses whenever they wanted and not be continually enrolled. Many of these students took developmental courses in their freshman year then waited to finish their math courses as a senior. This caused major problems as the students forgot everything they learned and still needed over a year of math courses to graduate, which some of them did not. After conducting this research the university implemented a policy for students to be continually enrolled in their math courses in order to improve their course success rate as well as to help them graduate.

College math courses should be taken in order, from the fall session to the spring session If at all possible, avoid taking math courses from the spring to fall sessions. There is less time between the fall and spring sessions for you to forget the information. During the summer break, you are more likely to forget the important concepts required for the next course.

It is a good idea to take summer math courses, unless the sessions are very short. If there is an extended summer session for 10 to 12 weeks then these sessions could be long enough for you to be more successful compared to waiting for three months. If you cannot take summer math courses then make sure you review the last chapter in your last math course to refresh your math memory. If you do not have your text then you can go to some of the math websites like www.purplemath.com and use their math review sections. That way you will be more prepared to make a good grade in your next math course.

The best plan to complete all your required math courses for graduation, and any additional courses required for your major, is to keep taking math courses each session (except for short summer sessions). You may want to take a break from math, but I know of hundreds of students who took a one or two session break and then failed the next math course. It does not matter if you like math or not, you need to continue taking math courses if you want to graduate.

Math as a Puzzle

A puzzle has many parts and they all fit together to make a picture. This is also true when you are learning math. You need all the concepts and rules to know how to solve a problem. Have you ever tried to put a puzzle together with one or more of the pieces missing? It becomes very frustrating especially if you think all the parts are there and after hours of work you find out that several pieces are missing. This is also true when you are half way through solving a math problem and find out you do not know or forgot the rules for the next step. In order to solve math problems you need to understand all the rules. In other subjects you may forget some of the "rules" and still pass the test, but in math, not knowing or forgetting *one* major rule can cause you to miss *many* problems.

Math as a Foreign Language

Another way to understand studying math is to consider it as a foreign language. Looking at math as a foreign language can improve your study procedures. Learning how to *speak* math as a language is the key to math success. Currently, most universities consider computer and statistics (a form of math) courses as foreign language courses. Some universities have now gone so far as to actually classify math as foreign language. In the case of a foreign language, if you do not practice the language, what happens? You forget it. If you do not practice math, what happens? You are likely to forget it, too. Students who excel in a foreign language must practice it *every* day. The same study skills apply to math because it is considered a foreign language.

Math instructors might as well be speaking French.

Like a foreign language, math has unfamiliar vocabulary words or terms, which must be put in sentences called *expressions* or *equations*. Understanding and solving a math equation is similar to speaking and understanding a sentence in a foreign language. Listen to yourself or others as they explain a math equation. They are taking mathematical symbols and translating them into words and sentences.

> **Example:** Math sentences use symbols (which are actually spoken words) in them, such as
>
> "=" (for which you *say*, "equals"),
> "-" (for which you *say*, "less"), and
> "a" (for which you *say*, "unknown").

The vocabulary in mathematics is very important. You must understand what the words mean in order to understand your teacher's explanation of the math. If the instructor starts talking about polynomials and you have no idea what a polynomial is, then you are lost. There is a true case of a student I worked with who memorized how to work the problems but failed his test. When I went over the test with him I asked him how to factor a polynomial. He asked me, "What is a polynomial?" I then asked him what a monomial was, and he did not know. I talked to his tutor and the rest of the tutor session was spent learning the language of mathematics by developing vocabulary note cards so he could understand what we were talking about. He had the ability to do math but could not understand the language.

Learn and practice using the math vocabulary like you were learning vocabulary in a German class

Learning how to speak math as a language is a key to math success. So, now that you know math is like a foreign language, what should you do? *First*, start a vocabulary list in the back of your notebook. Include the definitions and examples the instructor uses in class. Writing this vocabulary list helps you study too! *Second*, preview the chapter before the class in order to identify the vocabulary words that you will hear in class. You don't have to understand all of them while previewing the chapter, but familiarize yourself with the words. This will help you improve taking notes in class. We will talk more about this in Chapter 6, "How to Improve Listening and Note-taking Skills." *Third*, practice saying the vocabulary words out loud. Get comfortable with the words, their meanings, and how they connect with one another. *Finally*, when working math equations, say them out loud, using the words that the symbols represent.

Math — The Unpopular Subject

Unfortunately, math is not a popular topic, unless you are complaining about it. You do not hear the nightly news anchors on television talking in math formulas. They talk about major events to which we can relate politically, geographically and historically. Through television — the greatest of learning tools — we learn English, humanities, speech, social studies, and natural sciences, but we do not learn (or even hear about) math.

Math concepts are not constantly reinforced in our everyday lives like English, geography, history or other subject areas. Since it is not discussed, we don't know how to think about math. As a result, it requires more study time and study strategies to learn to think about and explore the world of math.

So, how can you learn how math relates to your everyday life? Take time to read the newspaper or news magazines like *Newsweek*. You will soon discover that math truly is an important part of life.

Math as a Sport

Learning math is similar to learning to play a sport such as basketball, track or football. In order to find success you must actively practice. You can listen and watch your coach all day, but unless you *practice* those skills yourself, you will not learn and probably won't even get into the game or meet.

> **Example:** In basketball, the way to improve your free throw percentage is to see and to understand the correct shooting form and then to actively practice the shots. If you simply listened to your coach describe the correct form and saw them demonstrate it, but you did not practice the correct form yourself, you would never improve.

Just like in sports, you must practice to get it right.

When I ran track, we had to practice the different starts as well as passing the baton. I was a sprinter and I liked practicing the starts. Also I ran either first or last on the relay team. I had to practice handing off the baton which meant gauging when to hand off the baton or when to start running full speed to get the baton when I was the anchor man. As the anchor man this relay took practice because if I started off too fast I would be out of the box before getting the baton and be disqualified. However, if I started too slowly I may lose the race. I could not just watch my other teammates and figure out when to start. Also in practice I had to run extra laps so I would be in shape to be in several events. I did not like running the extra laps but I did it for the team. Math is not a spectator sport. You must practice the skills in order to learn how to solve the problems and understand the rules.

Just like a runner has to endure running the extra lap, when learning to study, make yourself study an additional 20 minutes. You will develop discipline that will help you concentrate longer.

Math as a Musical Subject

Learning math is like playing a musical instrument. To be good at playing a musical instrument you need to understand the music theory and the rules of playing the instrument, then practice playing the instrument. You can see someone play the piano, cello or electric guitar, watch their hands and hear the sounds, but unless you practice you will not learn how to play. Imagine how many concerts you have attended or seen on television and how many people you have seen playing the piano. Could you now go play the piano, cello or electric guitar? No. You need to practice these instruments before playing them well, just like you have to practice math before you learn it.

Just like music, math requires daily practice.

Example: Suppose you want to play the piano, and you hire the best available piano instructor. You sit next to your instructor on the piano bench and watch the instructor demonstrate beginning piano-playing techniques. Since your piano instructor is the best available, you will see and understand how to place your hands on the keys and play. But what does it take to learn to actually play the piano? You have to place your hands on the keys and practice. Math works the same way. You can go to class, listen to your instructor, watch the instructor demonstrate skills, and you can understand everything that is said (and feel that you are quite capable of solving the problems).

However, if you leave the class and do not practice — by working answers successfully and solving the problems — you will not learn math.

Many of your other college courses can be learned by methods other than practicing. In social studies, for example, information can be learned by listening to your instructor, taking good notes, and participating in class discussions. Many first-year college students mistakenly believe that math can be learned the same way. Ask an experienced math student, and you will hear a different story.

After working with hundreds of students, I do not understand how many of them think homework is not an important part to learning math. Thinking someone can answer problems on a test just by watching the professor in class, is like thinking that someone who watches a musician play three minutes of Beethoven's Fifth can duplicate it on their piano without practicing. It's not going to happen. Face it, unless you are a math genius, you must practice (do your homework, review your notes) in order to learn math. This is not high school anymore where some students could just sit in class and pass the course.

! **Remember:** Math is different. If you want to learn math, *you must practice.* Practice not only means doing homework problems, but it also means spending the time it takes to understand the reasons for each step in each problem. •

So, how do you practice math? *First,* make sure you understand the math concepts and the basics. *Second,* practice the homework problems over and over until it comes to you naturally. *Third,* learn the vocabulary associated with the problems you are working. *Fourth,* try to "teach" the math to someone else.

Math as a Thinking Subject

Make sure to learn the questions you should ask when working through the problem.

Math is a thinking subject because you have to work through a step-by-step process in order to answer the problem. You do not just recall the answer. For example, in biology you may be asked about the difference between plant and animal cells, or you might have to answer a question like, "Do plants have cell walls?" This is a fact question that can be recalled from your memory. (Yes, you are correct. Plants have cell walls. Animals have cell membranes.) This is different from asking you to solve this equation:

$$2x - 5x + 10 = 6x - 8$$

You will have to think about the properties and rules that are needed to solve this equation. It is not just recalling one fact. (Again you are correct. The answer is $x = 2$.)

In a math class, you have to think from the minute the instructor begins talking. Note-taking is challenging because you have to think about the math as the instructor explains the problem, all while writing the information down in your notes. In most cases you are not just copying down facts. This could cause problems in note taking because you are concentrating on understanding the explanation while trying to write down each problem step. If this is a problem for you, then take time to read Chapter 6, "How to Improve Listening and Note-Taking Skills."

These students are thinking about math, not just memorizing it.

Also, students must think when reading the math textbook. That is why it takes longer to read the text. Remember when we said math is sequential? Well, here is another example. Math is a series of steps and combinations of rules and properties; math students have to think in between each step, remembering the rules and properties they have learned. When reading the math textbook, take time to think how each new concept connects with the previous one. This slows the reading process down significantly. Chapter 7, "How to Improve Your Reading and Homework Techniques" can help you in this area. Math, indeed, is a thinking subject.

Finally, you need to learn how to think like a math instructor. This means you need to think in a step by step way to solve problems. That means writing down each step of the problem without skipping steps, until the problem is solved. Some math instructors also look at answers as being only right or wrong. Partial credit may not be given just

You need to think like a math instructor.

Think how each new concept connects with the previous one. for showing your work, or for only providing the correct answer. Both the answer and the work are required in order to get credit for a problem.

Since math is a thinking subject, what should you do? *First*, reserve much more time to read a chapter or complete your homework. *Second*, during the evenings or days when you don't have time to complete the entire homework assignment, at least review your notes and do a couple of problems to keep the information in your brain. *Third*, you need to start thinking like a math instructor in your math course as well as when doing your homework.

Math as a Speed Subject

Math is a *speed subject,* which means, in most cases, it is taught faster than your other subjects. Math instructors have a certain amount of material that must be covered each session. They have to finish certain chapters because the next math course is based on the information taught in their courses. In many cases a common math department final exam is given to make sure you know the material for the next course. Instructors are under pressure to make sure you are ready for the final exam because it demonstrates how prepared you are for the next level in math. This is different from, let's say, a sociology course where if an instructor doesn't teach the last chapter it will not cause students too many problems in the next sociology or social science course. So don't complain to the math instructor about the speed of the course. Instead, improve your study skills so you can keep up!

Another way math is a speed subject is that most of the tests are timed, and many students think that they will run out of time. THIS CAUSES PANIC AND FEAR! This is different than most of your other courses where you generally have enough time to complete your

Practice doing problems within a time constraint tests or in your other courses that have multiple choice tests where you can start bubbling the responses on the Scantron sheet if you start running out of time. Students must not only understand how to do the math problems but also must learn the math well enough to complete the problems with enough speed to finish the test.

What makes me curious is, if students feel like they don't have enough time to complete the math test, why are most of them gone before the test time is over? Sure, students who have learned the math thoroughly may complete the test early. That makes sense. Some students leave, however, because they either don't know the material, want to leave the anxious environment, or carelessly work through the test.

So, since speed is an issue in learning math, what should you do? *First*, to use an analogy, start a daily workout program to stay in shape. Review, review, and review as you learn new material. *Second*, practice doing problems within a time constraint. Give yourself practice tests.

Math as the Only Socially Acceptable Course to Fail

In college, math has become the only socially acceptable course you can fail. Unfortunately this statement has become true in the United States, while in other counties like Japan, failing math is a family disgrace. Recently, a major toy company made a teenage girl doll that said, "Math is hard" as one of its statements. The underlying message is that math should be feared and hated, and that it is acceptable not to learn math. The result of this "popular" attitude is a reinforcement of the belief that it is all right to fail math.

Example: Student frequently get sympathy from others when they fail in math, while the same people will make fun of them for failing other courses. Students hear such statements as, "Don't worry about your grade in math; everybody flunks math. But your English scores really stink. You'd better get on track and work on doing better." Thinking that it is all right to fail math can lead to missing class and not completing your homework.

Now back to the toy company who made the doll that said, "Math is hard." Due to public outrage, the toy company was forced to take the doll off the shelves. Hopefully this is a sign of a change in the perception of Math here in the U.S.

Having a Bad Math "Attitude"

Students' attitudes about learning math differ from their attitudes about learning their other subjects, mostly due to bad experiences. In fact, some students actually *hate* math, even though these same students look forward to going to other classes.

Society, as a whole, reinforces students' negative attitudes about math. As stated before, it has become socially acceptable not to do well in math. If you had a bad attitude towards biology or psychology other students would wonder what was wrong with you. Bad attitudes toward math may also be reinforced by other non-math instructors, who also contribute to the problem.

Who has the bad math attitude?

Some students may have a bad math attitude because they are having difficulty learning math and wonder if they will ever have to use math in their lives or careers. However, in some cases students who do not use their math skills in their current major might switch to a major that requires more math and head into careers that make a lot more money. Don't use the excuse, "I won't ever need to know complicated math in the real world." Ultimately, it does not matter when the math will come in handy, because you need math to graduate regardless. Also, if you share this poor math attitude with your children then they may develop the same attitude.

A bad math attitude is only a problem if you base your behaviors on it

However, a bad math attitude does not have to be a major problem. Many students who hate math pass it anyway, just as many students who hate history still pass it. A bad math attitude is only a problem if you base your behaviors on it. If a bad math attitude leads to poor class attendance, poor concentration and poor study skills, then you have a bad math attitude and a *problem*. If you identify with these behaviors even a little, you need to read the chapter, "How to Take Control and Motivate Yourself to Learn Math," to understand the reasons for these behaviors.

! **Remember:** Passing math is your goal, regardless of your attitude .!

So, what can I do right now to change my attitude? First, listen to what you tell yourself about learning math. If you have a bad math attitude then "check your attitude at the door."

This means when you walk through the door leave your bad attitude outside the classroom and enter with a positive attitude. If you already have a positive attitude toward math then keep it during the lecture. A positive attitude can make it easier to learn math and concentrate. If you have a neutral attitude towards math, then work towards having a positive attitude. Second, if you have trouble changing your attitude then find someone you trust or a counselor and tell them what you are trying to do. They can be your conscience.

Differences Between High School and College Math

Math, as a college-level course, is almost two to three times as difficult as high school-level math courses. There are many reasons for the increased difficulty: course class-time allowance, the amount of material covered in a course, the length of a course, and the college grading system.

The first important difference between high school and college math courses is the length of time devoted to instruction each week. College math instruction for the fall and spring sessions is usually three hours per week; high school math instruction is usually provided five hours per week. Additionally, college courses cover twice the material in the same time frame as do high school courses. What is learned in one year of high school math is learned in one session (four months) of college math.

Simply put, in college math courses students receive less instructional time per week and instructors cover twice the material per course as in high school math courses. And, the responsibility for learning in college is the student's. As a result, most of the learning (and *practicing*) occurs outside of the college classroom.

Course Grading System

The course grading system for math is different in college than in high school.

> **Example:** While in high school, if you make a "D" or borderline "D/F," the teacher more than likely will give you a "D," and you may continue to the next course. However, in some college math courses, a "D" is not considered a passing grade, or, if a "D" is made, the course will not count toward graduation.

College instructors are more likely to give the grade of "N" (no grade), "W" (withdrawal from class), or "F" for barely knowing the material. This is because the instructors know students are unable to pass the next course if they learned only a part of the curriculum. No extra credit points for writing a report on the Pythagorean Theorem.

Most colleges and universities require students to pass one or two college-level algebra courses or the equivalent to graduate. In most high schools, you may graduate by passing one to three math courses, and these may not need to be algebra courses. In some college degree programs, you may have to take four math courses, and make at least a "C" in all of them to graduate.

The grading systems for math courses are very precise compared to the systems in English or humanities courses.

> **Example:** In a math course, if you have a 79 percent average and 80 percent is a "B," you will get a "C" in the course. On the other hand, if you made a 79 percent in English, you may be able to talk to your instructor and do extra credit work to earn a "B."

What should you not expect in a college math course? *First*, since math is an exact science and is not as subjective as English, do not expect to talk a math instructor into extra work to earn a better grade. *Second*, in college, there usually is not a "daily work" grade like often offered in high school. You still have to do your homework. Don't expect to do well without doing the homework even though it is not collected. *Third*, test scores may be the only grades which will count toward your final grade. Therefore, do not assume that you will be able to "make up" for a bad test score.

College Summer Session Versus Fall or Spring Sessions and the Difference Between Night and Day

College math courses taught during summer sessions are more difficult than those taught during fall or spring. The same amount of content is presented in fewer weeks, sometimes six, eight or twelve weeks. Students attending a six-week summer math session must learn the information and master the skills two-and-a-half times as fast as students attending regular, full-session math sessions. There is less time in between classes to study. In addition, each class is longer, making it harder to concentrate throughout the entire class.

Since math is a sequential learning experience, where every building block must be understood before proceeding to the next block, you can quickly fall behind, and you may never catch up. In fact, some students become lost during the first half of a math lecture and, therefore, never understand the rest of the lecture (this can happen during just one class session in the summer).

If you *must* take a summer math course, take a 10 or 12-week session so that you will have more time to process the material between classes.

Night classes present similar problems, depending on how they are scheduled. Some night classes meet once a week. These classes are very long, sometimes lasting four hours. An entire week goes by between classes, and it is very easy to put off studying or forget the material discussed in class. Other night classes are scheduled twice a week and there is little time after the first class to study for the next class, particularly if you work during the day.

> **Example:** If you do not understand the lecture on Monday, then you have only Monday night to learn the material before progressing to more difficult material on Tuesday. During a night course, you have to learn and understand the material before the break; after the break, you will move on to the more difficult material — *that night.*

Why Your First Math Test Is Very Important

Making a high grade on the first major college math test is more important than making a high grade on the first major test in other college subjects. The first major math test is the easiest and, most often, is the one that students are least prepared for.

Beginning college students often feel that the first major math test is mainly a review and that they can make a "B" or "C" without much study. These students are overlooking an excellent opportunity to make an "A" on the easiest test of the session. (Do not forget that this test usually counts the same as the more difficult remaining math tests.)

At the end of the session, these students sometimes do not pass the math course or do not make an "A" because of their first major test grade. In other words, the first test score was not high enough to "pull up" a low test score on one of the remaining major tests.

Studying hard for the first major college math test and obtaining an "A" offers you several advantages:

- A high score on the first test can compensate for a low score on a more difficult fourth or fifth math test, especially if all the major tests have equal value in the final grade calculations.

- A high score on the first test can provide assurance that you have learned the basic math skills required to pass the course. This means you will not have to spend time relearning the misunderstood material covered on the first major test while learning new material for the next one.

- A high score on the first test can motivate you to do well. Improved motivation can cause you to increase your math study time, which will allow you to master the material.

- A high score on the first test can improve your confidence for higher test scores.

Be serious about your first math test.

With more confidence, you are more likely to work harder on the difficult math homework assignments, which will increase your chances of doing well in the course. However, be careful not to let a good test score make you overconfident and become lazy about studying for the next test.

Use lessons from your first test experience to improve upon the next test.

What happens if after all your studying, you still make a low score on your first math test? You can still use this test experience to help you improve your next grade or to help determine if you are in the right math course. Your first math test, no matter what you make on it, can be used as a diagnostic test. Your teacher can review your test with you to see which type of math problems you got right and which ones you need to learn how to solve. It may be that you missed only a few concepts that caused the low score, and you can learn how to do these problems by getting help from the teacher, a learning resource center or the math lab. However, you need to learn how to do these problems immediately so that you don't fall behind in the course. After meeting with your teacher ask for the best way you can learn the concepts that are the bases of the missed problems and how to prepare for the next test. Even students who made a B on the first math test can benefit by seeing the teacher.

In some cases students may guess well on the math placement test or enroll in their next math course after being out of college for several years. Some of these students don't do well on their first math test because they have forgotten most of the concepts or did not know the material in the first place (guessed well on the multiple choice placement test). I have seen hundreds of these students over the years. If these students made below a 50 on their first math test, I suggested that it might be a good idea to drop back to a lower level math course. Even though it might be beyond the first week of drop and add, many colleges/universities will let you drop back to a lower math class after the first major math test. Students who drop back get a good foundation in mathematics that helps them in their next math courses. On the other hand, I have seen students who insisted on staying in the math course and repeated it several times before passing. Some of the students stopped taking the math course and dropped out of college. Dropping back to a lower level math course and passing it is the smartest move. These students went on to become more successful in their math courses. Remember: it does not matter where you start as long as you graduate. Discuss this option with your teacher.

Selecting a College Math Instructor

College and high school math instructors treat students differently. College instructors often do much less handholding than do high school teachers. High school math teachers will frequently warn you about your grades and offer help or makeup work. College instructors will expect you to keep up with how well or poorly you are doing. You must take responsibility for your own success and make an appointment to seek help from your instructor.

Students will often have to choose between a full-time or part-time instructor. Sometimes, due to the increase in the number of college math courses offered in the curriculum, there are more part-time math instructors than there are full-time instructors. You need to think about the following questions when choosing between a full-time or part-time instructor. In fact, you need to find out the answers to these questions if you are even choosing between two full-time instructors.

Choose a professor you can be comfortable with.

- What kind of reputation do the instructors have for working with students one-on-one outside of the class time?

- *Do the instructors usually keep office hours when you can visit and talk to them?* If they keep them early in the morning, when you can't get to campus, then see if there is another instructor with more convenient office hours.

- *Do the instructors help students online?* More and more instructors do this.

- Do the instructors create a comfortable class environment in which students feel free to ask questions?

- Do the instructors take time to stop their lectures and answer questions?

- Do the instructors allow students to practice problems in class?

- Do the instructors return your tests to you?

How do you find out the answers to these questions? *First*, most math departments keep sample syllabi, an instructor's "contract" of expectations, tests, and homework assignments. You can ask to see these. *Second*, the counselors or advisors might know something about the different teaching styles of the instructors. *Third*, good math students know who the supportive instructors are. *Finally*, you can try to find the instructors and directly ask these questions to them.

Learning Math Will Pay ($) Off

Now that we have learned how math is different, the difference between high school and college math, why your first math test is so important, and also how to select a math instructor, what do we want to gain from learning math? Another way to ask this question is, "What are your reasons for attending college?" Are you going to college to better yourself? Are you going to college to obtain the career you want? Are you going to college to make more money? I asked these questions to many students who are taking math and what do you think was the most popular response? You are right! Most students say they are going to college to make more money. Students also indicated that they want to like their careers and to make enough money to live a better life. It did not matter if these students were going for an

*The more math you take,
the more money you make.*

Associate of Science degree or an Associate of Arts degree, or a Baccalaureate degree. Their goals were to obtain their degree in the shortest amount of time and to obtain a high paying career.

Also students indicated that they want their career to be secure so they will not have to keep switching employment or have to be retrained. This is especially true of men and women who are returning to college to obtain better careers to support their family. Being clear on your college goal is a way to motivate your college success. So does taking math courses mean you can obtain a higher paying career, have more career options and have a chance at those popular careers? YES!

On the next two pages, you will see the top paying jobs for Associate of Science and Baccalaureate degrees. Associate of Science degrees are usually two-year degrees once you have been admitted to the program or once you have completed the prerequisite courses. Associate of Science degrees can be used in the allied health fields, as well as electronics and computer fields. The following graph demonstrates the 15 jobs with the best pay, fastest growth and the most openings for the 21st century. It also demonstrates their national annual salary (Farr and Ludden, 2004) and what math courses are required to obtain them. The center of the graph indicates the Associate of Sciences majors.

Do you see the pattern? Four of the five highest paying jobs (dental hygienists, diagnostic medical sonographers, registered nurses, electronics engineering technicians) require college algebra or statistics. Four of the five lowest paying jobs (veterinary technician, medical records technician, physical therapist assistant, and occupational therapist assistant) require mathematics courses below college algebra and statistics. Based on this information if you want the most job selections and highest paying career then passing more mathematics courses is your ticket to success.

Students who are going for a Baccalaureate degree either obtain an Associate of Arts degree at a community/junior college or are already attending a university. In most cases these students will make more money than the Associate in Science degrees. One way to look at these majors is to plot the graph by using salaries and the increasing amounts of math courses. The center of the graph will indicate the majors. The following graph demonstrates the 20 top careers with the best pay, fastest growth and the most openings for the 21st century. It also shows their national annual salary per year (Farr and Ludden, 2004).

Again look at the pattern. Five out of the five highest paying jobs (computer hardware engineer, computer software engineer, constructor manager, sales agent-securities, computer systems analysts) require business calculus or higher. In fact, of all nine careers that have salaries around $50,000 a year require business calculus or a higher math course. Four of the five lowest paying jobs (recreation worker, rehabilitation counselor, music arranger, social worker) require mathematics courses below college algebra and statistics. Based on this information, if you want the most job selections and highest pay then passing more mathematics courses is once again your ticket to success

By now, using your excellent number sense, you have figured it out. THE MORE MATH COURSES YOU TAKE, THE HIGHER PAYING CAREER YOU WILL GET! However, even taking the minimum math course(s) to graduate will lead to well paying careers. Learning mathematics is the key to your personal and career success.

Now that you know that taking more mathematics means more career choices and better pay, how can you accomplish that goal? Effective learning strategies for successful math study skills will lead to more math success. Math success can help you graduate and allow you to select majors in areas that will lead to high paying jobs and more job security. I want you to take math courses until you do not need any more courses for your major instead of stopping with a non-successful math course completion.

Taking more math can lead to more money.

Obstacles to Your Math Success

There is no obstacle you can't overcome.

Sometimes self-talk and statements by others may block your motivation to be successful in your math course. Don't get in the habit of saying, "When will I ever use this math?" or "Why do I have to take this math course because I will not use it in my job?" These statements may make you feel better when you are not successful in a math course. However, they could also lead to poor motivation and less studying. The real questions are: "Do I need this math course to graduate?" or "Do I need this math course as a prerequisite to enter my major?" For example, if you are a business major, in most cases you will need applied calculus to be accepted to the college of business. Being successful in applied calculus is your "ticket" to your business major and making that million dollars.

In some cases you may have to take some developmental math courses in order to be ready to take the required math courses. Don't be discouraged! Thousand of students have finished their developmental math courses and have

Best Jobs Requiring an Associate's Degree*

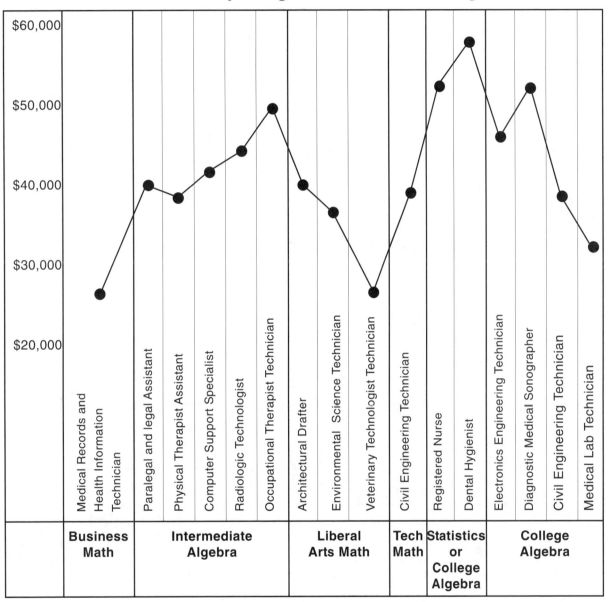

Best Jobs for the 21st Century, Third Edition © JIST Works

Best Jobs Requiring a Bachelor's Degree*

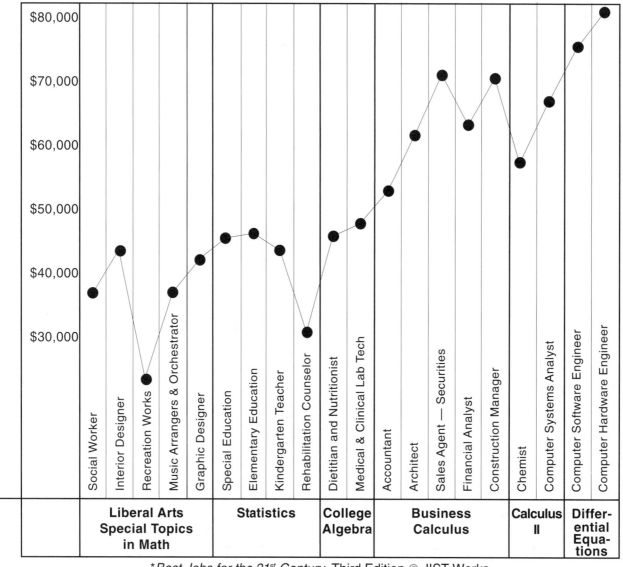

Best Jobs for the 21st Century, Third Edition © JIST Works
© Academic Success Press, Inc.

completed college algebra or calculus and are now in their careers. If you know your major, find it on the graph and find the highest required math course. If you cannot find your major or you don't have a major then talk to a counselor or take a course on selecting a major. YOU CAN BE SUCCESSFUL IN MATH AND OBTAIN THE CAREER YOU WANT.

<u>Summary</u>

- The skills required for learning math differ from the skills required for learning other courses.

- Math requires sequential learning, which means one concept builds on the next concept. You must build a firm and steady foundation with each chapter. This will help you be successful.

- Thinking of learning math like learning a foreign language or a musical instrument will help you change your math study skills.

- Math isn't just numbers; it is also vocabulary.

- Keeping a positive attitude about math will help you study more efficiently.

- Passing most courses requires reading, understanding and recalling the subject material. Math students must also learn how to think like a mathematician.

- Math is the only socially acceptable course to hate and fail. However, remember you can dislike math and pass it at the same time.

- You must practice math over and over and over just like learning how to shoot a free throw in basketball.

- When taking a math test, you not only have to understand and recall the material, you have to prove this to the instructor by correctly working the problems.

- In most other subject tests, you can just guess at the answers; you cannot guess at the answers in math tests because the answers on a math test must be precise and exact.

- Math courses are even more difficult because, in most cases, a grade of "C" or better is usually required to take the next course or, in some cases, just to pass the current course.

- There are major differences between high school and college math courses.

- The grading is exact and, in many cases, you cannot do extra credit work to improve your grade.

- Remember to study hard for your first test because it will be the easiest one and, therefore, the best opportunity to get a high grade.

- You need to be prepared to learn math in a different way.

• Learning more math can mean a better career and more money ($).

> ❗ **Remember:** Learning math takes different skills than learning your other ❗
> subjects.

Assignment for Chapter 1

1. Why is math considered to have a sequential learning pattern? _____

   _____

   _____

   _____

   _____

2. Describe several ways math is similar to a foreign language, and give two examples. __

   _____

   _____

   _____

   _____

   _____

   _____

   _____

3. a. Describe several reasons why learning math is like learning to play a sport.

   _____

   _____

   _____

   b. What happens if you don't practice your sport or math? _____

   _____

4. List three reasons why your first math test is so important. _____

   _____

   _____

   _____

5. How do attitudes toward math affect math learning? _____

_____

_____

6. How are high school and college math courses different? _____

_____

_____

_____

7. How do summer and fall session math courses differ? _____

_____

_____

_____

8. How does your math grading system differ from that of your other courses? _____

_____

_____

_____

9. How can you prepare for your first math test? _____

_____

_____

_____

10. a. How can learning more math pay off? _____

_____

b. Describe your two personal obstacles that may prevent you from learning more math.

_____

_____

c. How can you overcome the obstacles? _____

_____

_____

Assessing and Using Your Math-Learning Strengths 2

In Chapter 2
you will learn these concepts:

- A student's knowledge and intelligence, along with the quality of instruction and student characteristics, determine the level of success in a math class.
    - ✓ Ways to make sure you have the appropriate math knowledge for the class in which you enroll
    - ✓ Importance of placement in the correct math course
    - ✓ Characteristics of math instruction that affect student performance
    - ✓ Ways to enhance your math knowledge before beginning the math course
- A student's affective characteristics influence the level of success in the math class.
    - ✓ Improving chance of success through developing study skills
    - ✓ Taking the C3S General Study Skills Evaluation to determine your level of general study skills
    - ✓ Taking the Test Anxiety Inventory to determine your level of test anxiety
    - ✓ Taking the Math Study Skills Evaluation to determine your strengths and weaknesses in math study skills
    - ✓ Taking the Learning Modality Inventory for Math Students (Nolting, Kimberly, 2006) to discover how you best learn math
    - ✓ Finding an instructor who matches your learning style

Introduction

After exploring the characteristics of math, the second step to improving your effectiveness in studying math is to understand your unique study skills. Just as a mechanic does a diagnostic test on a car before repairing it, you need to do a diagnostic test to identify what study strategies need improvement. You do not want the mechanic to charge you for something that does not need repairing, nor do you want to work on learning areas that do not need improvement. You want to identify the learning areas that benefit you and the ones that need to be developed.

Ingredients for Success in Learning Math

Before we start exploring your learning skills for math, it helps to understand what contributes to academic success. Dr. Benjamin Bloom, a famous researcher in the field of educational learning, discovered that IQ (intelligence) and "cognitive entry skills" (knowledge about math) account for fifty percent of a student's course grade. See Figure 1 (Variables

Contributing to Student Academic Achievement) below. Quality of instruction represents 25 percent of the course grade, while "affective student characteristics" reflects the remaining 25 percent.

- *Intelligence*, for our purpose, is considered to be how fast a person can learn or re-learn math concepts.

- *Cognitive entry skills* refer to how much math people already know before entering a math course.

- *Quality of instruction* concerns the effectiveness of math instructors, lab assistants and tutors when presenting material to students in the classroom, math lab and while tutoring. This effectiveness depends on the course textbooks, curriculum, teaching style, tutoring style, teaching aids (videos, CDs, DVDs, websites, online homework) and other assistances.

- *Affective student characteristics* are characteristics people possess which affect their course grades — excluding how much math they knew before entering the math course. Some of these affective characteristics include anxiety, study skills, study attitudes, self-concepts, motivation and test-taking skills.

The first part of this chapter will explore these ingredients for success in a math class — appropriate math knowledge, low level of test anxiety, effective study skills, positive attitude for studying, motivation, test-taking and personal learning style.

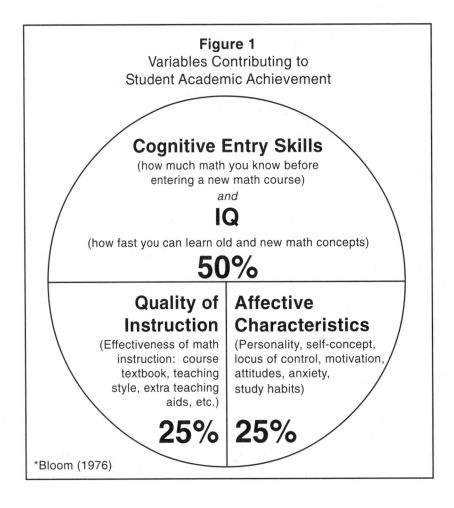

Figure 1
Variables Contributing to
Student Academic Achievement

Cognitive Entry Skills
(how much math you know before
entering a new math course)
and
IQ
(how fast you can learn old and new math concepts)
50%

Quality of Instruction
(Effectiveness of math instruction: course textbook, teaching style, extra teaching aids, etc.)
25%

Affective Characteristics
(Personality, self-concept, locus of control, motivation, attitudes, anxiety, study habits)
25%

*Bloom (1976)

What You Know About Math Affects Your Grades

Going into a class with a poor knowledge of math sets you up for earning low grades. A student placed in a math course that requires a more extensive math background than the student possesses will probably fail that course. Without the correct math background you may fall behind and never catch up. The following information is important to know in order to make sure that you are placed in the proper math course.

Placement Tests and Previous Course Grades

The math you need to know to enroll in a particular math course can be measured by a placement test. Most colleges/universities use a standardized test such as the ACT, SAT, Compass or Accuplacer to place students into math courses. However, some colleges/universities use their own placement test to place students. Also, the grades earned in the prerequisite math courses measure your level of math knowledge. However, a few students are still incorrectly placed in math courses by these resources. So, it is important to talk to your advisor and teacher to provide any other information that might assist in properly placing you into a math course.

Never enroll in a course you aren't ready for.

If the placement scores are questionable or borderline between two classes, ask the advisor if there is another diagnostic test you can take. Or, talk to one of the math instructors because they may be able to ask questions that will help determine correct placement into a math course. An inaccurate evaluation of math ability and knowledge can only lead to frustration, anxiety and failure; a proper placement will set you up for success!

A proper placement will set you up for success!

What if you think you are not ready for the course in which you enrolled? Without the correct math background, you might fall behind and never catch up. So, if by the second class everything looks like Greek, and you do not understand what is being explained, move to a lower-level course. In the lower-level math course you will have a better chance to understand the material and to pass the course.

Most students do not want to add another math course to their lives, but taking a course that is too difficult will most likely result in problems. You will either withdraw and then re-enroll next session or, worse, fail and then take it again. So, observe what is taking place in your math class and determine what is best for you! Be honest! You want to be successful! Remember the building blocks in chapter one? You want to build a firm foundation. Getting into the right math course is a major factor in building that foundation.

Some students are placed in the lowest level math course offered at their college or university. If you are one of these students, check your placement test score with your instructor or counselor to see if you are in the lower quartile (bottom 25% of the test scores). If you are, then ask the instructor or math lab supervisor if they have materials that you can work on that are below the course or textbook level. You also may be able to find some of these resources on the Internet. By learning or relearning this math information, you can improve your math knowledge, which is the basis for math success. Start working on these math lessons as soon as you can, even though they may be a lower level than the first chapter of your math text.

❗ Remember: It does not matter what level you are in math, as long as you ❗
learn the necessary math skills to be successful in the course.

Requests by Students for Higher Placement

Some students ignore their placement test scores entirely because they believe the placement scores are inaccurate. Based on this assumption, they try to encourage their advisors to move them to a higher-level math course. Even though there can be gray areas for a few students, most of the time placement scores are accurate. Also, many students try to enroll in a higher math course to avoid taking noncredit math courses, while other students do not want to repeat courses that they have previously failed. They just want to move on, thinking they can handle it. Some of these students do move on, but they may move on to further failure.

Why do students feel the need to do this? Some older students imagine their math skills are just as sharp as when they completed their last math course, which was five to ten years ago. But if they have not been practicing their math skills, they are just fooling themselves. Still other students believe they do not need the math skills obtained in a prerequisite math course to pass the next course. This is also incorrect thinking. Research indicates that students who were placed correctly in their algebra math course, and who failed it, will not pass the next algebra math course.

*Math success requires
a balance of strength and skill.*

I have conducted research on thousands of students who have either placed themselves or have convinced instructors to place them in higher-level math courses. The results? These students failed their math courses many times before realizing they did not possess the prerequisite math knowledge needed to pass the course. Students who without good reason talk their instructors into moving them up a course level are setting themselves up to fail.

What My Research Shows

To be successful in a math course, you must have the appropriate math knowledge. If you think you may have difficulty passing a higher-level math course, you probably do not have an adequate math background. Even if you do pass the math course with a "D" or "C," research indicates you will most likely fail the next higher math course. It is better to be conservative and pass a lower-level math course with an "A" or "B" instead of making a "C" or "D" in a higher-level math course and failing the next course at a higher level. This is evident when many students repeat a higher-level math course up to five times before repeating the lower-level math course that was barely passed. After repeating the lower-level math course with an "A" or "B," these students can pass their higher-level math course.

The above discussions about correct placement based on the math knowledge you bring to the math course are important since fifty percent of success in a math course is attributed to intelligence and current math knowledge.

What happens when you think you are in the correct math course and you fail the first major test? This means you are in academic trouble because you may not have the background to be successful in that course. Not understanding how to solve these test problems means that you are already behind in your math course or may have been misplaced because the first test in most cases is a review of the previous math course. My research and other math instructors' research show that students who fail their first math tests almost never successfully complete the course. In fact

> ***50 percent of success in a math course is attributed to intelligence and current math knowledge***

Seek help as early as possible.

some of these students keep taking the course over and over again instead of going back to a lower level course. If this is your case, ask the instructor whether you can have an administrative transfer to a lower level math course that he/she is teaching. If the instructor is not teaching a lower level course, ask for a recommendation of another instructor who is teaching the course and transfer to that course.

If you are attending a university that does not offer a lower level course, you may want to withdraw. (If you are on financial aid, make sure to see how withdrawing from one class affects your eligibility for financial aid.) Then next semester plan on taking a lower level math course at the community or junior college. After completing the lower level course, enroll in the university course.

> ***Make learning more productive by designing a study system***

If you are already at a community or junior college and failed the first test in the lowest level math course, talk to your math instructor and counselor. You may want to withdraw from the course and enroll in a math course at an adult high or at a vocational school that matches up more with your math knowledge. Another solution is to withdraw from the class and then hire a tutor and use some basic computer programs to build up your math skills, so you can be prepared to take the math course next semester.

You could also stay in the course and set up a plan with the instructor to build up your math skills by having a special program in the math lab or learning assistance center. This means you will have to build up your skills that were lacking on the first test while learning the current math. This is very difficult but can be done in most cases. However, you MUST spend a lot of time on this project because if you have not caught up by the second test you will most likely not pass the course.

Getting a good start is very important. It is not like other subjects where if you start off slow you can catch up by doing a lot of work. If you start off slow in a math course by making below a C on your first test, you may never catch up unless you follow these suggestions. Remember the goal is to complete your math courses even if it takes you longer. You will still graduate.

The Quality of Math Instruction Affects Your Grades

Quality of instruction accounts for 25 percent of your grade

Quality of instruction accounts for another 25 percent of your grade. Quality of instruction includes such things as classroom atmosphere, the instructor's teaching style, lab instruction, textbook content and format. All of these "quality" factors affect the ability to learn in the classroom.

Interestingly enough, probably the most important "quality" variable is the compatibility of an instructor's teaching style with the students'. First, you need to discover your learning style. Second, try to find an instructor who best matches your learning style. Sometimes this is difficult to find out, but a good place to start is to talk to the chair of the math department. The department chair knows the faculty. In addition, some advisors know the faculty teaching styles. You can also try to meet the instructor before the semester begins. The key is to start your inquiry early enough to get into the instructor's class that you want. If you cannot find an instructor to match your learning style, improving math study skills and using the math lab/learning resource center can compensate for most of the mismatch. You and your instructor might not be the best match, but it is still your responsibility to be successful in the course.

Quality of instruction is not out of your control

Use of the math lab or learning resource center (LRC) can dramatically improve the quality of instruction. With today's new technologies, students are able to select their best learning aids. These learning aids might be videotapes, CD-ROMs, computer programs and other math textbooks. Other learning resources help you learn the math outside of class when you are having difficulty understanding what is taking place in the classroom.

The quality of tutors is also a major part of the effectiveness of a math lab or learning resource center. A low student-to-tutor ratio insures more intensive assistance. Trained tutors are essential for good tutorial instruction because they know how to help students become better learners. Otherwise, the result is just a math study hall with a few helpers. The best way to work with tutors is to not only ask for assistance with the math concepts but to also inquire about good study strategies. These tutors have been successful in math and have some good strategies up their sleeves.

Most new math books come with solutions manuals and CD-ROMs, which make

Make the most of your instructor.

Your reaction to instruction determines your success

studying on your own much easier. If the textbook is still confusing, most libraries and resource centers have other math textbooks that you can use. Effective reading techniques for math books will be discussed in Chapter 7 to improve your learning.

Each math department designs its courses so that each course covers certain math concepts. Ideally, each course curriculum prepares students for the next level of math. However, sometimes the courses have gaps between them, or an instructor doesn't cover all the material required for the course, leaving students unprepared for the next course. If this happens, go to your instructor immediately to explain that you did not cover the math in your previous course. Your instructor will suggest a way for you to learn it.

Even though it seems that the quality of instruction is out of your control, it really isn't. The above suggestions can help you improve the quality of instruction you experience, even if it is outside of the classroom. Your reaction to it determines your success. Dropping a class because you do not like the instructor or because the teaching style does not match your learning style is not a valid reason. If you have a positive attitude towards learning math and your education as a whole, you can find ways to create a good instructional environment. Positive attitude is one of the affective student characteristics that attributes to the other 25 percent of success in a math course. The following information explores more affective characteristics that will determine your success in math.

How Affective Student Characteristics Influence Your Math Grades

Affective student characteristics account for about 25 percent of your grade. These affective characteristics include math study skills, test anxiety, motivation, locus of control, learning style and other variables that determine your personal ability to learn math.

Most students do not have this 25 percent of the grade in their favor. In fact, most students have never been taught *any* study skills, let alone how to study math, specifically. Students also do not know their best learning styles, which means they may study ineffectively by using those that are least effective. Until recently, little attention has been devoted to how students learn, so it is not unusual if you do not know what your learning styles are.

Affective student characteristics account for 25% of your grade.

However, later in this chapter you will have the opportunity to explore the ways you learn most effectively.

By improving your affective characteristics, you reap the benefits of a more productive learning experience and, subsequently, higher grades. Thousands of students have improved their math study skills, lowered their anxiety, and taken control of learning by using the strategies suggested in this book. The first step in improving how you study math is to determine what your learning style is for math.

Even students with good math background and grades will need to have good math study skills for a future math class. These students do well on several tests and maybe several courses, but eventually they enroll in a course that they start to have difficulty in. I have worked with hundreds of students who went from A's and B's in their previous math courses to F's in their next math courses. These students had good math backgrounds, but now they were in classes that required them to really study. They didn't know how. They had to learn math study skills to help them become better learners. In other words, even if you are now making A's on your tests, still learn these math study skills because they can help you now and in the future when the math classes become more difficult.

Your learning style is also an important part of affective characteristics. Knowing your modality learning style can improve your math learning efficiency. By using your most efficient math modality style (visual, auditory, hands-on) you can learn math faster and remember it longer. These learning strategies will be explained in detail later in Chapter 5 of this book.

How to Take the Math Study Skills Evaluation

To improve your math study skills, first you need to know which study skill behaviors you are doing right and which ones you need to improve. The Math Study Skills Evaluation was especially made for students who have difficulty in mathematics. It has helped thousands of students understand what they need to do to improve their grades. If you have not already done so, complete the Math Study Skills Evaluation at www.AcademicSuccess.com and click on Winning at Math Student Resources. Put *WAM* as the username and *Student* as the password to access the site. Click on Math Study Skills Evaluation (MSSE) and take the survey.

Be honest and write down your first response

Be honest when taking the Math Study Skills Evaluation and put down your first response. If you never did that response, then select the response that you would do. If you are not in a current math course, then select the responses that you would do if you had a math course.

First read the paragraph that explains the skills that need to be improved. Questions that you got right are not printed out on the report. Read the pages associated with the questions for which you answered "a" or "c." Then read the pages associated with the questions for which you answered "b."

Now let's discuss your total score. At the top of the computer program you should have a total score. Your total score indicates that you either have inadequate, good, or excellent math study skills. Scoring below 70 means that you have inadequate math study skills. Scoring between 70 and 79 means you have poor math study skills. Scoring between 80 and 89 means you have good math study skills and scoring above 90 means you have excellent math study skills.

The lower the survey score, the more opportunity you have to improve your math learning and grades. In fact, failing this survey is okay. Scoring below a 70 is not necessarily your fault because it means no one has taught you how to study math. Also scoring below a 70 or even an 80 means that your learning problems are mainly due to poor study skills and not your ability to learn math. By using the learning techniques in this book you can improve how you study math like thousands of students before you.

The exceptions to this concept are students who have disabilities. I have helped students with high Math Study Skills Evaluation scores who have continued to fail math. These students need extra accommodations to help them learn math. That is why Chapter 10, "How to Help Students with Disabilities Learn Math," was included in this book. Immediately refer to that chapter if you are a student with a disability.

How to Use the Math Study Skills Evaluation

To improve your study skills, make a plan of action

Now that you know your math study skills level it is time to design a plan of action. If you are in a math study skills course, it is simple—follow the syllabus. If you are using this book as part of a lab requirement, set up a schedule to complete the reading and homework assignments. If you are reading this book on your own, write out what you need to improve, how you will do it, and when you will finish. Use a calendar to record when you will read and learn the material based on the questions you missed on the survey. Research indicates that you need to be able to use the skills by midterm. This is usually by the seventh or eighth week of the semester or sixth week of a quarter system. Let your instructor and/or counselor know your plan so they might help you. Research has also shown that students who work on math study skills on their own also improve their grades. Now it is time for you to become more successful in mathematics.

Developing the Math Learning Profile Sheet

A more formal and more diagnostic assessment of your math learning can be conducted by assessing your test anxiety, your locus of control, and by reviewing the subtest scores of your Math Study Skills Evaluation. Complete the surveys and fill in the results in the Figure 2 (Math Learning Profile Sheet) by doing the following:

1. **Test Attitude Inventory** (next page) is a survey to assess college test attitudes and will indicate how much test anxiety you have compared to other college students. While you are taking the survey, answer the questions as if they relate to a math test. After taking the Test Anxiety Inventory, go to Appendix A and score the test. Plot your Total Score (T) above the Anxiety heading on the bottom of the graph. Use the left-hand side of the graph to put in the Total (anxiety) Score number.

   Take aim and improve your attitude and strategies to learn math.

   The anxiety score is measured in percentile norms, which compares you to other college students. For example, if you had a score of 50 percentile, then half the students tested have higher anxiety than you do and the other half have less anxiety than you. A score of 50 puts you right in the middle. High scores mean you have more test anxiety than other students and low scores mean you have less anxiety. A score between 1 and 25 means you do not have much test anxiety, a score between 26 and 50 means you have some test anxiety, and a score of between 51 and 74 means you have test anxiety that may be costing you a few points on your test.

   A score of 75 to 100 means you have strong test anxiety, and there is no doubt it hurts your math grades. Scores above 80 mean you have high test anxiety and need to reduce it as soon as possible by using the How to Reduce Test Anxiety CD, found on the inside back cover of this text. We will focus more on test anxiety in Chapter 3 (How to Reduce Math Anxiety and Math Test Anxiety).

Test Attitude Inventory

Please provide the following information:

Name _____ Date _____

Gender (*Please circle*): **Male Female**   Score: T_____ W_____ E_____

Directions

A number of statements which people have used to describe themselves are given on the following page. Read each statement and then circle the appropriate number to the right of the statement to indicate how you *generally* feel:

1 = Almost Never, 2 = Sometimes, 3 = Often, 4 = Almost Always.

There are no wrong or right answers. Do not spend too much time on one statement but give the answer which seems to describe how you generally feel. Please answer every statement.

	ALMOST NEVER	SOMETIMES	OFTEN	ALMOST ALWAYS
1. I feel confident and relaxed while taking tests	1	2	3	4
2. While taking examinations I have an uneasy, upset feeling	1	2	3	4
3. Thinking about my grade in a course interferes with my work on tests	1	2	3	4
4. I freeze up on important exams	1	2	3	4
5. During exams I find myself thinking about whether I'll ever get through school	1	2	3	4
6. The harder I work at taking a test, the more confused I get	1	2	3	4
7. Thoughts of doing poorly interfere with my concentration on tests	1	2	3	4
8. I feel very jittery when taking an important test	1	2	3	4
9. Even when I'm well prepared for a test, I feel very nervous about it	1	2	3	4
10. I start feeling very uneasy just before getting a test paper back	1	2	3	4
11. During tests I feel very tense	1	2	3	4
12. I wish examinations did not bother me so much	1	2	3	4
13. During important tests I am so tense that my stomach gets upset	1	2	3	4
14. I seem to defeat myself while working on important tests	1	2	3	4
15. I feel very panicky when I take an important test	1	2	3	4
16. I worry a great deal before taking an important examination	1	2	3	4
17. During tests I find myself thinking about the consequences of failing	1	2	3	4
18. I feel my heart beating very fast during important tests	1	2	3	4
19. After an exam is over I try to stop worry abuot it, but I can't	1	2	3	4
20. During examinations I get so nervous that I forget facts I really know	1	2	3	4

2. **The Locus of Control** web-based survey is an opinion survey that estimates how much control you believe you have over life events. "Internal" students take responsibility for their lives and their grades and therefore try to improve their learning skills. "External" students believe they have little control over their lives and grades and usually blame the college or others for their poor grades. Sometimes these students do not want to change and improve. Go to www.academicsuccess.com and click on Winning at Math Student Resources. Put in *WAM* as the username and *Student* as the password to access the site. Click on the Locus of Control survey and take the survey. Plot the Internal Locus number above the Locus of Control heading on the bottom of Figure 2 (Math-Learning Profile Sheet).

    The locus of control score is measured in percentile norms, which compares you to other individuals. For example, if you had a score of 50 percentile, then half of the other individuals tested have higher locus of control than you. A score of 50 puts you right in the middle. High scores mean you have more internal locus of control than other students, and low scores mean you have a lower locus of control. A score between

    1 and 25 means you may have an external locus of control

    26 and 50 means you may have some external locus of control

    51 and 74 means you may have internal locus of control

    75 and 100 means you have a strong internal locus of control

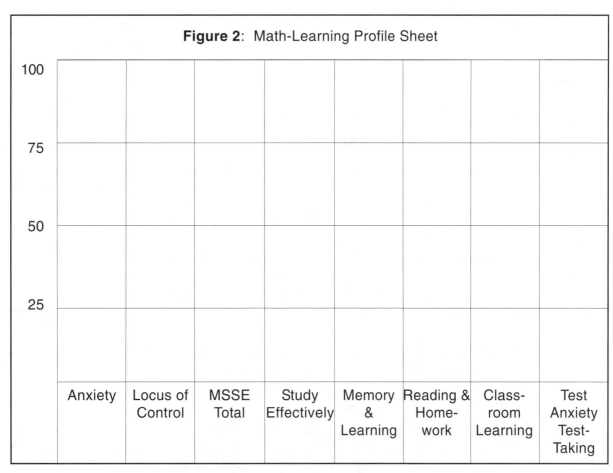

Figure 2: Math-Learning Profile Sheet

	Anxiety	Locus of Control	MSSE Total	Study Effectively	Memory & Learning	Reading & Home-work	Class-room Learning	Test Anxiety Test-Taking
100								
75								
50								
25								

Permission is granted to copy and enlarge this figure.

Many students who have difficulty in math may have an external locus of control, which could be based on their poor math attitude. Students with external locus of control can still find success in mathematics. If you do have a poor math attitude, it has already started to change after reading Chapter 1. To become more internal, you need to start accomplishing small goals that can lead to math success. These goals can be in the form of improving your math study skills based on the suggestions in this text. If you make a score of 20 or below, go ahead and read Chapter 9, "How to Take Control and Motivate Yourself to Learn Math." Other chapters in this book will also help you to become more internal.

3. **The Math Study Skills Evaluation** web-based survey measures your overall math skills with subtest scores. If you have not done so already, go to www.academicsuccess.com and click on Winning at Math Student Resources. Put in *WAM* as the username and *Student* as the password to access the site. Click on Math Study Skills Evaluation (MSSE) and take the survey. You will get a total score and subtest scores in the following areas:

Studying Efficiently,

Memory and Learning,

Reading and Homework,

Classroom Learning, and

Test Anxiety and Test-Taking.

The subtest scores for each section range from 0 to 100. These are percentage scores, not percentile scores like the Test Attitude Inventory and Locus of Control scores. The scores are divided into three ranges:

Needs Instruction (0–70),

Needs Review (71–89), and

Needs No Instruction (90–100).

Once you have completed all the surveys, plot the survey scores (if you have not done so already) on the Figure 2 (Math Learning Profile Sheet). A math-learning strengths and weaknesses profile can now be developed. Have your instructor or counselor explain the meaning of these assessments scores as they relate to how you learn math.

To better understand the Math Learning Profile Sheet, look at Figure 3, on the facing page, which features a 30-year-old married student who works part-time and has a family. According to the Math Learning Profile Sheet, she has extremely high test anxiety, internal locus of control, and poor math study skills, except in one area (Study Effectively). Despite her weaknesses, she still believes she can succeed in math and has a good attitude toward math.

Results: The student learned how to decrease her math anxiety and improve her study skills while attending my study skills class. She had failed her algebra course twice before taking my class. After taking my class, she took the algebra course again and passed with a "B"!

Figure 4, on the facing page, represents a student with a long history of failing math. His only positive scores were his low test anxiety and the Math Study Skills Evaluation subtest score in Test Anxiety and Test-Taking. He had poor study skills, poor attitude, and was external in his locus of control — all likely due to failing math so many times. This "external"

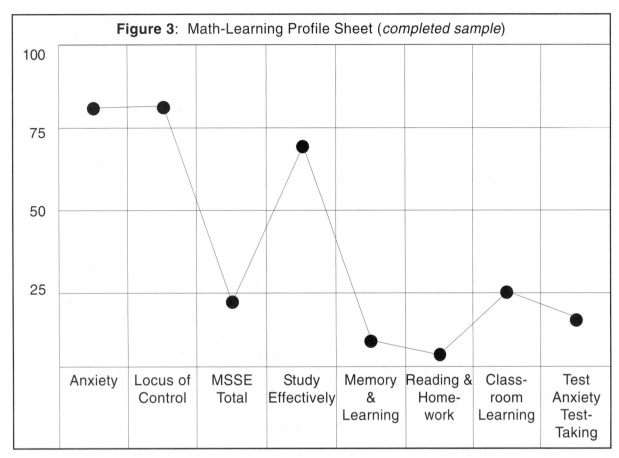

Figure 3: Math-Learning Profile Sheet (*completed sample*)

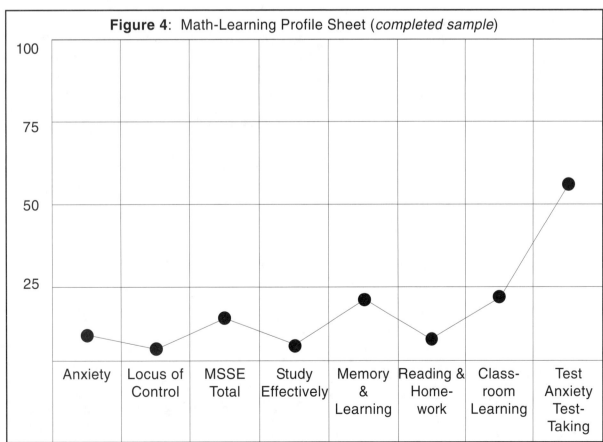

Figure 4: Math-Learning Profile Sheet (*completed sample*)

student had to begin believing he could pass math through improving his study skills. He also needed support from his teachers and counselors to become more "internal" to pass math.

> **Results:** The student improved his math study skills while attending a math study skills course, and by setting up short-term goals, he became more internal. With an increase in locus of control, he was willing to try some new learning techniques. He passed math that semester

Figure 5, below, represents a profile of many students that I have worked with in helping become more successful in math. This profile could be a male or female student who is returning to college having a history of math learning problems but making A's and B's in other courses. The profile's positive areas are locus of controls and math study skills (except the Test Anxiety/Test-Taking subtest). The major problem areas are extremely high test anxiety and Test Anxiety/Test-Taking along with average memory and Learning subtest scores. These students generally have high test anxiety, poor math test-taking and test assessment skills, along with average memory and learning skills. These students need to practice the short-term and long-term relaxation techniques on the How to Reduce Test Anxiety CD (inside back cover), complete Chapter 3 (How to Reduce Math Anxiety and Math Test Anxiety) and Chapter 8 (How to Improve Your Math Test-Taking Skills). In general, these students are motivated to become successful in math, they just need to reduce their math anxiety and improve their math test-taking skills. Almost all of these students have become successful in their math courses.

From these student profiles it is evident that each student has different reasons for being unsuccessful or not being as successful as they could be in math. Their problems usually

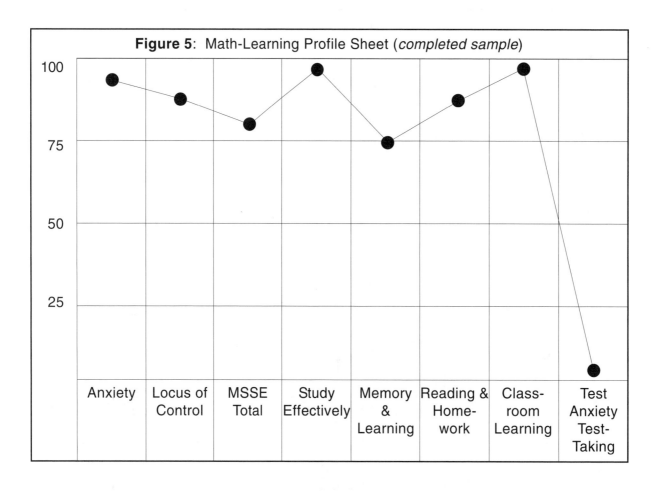

Figure 5: Math-Learning Profile Sheet (*completed sample*)

occur in the form of high anxiety and a combination of having an external locus of control and poor math study skills. These students made positive changes — and you can too — to improve your math success and grades. If you have not plotted your scores, go ahead and plot your scores on the blank Math-Learning Profile Sheet (Figure 2). Based on your scores, follow the steps below to develop your plan:

1. If your test anxiety is over 75%, then start practicing the relaxation techniques on tracks one and two of the How to Reduce Test Anxiety CD, and read Chapter 3.

2. If your anxiety is between 50% and 74%, then start practicing the relaxation techniques on track one of the How to Reduce Test Anxiety CD.

3. If your locus of control score is below 50%, then read Chapter 9 (How to Take Control and Motivate Yourself to Learn Math).

4. Based on the Math Study Skills Evaluation, read the pages that are associated with the questions that you answered with an "a" or "c," which are the areas in which you need the most help. Then read the pages that are associated with "b" as an answer.

5. Now, based on your scores, circle the above steps you plan on completing.

General Study Skills Evaluation: Anxiety, Locus of Control and Study Skills Plus/C3S

Just like we evaluated profiles of students who were having difficulty in mathematics, we can evaluate profiles of students who want to improve their grades in other college courses. Assessing your test anxiety, locus of control and general study skills can help identify the learning skills you need to improve. You already have scores from the Test Attitude Inventory and the Locus of Control web-based assessment. If your *Winning at Math* text has the Study Skills Plus, also known as C3S, then go to Appendix B and obtain the password, log on and take the survey. The Study Skills Plus web assessment is mainly included in *Winning at Math* texts that are used in study skills, college success, freshman seminar or college orientation courses. The Study Skills Plus is usually not included in the *Winning at Math* texts that are used in math courses or as part of a math lab/learning assistance center.

Figure 6 (The General-learning Profile Sheet), on the next page, is a more formal evaluation of your general learning skills. Completing the Test Attitude Inventory and the Locus of Control survey is required for all students. Completing the Study Skills Plus/C3S depends on if you have the website password in Appendix B or at the request of your instructor. Complete the surveys and fill in the results on the General-learning Profile Sheet (Figure 6) by doing the following:

1. **Test Attitude Inventory** — Plot your Total Score (T) above the Anxiety heading on the bottom of the graph above. Use the left-hand side of the graph to put in the Total (anxiety) Score number.

2. **Locus of Control** — Plot the Internal Locus number above the Locus of Control heading on the bottom of the graph.

3. **Study Skills Plus/C3S** — A web-based survey developed to assess general study skills, assess study skills weaknesses and to provide treatment in the form of an interactive web-based course. The web-based survey measures your skills in the following areas:

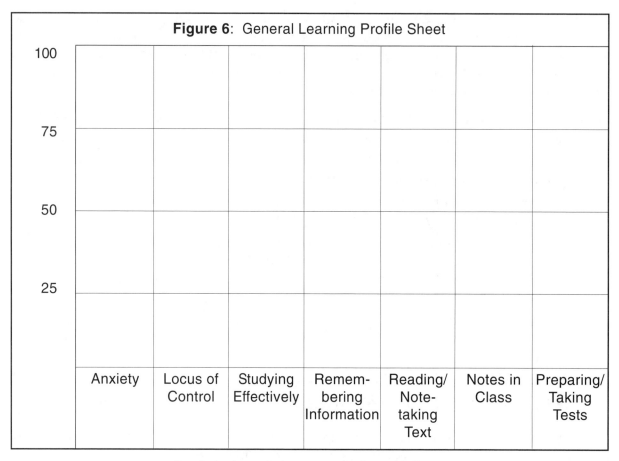

Figure 6: General Learning Profile Sheet

Permission is granted to copy and enlarge this figure.

Studying Effectively,

Remembering Information,

Reading and Taking Notes from Textbooks,

Taking Notes in Class, and

Preparing for and Taking Tests.

Use the password inAppendix B to log on to the Study Skills Plus Site and take the C3S Assessment.

The C3S scores for each section range from 0 to 100. These are percentage scores, not percentile like the Test Attitude Inventory and Locus of Control scores. The scores are divided into three ranges:

Need Instruction (Scores of 0–50),

Need Review (Scores of 51–80), and

Need No Instruction (Scores of 81–100).

Once you have completed all the surveys, enter the scores in Figure 6, above. Then connect the dots with a line. A general learning strengths and weaknesses profile is now developed. Have your instructor or counselor explain the meaning of these assessments scores as they relate to how you learn in general.

To better understand the General Learning Profile Sheet, look at Figure 7, below, which represents a profile sheet of a young male student who had difficulty in his courses. The student's profile graph indicates that he has high test anxiety, internal locus of control, low study skills in Study Effectively and Remembering Information, poor Reading/Note-taking Text study skills, and average study skills in Notes in Class and Preparing/Taking Tests. This student has the motivation (internal locus of control) to change his behavior to lower his test anxiety and to improve his study skills. His high anxiety may have prevented him from using his study skills. He first needs to start working on reducing his test anxiety, and if most of his test questions come from the text, he needs to improve his Reading/Note-taking Text study skills. Second, he needs to improve Studying Effectively and Remembering Information study

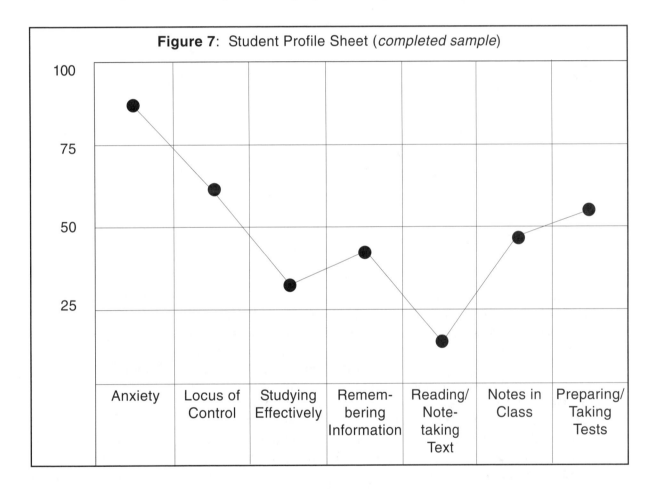

Figure 7: Student Profile Sheet (*completed sample*)

skills, all of which can be learned through the C3S program. This did improve his Reading/Note-taking Text skills and Studying Effectively skills and ultimately helped his grades.

Figure 8A (Student Profile Sheet), on the next page, represents the score from a woman returning to college after raising a family. However, even though she was confident about returning to school, she was studying about 25–30 hours a week and only making C's. The student's profile graph indicates low test anxiety, high internal locus of control and high marks in Studying Effectively, meaning she was motivated, had a good study environment and allowed herself appropriate study time. The low scores in the remaining C3S study skills areas meant that she was very inefficient in studying and test-taking. I call these students "wheel spinners" because they put a lot of time into studying but do not get anywhere (just like a car

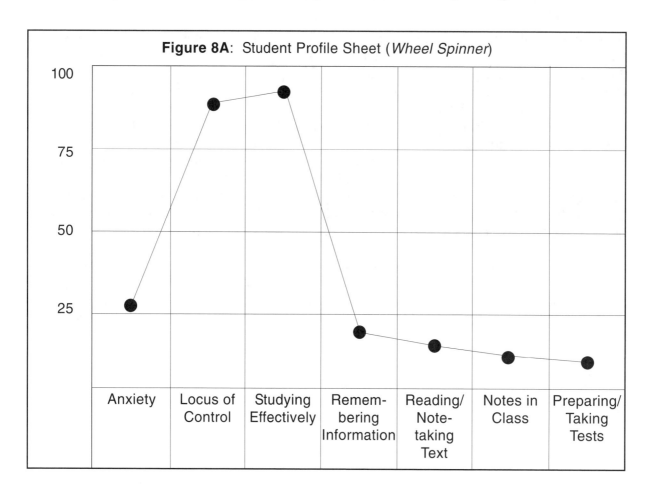

Figure 8A: Student Profile Sheet (*Wheel Spinner*)

spinning its wheels). This student was not taught study skills and was using the "trial and error" method of learning. In time she may have figured out the best way to study, but why wait and make low grades? After learning effective study skills and test-taking skills, she became more learning efficient and test-wise, which improved her grades.

Figure 8B (Student Profile Sheet), on the facing page, represents scores from a male student who had difficulty learning in high school, which carried over into his first semester of college. He had been attending classes and taking notes but did admit he was not doing much studying. The student's profile graph indicates high test anxiety and high external locus of control. This could mean that he has poor motivation to study, thinking that studying will not do much good anyway. The study skills are high in Notes in Class, average in Preparing/Taking Tests and low to very low in the other areas. This means the student has good note-taking skills and average test-taking skills but does not study. I call these students "the learned helpless." These students go through the motions of attending college but do not think they will be successful. They have the intelligence to be successful; however, they procrastinate in studying. This student needs to work on reducing his test anxiety by listening to the CD, *How to Reduce Test Anxiety* (inside back cover) and complete Chapter 3 (How to Reduce Math Anxiety and Math Test Anxiety). This chapter can be applied to any college subject. This student also needs to work on his low C3S study skills areas. He did see a counselor about his grades and his learned helplessness and did pass his courses. The next semester he continued to work on these concerns.

Just like the students who have difficulty in learning math, these students have different profiles that lead us to understand how to improve their overall learning. As mentioned be-

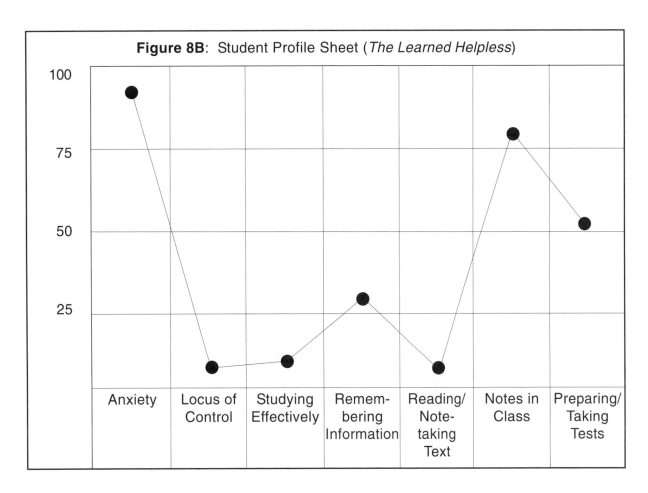

Figure 8B: Student Profile Sheet (*The Learned Helpless*)

fore, you can take your profile sheet, go to your counselor, advisor or instructor to have them understand your difficulties in learning. Then develop a plan to use the C3S and *Winning at Math* to improve your learning skills and test-taking skills, which can improve your grades. If you have difficulty in your math course, then use both profiles to develop a learning plan. I would suggest first working on your math-learning skills, because once you learn those skills they can transfer to your other courses. Then complete the plan by learning the skills in the C3S areas. Developing and completing these plans will improve your locus of control and college success.

How to Determine Your Learning Style

A learning style is a description of the cognitive, affective, and physiological factors that shape the way a student inputs material to be learned and then demonstrates the knowledge of the material. Learning styles also pertain to the best time of day to study, environmental factors that may improve learning (silence, music, lights) and how the brain best processes the material.

Research has shown that students who understand their learning styles can improve their learning effectiveness in and outside of the classroom. Many learning style inventories are available and students should talk to their instructors or counselors about taking one or more of them.

Taking Stock of Your Learning Style

There are different types of learning styles assessments. One type of learning style assessment focuses on learning modalities while other assessments focus on cognitive or environmental learning styles. In this chapter we will focus on modality learning styles.

Learning Modalities (using your senses)

Learning modalities focus on the best way your brain receives information, that is, learning *visually* (seeing), *auditorially* (hearing) or *kinesthetically* (touching, hands-on). If it is available, take a learning style inventory that measures *learning modalities*.

There are many ways to learn math Even better, take an inventory that measures learning modalities specifically for math, such as the *Learning Styles Inventory* (Brown & Cooper, 1978) or the Learning Modality Inventory for Math Students (Nolting, 2006). Other learning-style inventories can measure learning style, but they mainly focus on English or reading-learning modes. Sometimes students have different learning styles for math, so a learning-styles inventory that measures math learning styles would be best for you. Take the Learning Modality Inventory for Math Students, Appendix C, to better understand your math-learning style.

Based on the Learning Modality Inventory for Math Students, rank order your learning modality score by putting 1, 2 or 3 in the space below. Number one is for the learning style that is most like you. If you have a tie, then pick the style that you feel is best for you to learn math, and that will be the tie-breaker.

Auditory _____ Visual _____ Kinesthetic _____

Modality learning styles are neither good nor bad. They are concerned with how you best take in information. Different college subjects are best understood through certain learning styles. In the case of mathematics, most math instructors are visual learners. They tend to teach the way they learn best, which is through the visual mode. Most of these instructors will write on the board or use a Power Point presentation to help you learn math.

How to Improve Your Math Knowledge

Instructors always operate on the premise that you finished your previous math course just last week; they do not wait for you to catch up on current material. It does not matter if your previous math course was a month ago or five years ago, instructors expect you to know the previous course material — period.

Review Your Previous Math Course Material and Tests

There are several ways to improve your math knowledge. Review what was covered in your last math class before attending your present math course. Look closely at your final exam to determine your weak areas. Work on your weak areas as soon as possible so they can become building blocks (instead of stumbling blocks) for your current course.

If it has been some time since your last math course, visit the math lab or learning resource center to locate review material. Ask the instructor if there are any computer programs that will assess your math skills to determine your strengths and weaknesses for your course. Review math videotapes on the math course below your level. Also review any computer software designed for the previous math course. You can also go to www.academicsuccess.com and click on "Student Math Practice and Learning Sites." These sites can help you review certain math concepts by either working out problems or reviewing math videos. To review algebra, click on the Purple Math site and click on "How do you really do this stuff?" and review the topics from your previous math class. Use the Video Math Topics section and click on Morabito's math Home Page for videos on algebra topics. Review the other websites to help you improve your math knowledge.

Review the math book from your previous course before starting the next course

Another way to make sure you are ready for your next math class is to take all of the chapter review tests in the textbook from your last math class. If you score above 80 percent on one chapter review test, move on to the next chapter. A score below 80 percent means you need to work on that chapter before moving on to the next chapter. Get a tutor to help you with those chapters if you have trouble. Make sure you review all the chapters required in the previous course as soon as possible. If you wait more than two weeks to conclude this exercise, it may be too late to catch up (while learning new material at the same time).

Employ a Tutor

One last way to improve your cognitive entry skills is to employ a private tutor. If you have a history of not doing well in math courses, you may need to start tutorial sessions *the same week class begins*. This will give the tutor a better chance of helping you regain those old math skills.

You still need to work hard to relearn old math skills while continuing to learn the new material. If you wait four to five weeks to employ a tutor, it will probably be too late to catch up and do well or even pass the course.

You may be able to locate a tutor by asking your instructor or the coordinator of the math lab. There also are commercial tutor centers off campus that you can pay to obtain help. However, the new fad is online tutors who help you with math. Recently one of the major networks did a national news report on how high school students were being tutored online from India. Your textbook publisher may also offer free online tutoring. Make sure to ask for references and how the tutor was trained before hiring a tutor. Also, if you are planning to use an online tutor, make sure you can learn online. Some students have difficulty with learning math online.

! **Remember:** Tutorial sessions work best when the sessions begin during the !
• first two weeks of a math course.   •

Schedule Math Courses "Back to Back"

Another way to maintain appropriate math knowledge is to take math courses every term until you complete the necessary math requirements— even if you do not like math — so that you can maintain sequential (linear) learning.

I have known students who have made "B's" or "C's" in a math class, and then waited six months to a year to take the next math course. Inevitably, many failed. These students did not complete any preparatory math work before the math course and were lost after the second chapter. This is similar to having one semester of Spanish, not speaking it for a year, then visiting Spain and not understanding what is being said.

The only exception to taking math courses "back to back" is taking a six-week "kamikaze" math course (an ultra-condensed version of a regular course), which should be avoided. These types of courses do not allow enough time for students to rehearse the math enough to maintain it in long term memory.

If you are one of the unfortunate many who are currently failing a math course, you need to ask yourself, "Am I currently learning any math or just becoming more confused?" If you are learning some math, stay in the course. If you are getting more confused, withdraw from the course. Improve your math knowledge during the remaining part of the semester and reenroll in the class next semester.

Finding Your Best Instructor

Instructors want you to succeed.

Finding an instructor who best matches your learning style can be a difficult task. Most students are placed in their first math course by an academic advisor. Usually academic advisors know who are the most and least popular math instructors. However, advisors can be reluctant to discuss teacher popularity. And, unfortunately, students may want the counselor to devise a course schedule based on their time limits instead of teacher selection.

To learn who the best math instructors are, ask the academic advisor which math instructor's classes fill up first. This does not place the academic advisor in the position of making a value judgment; neither does it guarantee the best instructor, but it will increase the odds in your favor. Another strategy is to ask your friends who are serious about their classes. However, if a fellow student says an instructor is excellent, make sure your learning style matches your friend's learning style. Ask your friend, "Exactly what makes the instructor so good?" Then compare the answer to how you learn best. If you have a different learning style than your friend, look for another instructor, or ask another friend whose learning style matches your own more closely.

Most learning centers or student personnel offices will have counselors who can measure and explain your learning style. Then, if you have time, interview or observe the instructor teaching a class. This process is time consuming, but it is well worth the effort!

Once you have found your best instructor, do not change. Remain with the same instructor for every math class whenever possible.

! **Remember:** While carefully choosing your best instructor may be time-con- !
• suming, it will pay off with higher grades.   •

Summary

- Controlling math success is primarily based on improving the characteristics that affect your ability to learn math — your *affective* learning characteristics.

- The Math Study Skills Evaluation can help you discover how you can improve your math success.

- The major affective characteristics are study habits, anxiety and control over math.

- There are various ways to improve your math knowledge and math learning.

- Review your previous math material to have the math knowledge to start the course.

- Once placed in the appropriate math course, success is based on your ability to learn math.

- Understanding your learning modality style will improve your learning.

- Try to find an instructor who matches your learning style.

- Take your General Learning Profile Sheet to your counselor/advisor and develop a learning plan.

- Make sure you take math every semester (except for short summer sessions) until you complete all your math courses.

- Talk to your instructor or counselor about your Math-Learning Profile Sheets and develop a learning plan.

- Students with high math anxiety need to read Chapter 3 (How to Reduce Math Anxiety and Math Test Anxiety) and listen to the "How to Reduce Test Anxiety" CD.

! **Remember:** The first step in becoming a better math student is to identify your learning strengths and weaknesses. Now you can focus on what you need to improve. !

Chapter 2 Notes

Name: _____ Date: _____

Assignment for Chapter 2

1. How does math knowledge affect your math grades? _____

   _____

   _____

   _____

2. Using your Math Study Skills Evaluation, explain your strengths and weaknesses. _____

   _____

   _____

   _____

   _____

3. How long do you have to practice the study skills suggestions in this book to improve

   your math performance this semester? Why? _____

   _____

   _____

   _____

4. Based on your Math Learning Profile Sheet, list and explain the areas in which you need

   to improve. _____

   _____

   _____

   _____

5. Based on your General Learning Profile Sheet, list and explain the areas in which you

   need to improve. _____

   _____

   _____

   _____

6. How does your modality learning style match up with your instructor? _____

_____

_____

_____

_____

7. Explain your best modality learning style and five different ways you can improve your learning. _____

_____

_____

_____

_____

_____

8. List and describe three ways you can improve your math knowledge. _____

_____

_____

_____

_____

_____

9. What are the reasons to schedule math courses each term? _____

_____

_____

_____

_____

10. How can you find your best math instructor? _____

_____

_____

_____

_____

How to Reduce Math Anxiety and Math Test Anxiety

3

In Chapter 3
you will learn these concepts:

- Math anxiety is a learned behavior based on a person's past experiences with math. It affects the ability to learn in future math courses or to use math in real-life situations.
  - ✓ The defiinition and causes of math anxiety
  - ✓ The effects of math anxiety on learning
- Test anxiety interferes with the ability to demonstrate the full extent of a person's knowledge.
  - ✓ The definition, causes and types of test anxiety
  - ✓ The effects of test anxiety on learning and testing
- Math and test anxiety are learned behaviors that students are able to learn how to reduce and control.
  - ✓ Techniques students can use to reduce test anxiety
  - ✓ A CD to practice relaxation techniques

Introduction

Math anxiety is a common problem for many high school, college and university students. It is especially difficult for students in developmental courses who normally have more math anxiety than other students. However, there are students who are in higher level math courses that also struggle with this problem. It is very common for students to have anxiety only about math and not in their other subjects.

Most students think that math anxiety only affects them when taking a test, but it also affects other areas. It can affect the way you do your homework, learn in the classroom or through distance learning courses, and the way you choose a career. Students who have math anxiety may procrastinate in doing their homework or put off sitting down and completing an online lesson. This can lead to math failure. Students also select a major based on the amount of math that is required, which could lead to lower paying or dissatisfying careers. However, most students with math anxiety meet it face to face during the test, experiencing test anxiety as well.

Mild test anxiety can be a motivational factor in that it can make students properly prepare for a test. However, high test anxiety can cause major problems in both learning and test taking, as students avoid studying for the test when anxiety begins to afflict their thought processes. Reducing test anxiety is the key for many students to become successful in math. Such students need to learn the causes of test anxiety and how to reduce the test anxiety that affects their learning and grades.

Several techniques have proven helpful in reducing both math anxiety and math test anxiety. However, reducing them does not guarantee good math grades. It must be coupled with effective study skills and a desire to do well in math.

Understanding Math Anxiety

Definition of Math Anxiety

Math anxiety is a relatively new concept in education. During the 1970s, certain educators began using the terms "mathophobia" and "mathemaphobia" as a possible cause for children's unwillingness to learn math. Math anxiety is an extreme emotional and/or physical reaction to a very negative attitude toward math. There is a strong relationship between low math confidence and high math test anxiety.

Math anxiety is more common than you think.

Math anxiety is the feeling of tension and anxiety that interferes with the manipulation of numbers and the solving of math problems during tests. (Richardson and Sulnn, 1972). Math anxiety is a state of panic, helplessness, paralysis and mental disorganization that occurs in some students when they are required to solve math problems. This discomfort varies in intensity and is the outcome of numerous previous experiences students have had in their past learning situations (Tobias, 1976).

Anxiety slows down the learning process

It has been shown that math anxiety exists among many students who usually do not suffer from other tensions. Counselors at a major university reported that one-third of the students who enrolled in behavior therapy programs offered through counseling centers had problems with math anxiety (Suinn, 1970).

Educators know that math anxiety is common among college students and is more prevalent in women than in men. They also know that math anxiety frequently occurs in students with a poor high school math background. These students were found to have the greatest amount of anxiety.

Approximately half of the students in devlopmental math courses (designed for students with inadequate high school math background or low placement scores) could be considered to have math anxiety. However, math anxiety also occurs in students in high-level math courses, such as college algebra and calculus.

Today, math anxiety is accepted as one of the major problems students have in completing their math courses. It is real, but it can be overcome.

Types of Math Anxiety

Math anxiety can be divided into three separate anxieties: Math Test Anxiety, Numerical Anxiety and Abstraction Anxiety. Math Test Anxiety involves anticipation, completion and feedback of math tests. Numerical Anxiety refers to everyday situations requiring working with numbers and performing arithmetic calculations. Numerical anxiety can also include students who are trying to figure out the amount for a tip, thinking about mathematics, doing math homework or listening/seeing math instruction. Abstraction Anxiety deals with working with variables and mathematical concepts used to solve equations. Students can have all three math anxieties or only one anxiety. Most often, the students I have worked with have Math Test Anxiety and Abstraction Anxiety. These students don't have any anxiety working with numbers, but once they start learning algebra, they develop both conditions of math test anxiety and abstraction anxiety. This may have happened in high school or college.

The Causes of Math Anxiety

Since math anxiety is a learned condition, its causes are unique with each student, but they are all rooted in individuals' past experiences. Bad experiences in elementary school are one of the most common sources for students' math anxiety: coming in last in math races at the blackboard, watching a classmate next to them finish a problem twice as fast as they do, teachers saying, "That's okay. You just aren't good in math. You are better in English," or classmates and teachers calling them stupid. These words and experiences remain with people; they can still hear the words and eventually begin telling themselves the same thing. When these students walk into the classroom or open a math book, or take a test, these "mental tapes" play in their minds. When asked, many students indicated that they were made fun of when trying to solve math problems at the chalkboard. When they could not solve the problem, the teacher and/or students would call them "stupid."

Anxiety is a learned behavior; it can be unlearned

Math anxiety can begin as early as elementary school.

Teacher and peer embarrassment and humiliation become the conditioning experience that causes some students' math anxiety. Over the years, this math anxiety is reinforced and even increases in magnitude. In fact, many math anxious students — now 30, 40 and 50 years old — *still* have extreme fear about working math problems on the board. One 56 year old indicated that he had a great deal of fear that the instructor would call him to the board. Even if he knew how to do the problem, displaying that knowledge to his peers was very difficult.   Some students have said that they absolutely refused to go to the board.

Being embarrassed by family members can also cause math anxiety. According to students who have been interviewed on the matter, their parents tried to help them with math and this sometimes led to serious trauma. These students claim that the tutoring from their guardians, mainly their fathers, often resulted in scolding when they were not able to complete the problems. One student reported that his father hit him every time he got a multiplication problem wrong. Brothers and sisters can also tease one another about being dumb in math. This is particularly true of boys telling girls that they cannot do math. When people hear these statements enough times, they may start to believe them and associate these bad feelings with the word math. So, for students many years later just hearing the word "math" triggers a response of anxiety, consciously or unconsciously recalling the bad feelings, and becoming uneasy.

A good example of this is a student who I worked with who had completed her BS degree fifteen years ago at a college that did not require much math. She was returning to college to be an elementary school teacher, which required her to take math and a math placement test. As soon as I mentioned that she had to take math, she said, "I can't do math and I will have to wait a few days to get psychologically ready to take the math placement test." She indicated her old feeling of not being able to do math rushed through her and she almost had an anxiety attack. This is an extreme case but a true example of math anxiety. In most cases math anxiety is not this bad, but it is disruptive enough to cause learning and testing problems.

A Negative Math Experience

If you have math anxiety, try to remember the first time you had uneasy feelings about learning math. This does not include anxiety when taking a math test, which will be discussed later in this chapter. To help you remember this experience, check the appropriate response and answer the questions:

1. Was your first anxiety experience in math in:

    Elementary School _____ Middle School _____ High School _____

2. Can your recall the incident(s)? Yes _____ No _____

    Was it after . . .

	Yes	No
Being called on in class and getting the answer wrong?	___	___
Getting a poor grade on a homework assignment?	___	___
A parent saying he/she cannot do math and neither can you?	___	___
Another adult saying you cannot do math?	___	___
A fellow student telling you that you are no good in math?	___	___
A teacher telling you that you are no good in math?	___	___

    If your first negative math experience is not listed above the write it down here:

    _____

    _____

3. If you cannot remember a specific incident, then when was the last time you told yourself that you could not learn math?

    Today _____ Yesterday _____ Last month _____ Last year _____

    After answering these questions you may have a better idea of where your anxiety originated.

A Positive Math Experience

Some students with or without math anxiety may have had positive experiences with learning math as well.

Now, try to remember your first positive experiences with math. Was it when . . .

	Yes	No
A teacher, parent, or friend praised you for learning math?	____	____
You got a good grade on a homework assignment?	____	____
You got a good grade on a math test?	____	____
You made a good grade in a math course?	____	____

Other positive experiences were: _____

_____

_____

How did that make you feel? _____

_____

_____

Those who don't have math anxiety still have to understand it so they can help their classmates who need support. Also, if you do not have math anxiety now, you may develop it in the future.

One way to overcome math anxiety is to try to find out when it first occurred and how it is still affecting you. The math autobiography is an excellent way to review previous math experiences and to learn how to overcome math anxiety. By answering the previous questions you have already started your own math autobiography. By the end of this chapter you will obtain additional information that will help you write your own math autobiography by using Appendix D (Math Autobiography). It can be full of positive experiences, negative experiences, or a combination of both. Just remember, if you have math anxiety, the suggestions in this chapter and the rest of this textbook can help you reduce it. The first step has already been taken by understanding how it developed in the first place.

Now if you have math anxiety, tell yourself, "I can reduce my math anxiety and there is no reason to continue to be math anxious. It may take some time, but I don't have to be trapped by previous math experiences." The remaining part of this chapter will have additional examples of how you can reduce math and test anxiety.

How Math Anxiety Affects Learning

Math Anxiety can cause learning problems in several ways. It can affect how you do your homework and your participation in the classroom and study groups. Let's first start by looking at how math anxiety could affect your homework. Students with high math anxiety may have difficulty starting or completing their homework. Doing homework reminds some students of their learning problems in math. More specifically, it reminds them of their previous math failures, which causes further anxiety. This anxiety can lead to total avoidance of homework or "approach-avoidance" behavior; students start their homework, then they quit and return later, then quit again.

Anxiety can lead to total avoidance of homework

Total homework avoidance is called procrastination. The very thought of doing their homework causes these students anxiety, which causes them to put off tackling their homework. This makes them feel better for a short amount of time — *until test day.*

Math anxiety can also affect your classroom participation and learning. Usually students with math anxiety are afraid to speak out in class and ask questions. They remember that in the past they were made fun of when giving the wrong answer. They are also afraid of asking a question that others, including the teacher, will consider dumb. So they sit in class fearful of being asked a question, looking like they understand the lecture so they will not be called on. They also take a lot of notes, even though they don't understand, to give the illusion of comprehension. If you are one of these students, these are hard habits to break. However, these habits may cause you to be unsuccessful in your math class. Here are some suggestions to break these habits:

1. *Make an appointment to talk to your math instructor. Math instructors want you to talk to them.* When I do my consulting around the country one of the major complaints I get from math instructors is that the students don't come and see them. Make an appointment to see your math instructor before the first major test to discuss you math history and to ask for learning suggestions. In most cases it is easier to talk to the instructor before you get your first grade.

2. *Before class, ask the instructor to work one homework problem.* You might want to write the problem on the board before the instructor arrives. This is less stressful because you are not asking the question in front of the whole class. In fact, one of my good friends, Dr. Mike Hamm, suggests that his students put the problems they do not know on the board before class. Other students go to the board and solve the problems. Dr. Hamm then solves the ones the students cannot do.

3. *Prepare one question from your homework and ask it within the first 15 minutes of class.* Instructors are more likely to answer questions in the first part of class when they have time instead of the end of class when time is running out.

4. *Ask a question that you already know the answer.* That way if the instructor starts to ask you a question about the problem, you will know the answer. This is good practice for asking those questions to which you don't know the answers.

5. *Use email to send questions to your instructor.* This way you can still get the answer with very little anxiety.

Don't let anxiety keep you from studying with other students

By using these suggestions you can reduce your math anxiety and learn more mathematics. A question unanswered could be a missed test question. Remember: The instructor's job is to answer your questions and you are paying for the course.

Math anxious students sometimes avoid doing additional math outside of the classroom. They avoid study groups and Supplemental Instruction. It is like asking a person with aquaphobia (fear of water) to take a vacation at the beach. However, a person with aquaphobia can go to the beach and enjoy himself or herself and not get wet. In other words, students can still attend study groups and Supplemental Instruction and just listen. When they are ready to get their feet wet, they can ask a few questions. Don't let these great opportunities go by.

Math anxiety can affect how you learn mathematics. It can be overcome with your effort. You don't have to live in the past with your math fears. Today is a new day and you can change how math affects you. The next step is to understand how test anxiety can affect your demonstration of math knowledge.

How to Recognize Test Anxiety

Test anxiety has existed for as long as tests have been issued to evaluate student performance. Because it is so common and because it has survived the test of time, test anxiety has been carefully studied over the last fifty years. Pioneering studies indicate that test anxiety generally leads to low test scores.

At the University of South Florida (Tampa), Dr. Charles Spielberger investigated the relationship between test anxiety and intellectual ability. The study results suggested that anxiety coupled with high ability can improve academic performance; but anxiety coupled with low or average ability can interfere with academic performance. That is:

Anxiety + High Ability = Improvement

Anxiety + Low or Average Ability = No Improvement

Test anxiety can be unlearned.

Test anxiety is a *learned* response; a person is not born with it. An environmental situation brings about test anxiety. The good news is that, because it is a learned response, it can be *unlearned*. Test anxiety is a special kind of general stress. General stress is considered "strained exertion," which can lead to physical and psychological problems.

Defining Test Anxiety

Test anxiety is like being in a burning house with no way out

There are several definitions of test anxiety. One definition states, "Test anxiety is a conditioned emotional habit to either a single terrifying experience, a recurring experience of high anxiety, or a continuous condition of anxiety" (Wolpe, 1958).

Another definition of test anxiety relates to the educational system. The educational system develops evaluations, which measure one's mental performance, which creates test anxiety. This definition suggests that test anxiety is the *anticipation* of some realistic or nonrealistic situational threat (Cattell, 1966). The "test" can be a research paper, an oral report, work at the blackboard, a multiple-choice exam, a written essay or a math test.

Math test anxiety is a new concept in education. *Ms. Magazine* (1976) published "Math Anxiety: Why is a Smart Girl Like You Counting on Your Fingers?" and coined the phrase "math anxiety." Additional studies on the graduate level discovered math anxiety was common among adults, as well as children. Educators did not focus on math anxiety as a state of mind but as a skill deficiency, until the *Ms. Magazine* article appeared.

One of my students once described math test anxiety as "being in a burning house with no way out." Another one of my students described math test anxiety as "a sick feeling I get on test days that makes me feel like a little child and then I forget everything."

No matter how you define it, math test anxiety is real, and it affects millions of students.

The Causes of Test Anxiety

The causes of math test anxiety can be different for each student. It could possibly have first occurred in middle or high school. However, for many students it first occurs in college when passing tests is the only way to pass the course. Homework and extra credit in most college courses don't count toward your grade. Now students must have a passing average and in some cases must pass the departmental final exam. Additional pressure also exists because not passing algebra means you won't graduate and you might not get the job you want. As you can see, there are more reasons to have math test anxiety in college than in high school.

If you have math test anxiety, I want you to try to remember the first time it surfaced.

1. Was your first math test anxiety experience in:

    Elementary School _____ Middle School _____ High School _____ College _____

2. Can your recall the incident(s)?   Yes _____   No _____

    Was it after . . .

	Yes	No
Your first algebra test?	___	___
Your first math test after being out of school for a long time?	___	___
You decided to get serious about college?	___	___
In a college algebra course that was required for your major?	___	___
When an instructor said that you must pass the next test to pass the course?	___	___
When you needed to pass the next test to stay in the course and maintain your financial aid?	___	___
Your parents asking you why you failed your last math test?	___	___
Your children asking you why you failed your last math test?	___	___

    If your test anxiety experience is not listed above then what was the experience?

    _____

    _____

3. If you cannot remember a specific incident when you had test anxiety, do you expect to have any major test anxiety on your next math test? Yes _____ No _____

It is also possible for students with math test anxiety to have positive experiences taking a math test. Now try to remember your first positive experience when taking a math test. Was it in:

Elementary School _____   Middle School _____   High School _____ College _____

Was it after . . .

	Yes	No
Studying many hours for a test?	____	____
Joining a study group?	____	____
Developing a positive attitude about passing the test?	____	____

Other experiences (explain): _____

_____

_____

_____

Now think back to your last positive experience with a math test. How did it make you feel?

_____

_____

_____

Since we have already explored your experiences with taking math tests, let's look at some of the direct causes of your math test anxiety. If you do have test anxiety, what is the main cause? If you don't know, then review the eight causes of test anxiety on the next page. Does one of these reasons fit you? If you don't have test anxiety, what would be a reason that could cause test anxiety?

By the end of the chapter you will be ready to finish your math autobiography by completing Appendix D. You should include positive test experiences, negative test experiences, or a combination of both. If you have math test anxiety, following the suggestions in this chapter and the rest of the book can greatly reduce it. The first step was already taken by understanding how you developed math test anxiety. The second step is writing the reasons.

I don't want to fail my next math test, but I'm just not good at it.

The causes of test anxiety can be different for each student, but they can be explained by eight basic concepts. See Figure 9 on the next page.

Examples: Students with worry anxiety have told me many things after not being able to solve problems "What is wrong with me?" "I did these types of problems before." "I just cannot get math!" "Math is awful!" "I hate math!" "I don't need it for my career so why am I taking the course." "I am going to fail this test and this course." I might as well drop this course and quit college." "I am dumb."

These types of statements make you have more worry anxiety and divert your attention away from the test, leaving you less time to complete the problems you *can* do. Later on in the chapter we will discuss how to get rid of these types of statements.

Students may have different levels of emotional anxiety and worry anxiety. The treatment depends on the levels of your type of test anxiety. Go to Appendix A (Scoring the Test Attitude Inventory) to measure the levels of your type of anxiety. The levels are measures in "percentile norms," which means your level of anxiety is compared to other college students. The percentage level of my anxiety falls under (fill in percentages from your anxiety levels below):

Total worry _____ Worry anxiety _____ Emotional anxiety _____

Figure 9
The Causes of Test Anxiety

1. Test anxiety can be a learned behavior resulting from the expectations of parents, teachers or other significant people in the student's life.

2. Test anxiety can be caused by the association between grades and a student's personal worth.

3. Test anxiety develops from fear of alienating parents, family or friends due to poor grades.

4. Test anxiety can stem from a feeling of lack of control and an inability to change one's life situation.

5. Test anxiety can be caused by a student being embarrassed by the teacher or other students when trying to do math problems.

6. Test anxiety can be caused by timed tests and the fear of not finishing the test even if the student can do all of the problems.

7. Test anxiety can be caused by being put in math courses that are above the student's level of competence.

8. Students leaving the room before the test time is up.

What are the causes of your test anxiety?

Low levels of anxiety are between 1 and 25.

Moderately low levels of anxiety are between 26 and 50.

Moderately high levels of anxiety are between 51 and 75.

High levels of anxiety are between 76 and 99 percentile.

What is your level of anxiety for each area? Students who have high test anxiety have both emotional and worry anxiety.

The Different Types of Test Anxiety

The two basic types of test anxiety are emotional (educators term this "somatic") and worry (educators term this "cognitive"). Students with high test anxiety have *both* emotional and worry anxiety.

Signs of emotional anxiety are upset stomach, nausea, sweaty palms, pain in the neck, stiff shoulders, high blood pressure, rapid shallow breathing, rapid heartbeat or general feelings of nervousness. As anxiety increases, these feelings intensify. Some students even run to the bathroom to throw up or have diarrhea. Even though these *feelings* are caused by anxiety, the physical response is real. These feelings and physical inconveniences can affect your concentration, your testing speed, and it can cause you to completely "draw a blank."

Worry anxiety causes students to think about failing the test. These negative thoughts can happen either before or during the test. This negative "self-talk" causes students to focus on their anxiety instead of recalling math concepts by telling themselves that they will fail the test.

The Effects of Anxiety on Learning and Testing

The effects of anxiety on student learning and testing can best be explained by reviewing the Stages of Memory discussed in Chapter 5. The Stages of Memory are Sensory Input, Sensory Register, Short-term Memory, Working Memory, Abstract Reasoning, Long-term Memory and Memory Output. When students are reading a math textbook or learning mathematics in the classroom their anxiety can affect their Sensory Register and Short-term Memory. Anxiety can interfere with how fast people process information and can decrease the amount of information they can hold for a short period of time. This means that less information is processing into their Working Memory where mathematics information is combined and learned. Also, anxiety

He is anxious, so he went to the library to read books instead of reviewing his math.

affects Working Memory by decreasing the amount of information that can be processed at the same time. The result is less information being transferred into Working Memory, and the information is further decreased or misunderstood as it transfers from Working Memory into Abstract Reasoning and Long-term Memory. The results can be poor Memory Output such as not understanding what you read or not answering a question during class.

During tests, anxious students focus on their anxiety instead of math

This process also describes some of the learning problems students with high anxiety have when reading the text or listening to a lecture. These students indicate that they read the same section over and over again but still cannot understand a word it says. Some of the students also mention that they feel more anxious after they read the text. Students listening to the lecture indicate that after following a few problem-solving steps they got "lost" and when called on in class had no idea what the instructor was talking about. Other study skills or disability problems may also cause these learning problems, but the math anxiety at the very least confounds the learning problem.

While doing their homework and taking tests students have described similar Memory Output problems. Some students with high anxiety say that when they first look at the test it looks like Greek. This could be caused by the anxiety affecting the Sensory Input that recognizes visual input to be processed into short-term memory. However, in most cases, as stated in Chapter 5, Working Memory is mainly used when solving homework problems or problems on a test. The Working Memory recalls information from Abstract Reasoning, Long-term Memory or both to solve the problem. The anxiety slows down this process.

The most recent research indicates that test anxiety strongly affects Working Memory. Authors Ashcraft and Kirk (2001) indicate that math anxiety temporarily disrupts mental processing in Working Memory that causes poorer math achievement. Math anxiety uses up Working Memory resources that make it harder to learn math. During tests, math test anxiety decreases the amount of Working Memory space, which means less information can be received and used from Long-term Memory and Abstract Reasoning. It would be like using a calculator (Working Memory) in which half of the keys are not functioning. The result is a slow down in performance and a decrease in accuracy, resulting in poorer grades.

Anxiety can cause mental blocks

The effects of test anxiety range from a "mental block" on a test to avoiding homework. One of the most common side effects of test anxiety is getting the test and immediately forgetting information that you know. Some students describe this event as having a "mental block," "going blank," or indicating that the test looks like Greek. After five or ten minutes into the test, some of these students can refocus on it and start working the problems. They have, however, lost valuable time. For other students, anxiety persists throughout the test and they cannot recall the needed information. It is only after they walk out the door that they can remember how to work the problems. When this happens, they often get mad at themselves, which increases their fears that the same thing will happen on the next test.

Test anxiety gets so bad that students would rather leave early and receive a lower grade than to stay in that "burning house"

Sometimes students with math test anxiety do not "go blank," but it takes longer to recall formulas and concepts and to work problems. The result is frustration and loss of time, leading to *more* anxiety. Since, in most cases, math tests are *speed* tests (those in which you have a certain amount of time to complete the test), you may not have enough time to work all the problems or to check the answers if you have mentally slowed down. The result is a lower test score because even though you knew the material, you did not complete all of the questions before the test time ran out.

Not using all of the time allotted for the test is another problem caused by test anxiety. Students know that they should use all of the test time to check their answers. In fact, math is one of the few subjects in which you can check test problems to find out if you have the problems correct. However, most students do not use all of the test time, and the results are lower test scores.

Why? Students with high test anxiety do not want to stay in the classroom. This is especially true of students whose test anxiety increases as the test progresses. The test anxiety gets so bad that they would rather leave early and receive a lower grade than to stay in that "burning house."

Students have another reason for leaving the test early — the fear of what the instructor and other students will think about them for being the last one to hand in the test. These students refuse to be the last group to finish the test because they feel the instructor or other students will think they are dumb. This is middle-school thinking, but the feelings are still real — no matter the age of the student. These students do not realize that some students who turn in their tests first fail, while many students who turn in their tests last make "A's" and "B's."

Another effect of test anxiety relates to completing homework assignments. Students who have high test anxiety may have difficulty starting or completing their math homework. They think about previous tests or begin worrying about the next test and whether they are going to stress out in front of everyone.

> **Example:** Some students begin their homework and work some problems successfully. They then get stuck on a problem that causes them anxiety, so they take a break. During their break the anxiety disappears until they start doing their homework again. Doing their homework causes more anxiety which leads to another break. The breaks become more frequent. Finally, the student ends up taking one long break and not doing the homework. Quitting, to them, means *no more anxiety* until the next homework assignment.

Figure 10
The 12 Myths About Test Anxiety

1. Students are born with test anxiety.
2. Test anxiety is a mental illness.
3. Test anxiety cannot be reduced.
4. Any level of test anxiety is bad.
5. All students who are not prepared will have test anxiety.
6. Students with test anxiety cannot learn math.
7. Students who are well prepared will not have test anxiety.
8. Very intelligent students and students taking high-level courses, such as calculus, do not have test anxiety.
9. Attending class and doing my homework should reduce all of my test anxiety.
10. Being told to relax during a test will make you relaxed.
11. Doing nothing about test anxiety will make it go away.
12. Reducing test anxiety will guarantee better grades.

The effects of math test anxiety can be different for each student. Students can have several of the mentioned characteristics that can interfere with math learning and test taking. However, there are certain myths about math that each student needs to know. Review Figure 10, The 12 Myths About Test Anxiety, above, to see which ones you believe. If you have test anxiety, which of the mentioned characteristics are true of you?

Now that we understand how math anxiety and math test anxiety affect learning and testing, it is time to learn how to reduce your test anxiety. Tell yourself, "I can reduce my math test anxiety. It may take some time, but I can reduce my math test anxiety."

How to Reduce Math Anxiety and Math Test Anxiety

To reduce math anxiety and math test anxiety, you need to understand both the relaxation response and how negative self-talk undermines your abilities. These anxiety reduction techniques and positive self-statements can be used before or during your homework, math class or taking a test. These techniques need to be practiced several times before they will become effective. If you have extremely high math anxiety or math test anxiety you will need to practice the long-term relaxation techniques.

Relaxation Techniques

The relaxation response is any technique or procedure that helps you to become relaxed and will take the place of an anxiety response. Someone simply telling you to relax or even telling yourself to relax, however, without proper training, does little to reduce your test anxiety. There are both short-term and long-term relaxation response techniques which help control emotional (somatic) math test anxiety. These techniques will also help reduce worry (cognitive) anxiety. Effective *short-term* techniques include The Tensing and Differential Relaxation Method and The Palming Method.

Short-Term Relaxation Techniques

The Tensing and Differential Relaxation Method

The Tensing and Differential Relaxation Method helps you relax by tensing and relaxing your muscles all at once. Follow these procedures while you are sitting at your desk before taking a test:

1. Put your feet flat on the floor.

2. With your hands, grab underneath the chair.

3. Push down with your feet and pull up on your chair at the same time for about five seconds.

4. Relax for five to ten seconds.

5. Repeat the procedure two to three times.

6. Relax all your muscles except the ones that are actually used to take the test.

*This technique can help
you reduce anxiety.*

Deep Breathing

Deep Breathing is a technique that can reduce your test anxiety. Follow these steps to Deep Breathing:

1.   Inhale slowly and deeply though your nose by filling up the bottom of your lungs first.

2.   When you have a full breath stop for a few seconds and hold your breath.

3.   Exhale slowly through your mouth pretending like you are whistling out the air. Be sure to exhale fully and let your whole body relax.

4.   Wait a few seconds and then start to inhale as stated in number 1.

After practicing deep breathing it should become a very natural process. You may want to repeat the steps five times and then take a break. You may then want to do one more set. If you start to get light-headed while practicing, then stop for a few minutes. You were probably breathing in and out too fast. Practicing this breathing technique will make it easier to use right before or during the test if needed. This technique will help some students to relax, while other students may prefer other short-term techniques.

Visualization

Have you ever daydreamed in class or during a workshop? I have asked this question to thousands of students and the answer is always yes. Then I ask them what happens when they daydream? The answer is that their minds leave the room and the body thinks it is where the mind has gone. Then I ask what would happen if you daydreamed about some relaxing place? Your mind would tell your body to relax. This process is called visualization, or using visual images in your mind to reduce test anxiety. This technique has been used for hundreds of years. Athletes also use this technique to reduce their anxiety and to improve their game performance. You can imagine anything or any place in order to reduce your test anxiety.

Follow these steps to practice visualization:

1.   Find a comfortable place to sit.

2.   Close your eyes and think about a relaxing place, real or imaginary.

3.   Imagine yourself in that place, making sure to see it though your own eyes, not seeing yourself from afar.

4.   What type of sounds do you hear? What do you smell? Are you feeling the sand between your toes or maybe the cool air? Make the scene as real as possible.

5.   Now visualize that scene for one to two minutes.

6.   Open your eyes and continue to feel relaxed.

You need to develop two scenes and practice them every day until you can relax your self in a few minutes. Then you will be ready to use them on the test.

The Palming Method

The palming method is a visualization procedure used to reduce test anxiety. While you are at your desk before or during a test, follow these procedures:

Visualize yourself relaxing.

1. Close and cover your eyes using the center of the palms of your hands.

2. Prevent your hands from touching your eyes by resting the lower parts of your palms on your cheekbones and placing your fingers on your forehead. Your eyeballs must not be touched, rubbed or handled in any way.

3. Think of some real or imaginary scenes that are relaxing to you. Mentally visualize this scene. Picture the scene as if you were actually there, looking through your own eyes.

4. Visualize this relaxing scene for one to two minutes.

Practice visualizing this scene several days before taking a test and the effectiveness of this relaxation procedure will improve. Track One of the CD, *How to Reduce Test Anxiety* (Nolting, 1987), further explains test anxiety and discusses these and other short-term relaxation response techniques. Short-term relaxation techniques can be learned quickly but are not as successful as the long-term relaxation techniques. Short-term techniques are intended to be used while learning the long-term technique. The *How to Reduce Test Anxiety* CD is in the back of this text.

Long-Term Relaxation Techniques

The Cue-Controlled Relaxation Response Technique is the best long-term relaxation technique. It is presented on Track Two of the CD, *How To Reduce Test Anxiety* (Nolting, 1987). Cue-controlled Relaxation means you can induce your own relaxation based on repeating certain cue words to yourself. In essence, you are taught to relax and then silently repeat cue words, such as "I am relaxed." After enough practice, you can relax during math tests. The Cue-Oriented Relaxation Technique has worked with thousands of students. For a better understanding of test anxiety and how to reduce it, listen to *How to Reduce Test Anxiety* (Nolting, 1987).

Managing Self-Talk

Imagine two students taking their first math test during the semester, and half way through the exam they start missing several problems. One student starts saying to himself that he is going to fail the test and might as well turn in his paper and quit. The other student says to herself, "I might miss these problems but that is not a reason to give up and leave. I will just try as hard as I can on the other problems and I can pass." One student feels a lot of anxiety and the other student remains calm and develops a plan. In both cases, the situation is the same but the feelings in response to the test situation are extremely different due to their internal dialog or self-talk. Which student are you?

Cognitive psychologists claim that what we say to ourselves in a response to an event mainly determines our mood or feeling about that event. Sometimes we say these statements to ourselves so quickly and automatically that we don't even notice. We then believe the situation is causing the feeling, when it is actually our interactions or thoughts about the event that are controlling our emotions. This sequence is represented by the following time line:

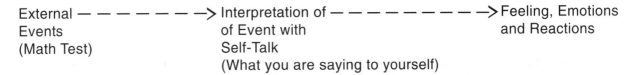

External — — — — — —> Interpretation of — — — — — — — — —> Feeling, Emotions
Events   of Event with   and Reactions
(Math Test)   Self-Talk
                                          (What you are saying to yourself)

Based on this psychological theory, in most cases you are responsible for what you feel. You have a choice to have positive or negative self-talk while doing your math homework or during a math test. This can determine how you feel during the test and control some of your anxiety. Some students see a math test as an opportunity to show their knowledge of the subject and are excited about that, while others see the same test as a potential failure that will lead to anger and dissatisfaction. The realization that you are responsible for your own feelings can be very powerful once you fully accept it. Some points about self-talk are:

— Self-Talk is like a telegraphic message, where one or two words can bring up many different thoughts and feelings.

— Self-Talk is like a bad CD. It keeps playing the same word over and over again.

— Self –Talk happens automatically. You don't even think about what you are saying to yourself.

— Negative self-talk during anxious situations is usually illogical, though it might seem rational at the time.

— Self-Talk can increase or decrease test anxiety. It just depends on what you are telling yourself.

— Positive self-talk can increase appropriate behavior. Telling yourself that you can do your homework can lead to actually doing your homework.

— Negative self-talk can cause avoidance and procrastination. Students who tell themselves that they are not good in math don't want to do their homework.

— Negative self-talk is a bad habit. You are not born with these habits and it can be changed into a good habit.

With practice your can control your self-talk to improve your math success.

Negative Self-Talk

Students who have high test anxiety usually use negative self-talk. This negative self-talk can increase the student's test anxiety and may cause them to fail. It is totally possible for students with negative self-talk to change this bad habit.

To change the negative self-talk habit, it is beneficial to understand the different types of negative self-talk. If you have negative self-talk, then review the different types to see which one matches you best. You may be exactly one type or a combination of different types.

1. **The Worrier** (increases anxiety). The Worrier always looks out for the worst-case situation. They are scared of failure. When they feel a little bit of anxiety, they blow it out of proportion and give up, believing there is nothing that can help them pass. In some extreme cases, they drop out of college believing they will never be able to pass a math course. The worrier's favorite question is, "What if . . . ?" For example, "What if I fail this test and then this class? I will not graduate and be in this dead-end job forever or all my friends will make fun of me and call me dumb." The Worrier can eventually give in to fear and sabotage his/herself in self-defense from disappointment.

> **Example:** A student is taking his/her math test and comes to one problem that he/she cannot do. The student tells him/herself that all the rest of the problems are going to be just as hard so they might as well start panicking now. This leads to some anxiety, which the student magnifies, causing them to give up on the test and leave.

2. **The Victim** (increases depression). The Victim wants to feel helpless and hopeless. They create anxiety by telling themselves that no matter what they do, they will not be successful in math. The Victim believes that there is something wrong with them that is not curable. They do not blame other factors that they can change, such as decreasing anxiety and improving his/her math study skills. They want to doom themselves and get into a learned helplessness mode that eventually stops them from even trying. The Victim's favorite statement is, "I can't. I will never be able to no matter how hard I try . . ." The Victim's goal is to be depressed enough to quit trying.

> **Example:** I had a student who was referred to me by a chemistry instructor after he did not complete a pre-algebra course. He indicated that he had failed or barely passed every math course he had taken since middle school. He told me he could not learn math at all and wished he could get a degree without taking math. We set up some time to work together and he received help from our tutors and study coaches. He kept telling everyone he could not do math. We assessed this student and found out that he had the exact opposite learning styles as most math instructors. I told him we could teach him by using a hands-on approach or by using manipulatives. He did not believe me. I had a meeting about this student with his professor, and I explained he believed he was a victim of math and did not want to give up that title because it meant he could and would always fail at math. To give up that label would mean he was wrong all these years and that he would have to admit he could in fact be successful in math. In our last tutoring session he was solving linear equation using Hands on Equations. In fact, after about three problems he drew pictures on the board representing how to solve the equation. He was now doing algebra and the victim cycle was broken.

3. **The Critic** (wants low self-esteem). The Critic wants to judge and evaluate his/her behaviors in order to put his/herself down. They look for flaws, and if they don't have any, they create some. They put themselves down when they notice other students not showing any anxiousness. They ignore their success, and instead of being proud

of their accomplishments, they believe them to be a fluke. The Critic's favorite statement is, "You are too stupid to learn math!" If they did pass the test then they would say afterward, "You could have made a better grade. Look at all those careless errors." The Critic's goal is to promote low self-esteem so that they will stop learning math.

> **Example:** A student I worked with was repeating a math course. The student indicated that he could not do math, but nonetheless, he made a B on his first test. He was shocked by the grade and, despite starting so well, was convinced that he would fail the next exam. I asked him why and he told me that the problems he missed on this test would cause him to fail the next test. Thinking this way breeds negativity that can often lead to students setting themselves up for failure.

4. **The Perfectionist** (wants more stress and pushes you too far). The Perfectionist is closely related to the Critic, but instead of putting themselves down for missing problems, they use the experience to push themselves toward success. The Perfectionist cannot stand mistakes or poor grades. They drive themselves to near exhaustion making sure that they understand every single concept. Self-worth means nothing to them, because they will never be happy with anything less than perfection. This can eventually lead to failure when someone passes his/her "breaking point". Even a grade such as a 92 is not good enough for them. In some cases it can drive them towards causing harm to themselves.

> **Example:** A student was making A's on her math tests until she made a C on her last test before the final. When she went to take the finial exam she had a panic attack. It caused her so much anxiety that she could not take the test. She started crying outside the math office where a faculty member started talking to her. She was then referred to me and we talked about her anxiety. She told me that she must make an A in the course and would not settle for a B. She was afraid to take the final because she thought a poor grade would cause her to lose her A. Then her thoughts caused so much anxiety that she became physically ill and could not take the test. We started working on her test anxiety as well as her self-talk. She took the final a few days later and made a B in the course, which she was fine with.

After reading about these different types of personalities which one can you most relate to? The person inside of you may be a combination of two different types, but there usually is one personality that dominates your perception of math. The next step is to learn how to cope with these problems and to begin using your personality type to become successful.

Examples of Negative Self-Talk:

- "No matter what I do, I will not pass this course."
- "I failed this course last semester, and I will fail it again."
- "I am no good at math, so why should I try?"
- "I cannot do it; I cannot do the problems, and I am going to fail this test."
- "I have forgotten how to do the problems, and I am going to fail."
- "I am going to fail this test and never graduate."
- "If I can't pass this test, I am too dumb to learn math and will flunk out."

Positive Self-Talk

You can counter and control negative self-talk in several ways. Negative self-talk can easily be replaced with positive self-talk. You can also develop thought- stopping techniques that can reduce or eliminate negative self-talk. Try all the following ways to discover which one, or combination of two techniques, work best for you.

The first technique is to develop positive self-talk statements to replace any negative self-talk. Suggestions for writing positive self-statements are:

1. Use the first person tense. For example, "I can control my anxiety and pass this test."

2. Avoid using negatives in the statement. For example, don't say, "I will not get nervous during this test." Instead say, "I will calm myself down during the test.

3. Make the statements positive and realistic. For example, you can say, "I will be successful on this test", instead of saying, "I will make a 100 on this test."

- **The Worrier**, who asks, "What if I fail the test?" can counter with, "If I fail the test I will just do better on the next one."

- **The Victim**, who believes things are hopeless says, "No way will I ever pass math." They can counter with "I used a different way to study and take the test so I can pass the course this time."

- **The Critic**, who puts themselves down by saying, "I cannot reduce my test anxiety and will fail." They can replace this by saying, "I know I have test anxiety but I have learned to control it."

- **The Perfectionist**, who says, "I must make an A or I am a failure," can instead say, "I don't need an A to be successful. I just need to pass this course so I can take the next one and graduate."

These are examples of positive self-talk that can control anxiety. Some additional positive self-talk statements are listed below.

Examples of Positive Self-Talk:

- "I failed the course last semester, but I can now use my math study skills to pass this course."

- "I went blank on the last test, but I now know how to reduce my test anxiety."

- "I know that my poor math skills are due to poor study skills, not my own ability, and since I am working on my study skills, my math skills will improve."

- "I know that, with hard work, I will pass math."

- "I prepared for this test and will do the best I can. I will reduce my test anxiety and use the best test-taking procedures. I expect some problems will be difficult, but I will not get discouraged."

- "I am solving problems and feel good about myself. I am not going to worry about that difficult problem; I am going to work on the problems that I can do. I am going to use all the test time and check for careless errors. Even if I do not get the grade that I want on this test, it is not the end of the world."

Now you can develop your own positive self-talk. Develop three positive self-talk statements that are not in this book, making sure to use the word I in each statement.

Statement 1: _____

_____

_____.

Statement 2: _____

_____

_____.

Statement 3: _____

_____

_____.

Thought-Stopping Technique

Many students have difficulty controlling their negative self-talk. These students have tried to tell themselves to eliminate the negative self-talk, but no matter what they try it persists. These students need a thought-stopping technique to break this bad habit.

Thought-stopping entails focusing on the unwanted negative self-talk, and then suddenly stopping those thoughts with some type of internal or external action. Actions such as yelling to yourself, "Stop that," or making a loud noise such as slapping a desk, can effectively interrupt the negative self-talk. In a homework situation you may want to slap the desk, but obviously doing this in the classroom would be inappropriate.

To stop your negative thoughts in a classroom while listening to a lecture or during a test, silently shout to yourself, "Stop thinking about that." After your silent shout, either relax yourself or repeat one of the positive self-talk statements that you have made up. You may have to shout to yourself several times to control your negative self-talk. After every shout, use a different relaxation technique, such as positive visual scenes or positive statements that will help control your anxiety.

The way stop-thinking works is by interrupting the worry response before it can create the type of anxiety that gets out of control. During the interruptions you can gain control and replace the negative self-talk with positive responses. Students with high worry anxiety need to practice these techniques at least a week before the test several times a day. Then they need to keep practicing it once a day until the negative self-talk disappears. If needed obtain additional help from the counselor or college psychologist to help you with stopping negative self-talk.

Writing Your Math Autobiography

During this chapter we have discussed writing your math autobiography and how it can help reduce or help prevent math anxiety or math test anxiety. The autobiography relates to how you remember and feel about past math experiences. It can also help explore how these past feelings and events may have shaped your current life. Math autobiographies can be a good healing tool that can help you let go of negative experiences.

Use Appendix D as a guide to writing your math autobiography. Depending on your instructor, you may be able to hand in Appendix D as your autobiography. Remember: The autobiography is a tool to help you to become a better math student and to help reduce your math and test anxiety. If need be, you can share and discuss your math autobiography with a counselor or college psychologist.

Summary

- General test anxiety is a learned behavior developed by having emotional and/or worry (somatic and/or cognitive) responses during previous tests.

- General test anxiety is a fear of any type of test.

- Math anxiety is usually caused by previous experiences.

- Math anxiety affects learning in class and doing your homework.

- Math test anxiety is a subclass of general test anxiety that is specific to one subject area.

- Math test anxiety, like general test anxiety, can decrease your ability to perform on tests.

- Your ability to complete the test decreases by blocked memory and an urgency to leave the test room before checking all your answers.

- To reduce test anxiety, you must practice relaxation techniques and develop your own positive self-talk statements.

- Reducing your math test anxiety does not guarantee success on tests; first you have to know the appropriate material to recall during the test and have good test-taking skills. Increasing productive study time also builds in positive experiences that can support you through the test.

- To substantially reduce high test anxiety, follow the instructions presented on Track Two of the CD, *How to Reduce Test Anxiety* (Nolting, 1987). The CD is attached to the back of this text.

! **Remember:** Reducing test anxiety will not happen overnight — it will take ! time and practice.

Name: _____ Date: _____

Assignment for Chapter 3

1. Create your personal definition of math anxiety:

   _____

   _____

   _____

   _____

2. Describe two ways math anxiety can affect learning:

   Way one: _____

   _____

   Way two: _____

   _____

3. Describe how you know if you have math anxiety or math test anxiety.

   _____

   _____

   _____

4. List and explain the two different types of test anxiety.

   Type one: _____

   Type two _____

5. Explain two ways test anxiety can affect your test grade.

   Way one: _____

   _____

   Way two: _____

   _____

6. Describe your best short-term relaxation technique. Practice your short-term relaxation technique.

_____

_____

_____

7. List and describe one of the four negative self-talk personalities that matches you the best.

_____

_____

_____

8. Describe how you would use the thought-stopping techniques with positive self-statements.

_____

_____

_____

_____

_____

9. Listen to the CD *How to Reduce Test Anxiety* (Nolting, 1987) and practice the "Cue-Controlled Relaxation Technique" every day until it takes you two minutes or less to relax before a test.

10. Go to Appendix D and complete the math autobiography.

How to Create a Positive Study Environment and Manage Your Time

4

In Chapter 4
you will learn these concepts:

- A productive study environment involves finding the most beneficial time to study, the best place to study, and identifying the best types of studying for you.
  - ✓ How to choose the best study environment for you
  - ✓ The best order in which to study subjects
  - ✓ Benefits of study breaks
  - ✓ How to use the math lab or learning resource center
  - ✓ Ways to use study groups and Supplemental Instruction
  - ✓ Best times to study math
  - ✓ Development of a study schedule
  - ✓ Steps to prioritizing your time
  - ✓ Steps to creating a weekly study plan
  - ✓ Ways to manage work and school

Introduction

A positive home and college study environment can improve your learning experiences. Traditional study environments include an on campus study area (library) and an off campus study area. Study environments have been expanded to include math labs, Learning Resource Center (LRC), study groups, Supplemental Instruction, collaborative learning computer programs and websites.

These new study environments require students to learn how to use resources in the math lab/LRC such as: computer programs, CD-ROMs and assessment instruments.

The learning environment in the classroom has also changed, and it now emphasizes more collaborative learning. Students now have to learn how to benefit from their collaborative classroom learning experiences and how to make the best use of the math lab or LRC. Learning outside the classroom has also changed. Students need to learn how to effectively use collaborative learning, study groups and Supplemental Instruction. To maximize learning, students need to learn how to effectively use their new study environments and learning resources.

Another way to maximize your learning is to effectively manage your time. In high school, teachers and parents manage the student's time. In college, students suddenly have more activities (work, social, study) and less time to fit them all in (and no teachers or parents handy or willing to schedule their time for them).

When freshman college students are asked to give their number one reason for poor grades, they indicate that they do not have enough time to study. When students are asked how much time they study per week, most do not have any idea.

Students who do not effectively manage their study time may fail math courses. As pointed out in Chapter 1, math requires much *practice* (the same as mastering a sport or musical instrument) for the student to perform well on tests. Therefore, developing a good plan for studying math can be an important key to getting good grades.

How to Choose Your Best Study Environments

Your study environment is the key to efficient learning. Some study environments have too many distractions. Don't pick Grand Central Station at your house as a study area because it will cause lack of concentration and lost study time. Other study environments may be quiet, but you may not have the necessary materials around you to supplement your studies.

Creating a positive study environment may take some time, but it will improve the quality of studying. Choosing an appropriate study place may seem trivial, but it can significantly enhance learning. When you start studying, choose a specific place whether at home, at college, at the math lab or LRC.

Studying can be difficult at times.

Claim your study spot.

Choosing a Place to Study

While studying in your home, choose one place, one chair, one desk or table as your study area. If you use the kitchen table, choose one chair, preferably one that you do not use during dinner. Call this chair "my study chair." If you study in the student cafeteria, use the same table each time. Do not use the table at which you play cards or eat.

By studying at the same place each time, a conditioned response will be formed. From then on, when you sit down at your study place your mind will automatically start thinking about studying. This conditioned response decreases your "warm up" time. "Warm up" time is how long it takes to actually begin studying after you sit down.

Another aspect of the study environment involves the degree of silence you need for studying. In most cases, a totally quiet room is not necessary. But if you can only study with total silence, keep this in mind when selecting your study places and times.

Most students can study with a little noise, especially if it is a constant sound, like their MP3 players. In fact, some students keep on a mellow radio station or a fan to drown out other noises. However, do not turn on the television to drown out other noises or to listen to while studying. That will not work! Why? Because you are likely to get distracted. For most efficient studying, select a study area where *you* can control the noise level.

Setting Up Your Study Area

Signs should surround your home study environment that "tell" you to study. One sign should be your study schedule. Attach your study schedule to the inside flap of your notebook and place another copy in your study place at home. Place your study goals and the rewards for achieving those goals where they can be easily seen. You will make up a study schedule later on in this chapter.

Do not post pictures of your girlfriend, boyfriend, bowling trophies, fishing trophies or other items in your study area; these could be distracting. Instead, post pictures indicating your goals after graduation. If you want to be a nurse, doctor, lawyer or business person, post pictures that represent these goals. The study area should always reinforce your educational goals.

Keep only what you need in your space.

When sitting down to study have ready the "tools of your trade": pencils, paper, notebook, textbook, study guide and calculator. Anything you might need should be within reach. In this way, when you need something, you can reach for it instead of leaving your study area. The problem with getting up is not just the time it takes to get the item, but the time it takes to "warm up" again. After getting milk and cookies and sitting down, it takes another four to five minutes to "warm up" and continue studying.

In most colleges and universities there will be more than one place to get additional help in math. Visit all the places you hear about, each at various times so you can see how they operate with different personnel and under crowded or sparse conditions. Ask more than one person at each location what materials they have to help you.

The Best Way to Study Subjects

When studying, arrange your subjects in the order of difficulty. In other words, start with your most difficult subject — which is usually math — and work toward your easiest course. By studying your most difficult subject first, you are more alert and better motivated to complete the work before continuing on the easier courses, which may be more interesting to you. If you study math last, you will probably tire easily, become frustrated and you may quit.

However, you are less likely to quit when you study a subject that interests you.

! Remember: Study math first **!**

Mix the Order of Study

Another approach to improving the quality of your study is to mix up the order of studying different subjects.

> **Example:** If you have English, accounting and math to study, then study them in the following order: 1] math, 2] English, and 3] accounting. By studying the subjects in this order, one part of your brain can rest after studying math while the other part of your brain is studying English. Now your mind is "fresh" when you study accounting.

Decide When to Study

Deciding when to study different types of material is part of developing a positive study environment. Your study material can be divided into two separate types. One type is new material and the other type is material that has already been learned.

The best time to review the material you have already learned is right before going to sleep. By reviewing materials for the test the night before, you will have less brain activity and fewer physical distracters that might prevent you from recalling the material the next day.

> **Example:** If you have an 8:00 test the next morning, you should review the material the night before. If you have a 10:00 test the next day, review the material both the night before and the day of the test. Reviewing is defined as reading the material to yourself. You also might review a few problems you have already solved to keep your mind alert, but do not try to learn any new material the night before the test.

When to Learn New Material

Learn new material during the first part of the study period

Learning new material should be done during the first part of the study period. Do not learn new material the night before a test. You will be setting yourself up for test anxiety. If you try to cram the procedures to solve different types of equations or new ways to factor trinomials, you will end up in a state of confusion. This is especially true if you have major problems learning how to solve new equations or factoring. The next day you will only remember *not* being able to solve the equation or factor the trinomials; this could distract you on the test.

Most students get tired after studying for several hours or before going to bed. If you are tired and try to study new material, it becomes more difficult to retain. It takes more effort to learn new material when you are tired than it does to review old material. When you start getting tired of studying, the best tactic is to begin reviewing previously learned material.

Find the Most Efficient Time to Study Math

The most efficient time to study is as soon as possible after the math class is over. Psychologists indicate that most forgetting occurs right after learning the material. In other words, you are going to forget most of what you have learned in the first hour after class. To prevent this mass exodus of knowledge, you need to recall some of the lecture material as soon after class as is practical.

The easiest way to recall the lecture is to rework your notes. Reviewing your notes will increase your ability to recall the information and make it easier to understand the homework assignments (see Chapter 7).

Choosing Between Mass and Distributive Learning

There are two different types of learning processes: "mass learning" and "distributive learning." Mass learning involves learning everything at one time. Distributive learning is studying the same amount of time as mass learning — with study breaks.

> **Examples:** *Mass learning* — you would study three hours in a row without taking a break, then quit studying for the night. *Distributive learning* — you would study for about 50 minutes with a 10 minute break, study for 50 more minutes with a 10 minute break, and finish with 60 minutes of studying before stopping.

The Benefits of Study Breaks

Study breaks help you study for a longer time, and you get more done

Psychologists have discovered that learning decreases if you do not take study breaks. Therefore, use the distributive learning procedures (described above) to study math.

If you have studied for only fifteen to twenty minutes and feel you are not retaining the information because your mind is wandering, take a break. If you continue to force yourself to study, you will not learn the material. After taking a break, return to studying.

If you still cannot study after taking a break, review your purpose for studying and your educational goals. Think about what is required to graduate. It will probably come down to the fact that you will have to pass math. Think about how studying math today will help you pass the next test; this will increase your chances of passing the course and of graduating.

Write on an index card three positive statements about yourself and three positive statements about studying. Look at this index card every time you have a study problem. Use every opportunity available to reinforce your study habits.

The Best Way to Use Your Math Lab or Learning Resource Center

Learning how to use your math lab or learning resource center (LRC) can improve your learning, and in turn, your grades. Many students are unaware of the tutorial and learning

*The math lab really helps
me with my math.*

resources offered at their college or university. Some students find out about these resources after they are failing, which in most cases is too late. You need to find the location of learning resources and how to utilize them as soon as possible after course registration.

Some colleges and universities have math labs, LRCs, Academic Enrichment Centers, computer labs, Student Support Services, Disabled Student Services or other specialized labs to help students. You should ask your instructor or counselor where to get help in math.

Do not forget to ask your fellow students for recommendations to get help in math. Sometimes the students know the best places to get the guidance you need.

1. *Videos* — Locate the videotapes that correspond to the section of the text you are learning. You may have to switch to different videotape resources based on the section of the text you are studying. Have the book open to the section of the text to be discussed on the video, and have paper and pencil ready to take notes. Use the fast forward button to bypass what you have mastered. When you reach the section that gives you difficulty, slow down and watch that section several times.

    ! **Remember:** Nobody cares how many times you rewind the tape. **!**

2. Computer Programs/CD-ROMs — Locate the computer program that best goes with your text. It may be the computer software offered by the textbook publisher or some commercially bought software. Ask if you can copy it and use it at another location or on your own computer.

    Review the other available software programs to find the one that fits your needs. The newer computer programs are more user friendly, but some of the older programs are more effective.

3. *Web Based Support Materials* — Most book companies have web supported materials to support student learning. These support areas could be an online tutor service, call-in tutor service, or extra homework problems and their solutions. Ask your instructor or lab supervisor about these support materials. If your text does not have these support materials, then you can go to the web and find them yourself. The main difference is that you may have to pay for the services.

4. *Supplemental Texts* — Most textbooks offer supplemental texts. The supplemental text may be a study guide or solutions manual. Review the supplemental text for intermediate steps needed to solve the homework problems. Make sure it explains how each step was obtained.

    You can check your homework, step-by-step, to find your errors. If you notice any step that you often miss, write it down and ask yourself if there is some concept involved that you do not understand. Talk to your instructor or tutor if the problem persists.

5. *Old Textbooks* — Math is a universal language, but different textbooks describe the same topic with different English. You may understand another text better than your

current text. Some textbook authors are better at explaining a topic than others. This is especially true if you are bilingual or raised in a different part of the country. If you can locate a math textbook on the same level and describing the same topic, it may be very helpful.

6. *Tutoring* — Most students believe that tutoring is the best learning resource. However, research has shown that the sessions are useless if the tutor is untrained. Try to work with a trained tutor who has had your course. Explain to the tutor your learning style and suggest that he/she tutor you based on your learning style.

Will it never end?

> **Example 1:** If you are an auditory learner, then have the tutor orally explain to you how to solve the problem. Then repeat back what the tutor said (in your own words). Use a tape recorder to tape the tutor's explanation so you can play it while doing your homework. Make sure the tutor does not just work the problem for you without explaining the reasons for each step.

Try not to schedule your tutoring sessions around lunch time since it is usually the busiest time of the day. Have your questions ready from your previous homework assignments. Focus on the concepts you do not understand, not just on how to work the problem. The more specific you are about your homework problems, the more tutorial help you will receive.

Do not expect miracles! If you tell your tutor, "I have a test in twenty minutes and do not understand anything about chapter six!" — about all the tutor can do is offer to pray for you. However, past experiences have shown that those who have previously helped themselves to tutoring are most likely to be rewarded with good grades.

> **Example 2:** If you are a visual learner, then have the tutors write down the steps to solve the problem. Also write down the reasons for each step or reference text pages for the reasons. If the tutor cannot write it down for you then write down the steps yourself and ask the tutor to review the steps.

❗ Remember: Make sure you get help early. It will be too late if you wait until you are failing a course to get help. ❗

Trained tutors can help your grades.

7. *Practice Tests* — Use practice tests to find out what you do not know before the real test. Ask if the math lab/LRC offers practice tests. Take these practice tests at least two days before the real test. This will give you at least one day to find out how to work the missed problems and another to review for the test.

   The more realistic practice tests you can take, the better you will do on the real test. Make sure the practice tests are timed and do not use any of your notes or the text.

8. *Assessment Instruments* — Assessment instruments can be used to place you into the correct course, locate your math weakness and help you understand your learning strengths and weaknesses. If you are not sure that you have been placed into the correct course, ask to take a placement test. Being placed into the correct course is *a must* to pass math. Ask if the lab has diagnostic math tests to locate your weaknesses. Ask about other assessment instruments, which can be used to help improve your learning.

9. *Other Helpful Items — Manipulatives, Models, Posters, Graphing Calculators.* If a picture is worth a thousand words, a model is worth a million for the kinesthetic/tactile learner.

   Ask for what may be called "manipulatives" or "3-D models." Manipulatives and models are concrete representations of a concept that you can physically touch. A good example of a manipulative is the Hands On Equation. The Hands on Equation uses a simulated balance beam with top like objects to represent variables and dice to represent numbers. Your math lab can order the Hands On Equations by going to www.Borenson.com. Some students have made their own manipulative by using magnetic plastic numbers and letters that are put on a metal board from child games. Students have also gone to sign shops and purchased the numbers and letters. The students can then set up an equation by using the manipulative and move the numbers and letters around to solve it. Students have also used the letters to represent rules such as the distributive property by manipulating them to understand the rule.

   > **Example:** On the board put down $a(b + c) =$. Then on the other side of the equation take additional letters and place them to represent $ab + ac$. Now you have $a(b + c) = ab + bc$. Now do the steps over again until your learn it. Then put numbers in to represent the letters. Such as $2(3 + 4) = (2)(3) + (2)(4)$. Now do the multiplication on each side of the equation and you will get $14 = 14$.

You can also use these manipulatives to understand more difficult mathematical problems. The calculator is another excellent learning tool for students beginning in pre-algebra and developmental algebra. Graphing calculators match the dynamic cognitive and the kinesthetic/ tactile (hands on) learning styles. Use the graphing calculator to see what happens when you add numbers to the equation. You can see the graph move and then understand the effects. This is an excellent way for trial-and-error learners (dynamic) to understand the equations. If you are in high-level courses, ask for connections intended for uploading graphing calculator programs from a computer. However, some colleges/universities would rather you learned developmental math without using a calculator.

Know how to use your calculator.

In general, learning math is a lot like learning to ride a bicycle. You can watch someone else do it, but you only learn by trying it yourself. You must believe in yourself and keep at it. Even if you start off wobbly, as long as you keep peddling, you are riding. But if you do not believe in yourself enough to keep peddling, you will fall. In time, you will be steady enough to take off the training wheels and wonder why you ever thought they were necessary. Even if you get rusty after a long absence, you will never again need training wheels.

Math is also something you learn by trying it yourself. Others can assist you with techniques, but you need to learn on your own. As long as you keep trying, you are learning to think mathematically, and you will be able to do it. In the future, even after a long time away from math, you will remember that you were able to master math before and with a little review you still can.

How to Enhance Collaborative Classroom Learning and Study Groups

Collaborative learning is a mode of learning that involves student participation in a small group to complete a desired task, assignment or project. In a math class, collaborative learning would be a small group of two to six students working together to solve math problems. Due to math reforms, math classes will now include more collaborative learning as a mode of instruction.

> **Example 1:** You develop a study group that is preparing for an upcoming test. Each group member makes up several sample test questions on note cards and the group discusses the answers.
>
> **Example 2:** You are in the math classroom and the class is divided into groups of four. Each group is assigned a different word problem to solve. The student recorder listens to the group discussing the problem and writes down the solution steps. Each group shares the solution with the other groups.

There are different types of collaborative learning exercises, which your instructor may use. Your instructor may combine traditional instruction and collaborative learning exercises. Collaborative learning has some benefits over traditional instruction.

The Benefits of Collaborative Learning

- Less fear of asking questions when compared to asking questions in the classroom.
- You may have a group learning style that enhances your learning.
- Sometimes an explanation of a concept or problem is more effective coming from a group member than from the instructor.
- Your instructor is free to walk around and individually help group members with difficult questions.

Groups can help you learn.

- The group can make up test questions and quiz each other.
- Learning groups can lead to after-class study groups.
- Collaborative learning prepares you for the business and industry work force. Experience with groups and team building is important to a prospective employer.

Being a good collaborative learner can be different from being a good individual learner. To benefit from collaborative learning, you may have to learn some new skills.

Characteristics of Good Group Members

- Completing any necessary preparation work prior to your group meeting. Little is accomplished in a group meeting if individual commitments are broken.
- Being supportive and acknowledging participation of fellow group members' ideas even if they are different from yours.
- Encouraging the group to stay on task. If discussion strays, lead the group back toward your team goal.
- Keeping a good balance between being an active participant and a good listener. Both of these characteristics are critical to a positive collaborative learning environment. Speak for yourself and let the others speak for themselves.
- Accepting help and suggestions from other members without feeling guilty.
- Accepting group members who try even if they cannot solve the problems.
- Bringing closure to a team session by summarizing the group's efforts. Reach consensus (everyone agrees) on any group decisions involving completion of your tasks.

Since this may be a new learning experience, some group members may not participate or may become disruptive. If a group member on your team is not participating or is being disruptive, follow the five steps below, in order.

SI can help improve your grades.

Supplemental Instruction

Supplemental Instruction (SI) is an academic support program in which a student who has already passed a particular course successfully attends the course of the same instructor the next semester. The SI leader models effective classroom learning and facilitates study groups for current students. In these study groups, students learn how to study for that class while learning the course work. The SI leader is trained in effective learning strategies and also knows what it takes to get a good grade in that course with that particular instructor.

Colleges and universities, in many countries, use Supplemental Instruction. If you have SI in your class, the SI leader will introduce himself or herself on the first day of class. Take advantage of this learning opportunity. If you do not have SI in your class, sometimes you can find a tutor who will work with a group from your class in a similar way.

How to Develop a Study Schedule

Before starting to develop a study schedule let's look at studying and learning effectiveness based on educational psychology. Educational psychologists have conducted research on studying and memory and found out the best time to study math is right after your math course. In fact they found out that you might lose up to 50% of the information learned in the math class by the next day. This means that the closer you can schedule doing your math homework, reviewing your math notes or reading the text after class, the easier you can learn your math. If possible when working out your schedule leave a one or two hour space right after your math class for studying. Better yet schedule

I really should study.

those times to go to the math lab or learning resource center to study and work with a tutor. If you have back-to-back classes, then schedule studying math as soon as possible after the last class. Even if your schedule has very few breaks, spend at least a few minutes reviewing your notes the same day. Remember, studying right after class is the best way to learn math.

Educational psychologists have also conducted research to see what you remember most clearly the next day after studying several subjects. The research indicates that the subject you studied last is what you remember best the next day. They also found out that if you study math and then watch a movie, the next day you will remember less about mathematics. In other words, seeing that movie will interfere with you remembering your math. This means that you may want to review your math before going to bed if you are going to have a test on it the next day.

Educational psychologists have also done research on your biological clock and how to develop habits. All of us have a biological clock that responds to the best and worst times to learn material. The first biological clock is based or late night people. This also applies to learning. Most of us learn best at different times of the day. If you are a morning person, then don't schedule your studying late at night. On the other hand, if you study best at night, then schedule your class late in the morning. Try to schedule your study times to match your daily biological clock. It will take about two weeks to develop this new schedule into a habit. Now let's look at how you can develop a study schedule while keeping these important points in mind.

There are two basic reasons for developing a study schedule: To schedule your study time and to become more efficient at studying.

You need to learn to set aside a certain amount of study time each week. You should emphasize the number of hours, *per week*, you are going to study instead of the number of *daily* study hours. How many hours do *you* study per week? Ten hours, 15 hours, 20 hours, 30 hours? Without knowing the amount of your study hours per week, you will not know if you are studying at a productive rate.

> **Example:** If your goal is to make a B average, and with studying 15 hours per week you make all B's on your tests, then the goal has been met. However, if you study 15 hours per week and make all D's, then you need to increase your study time and or your study methods. By monitoring your grades and the number of hours you study per week, you can adjust your study schedule to get the grades you want.

The second reason for developing a study schedule is to use time more efficiently. *Efficient* study means knowing *when* you are supposed to study and when you do *not* have to study. This approach will help keep you from thinking about other things you should be doing when you sit down to study. The reverse is also true. When doing other, more enjoyable things, you will not feel guilty about not studying.

> **Example:** You are at the mall on a Sunday afternoon, shopping for clothes, when you start feeling guilty. You have not started studying for that math test on Monday. If you had created a study schedule, you could have arranged to study for the math test on Saturday and still have been able to enjoy the mall on Sunday.

A study schedule should be set up for two reasons: To determine the amount of study time you need, per week, to get the grades you want and to set up peak efficient study times.

How to Prioritize Your Time

To develop a study schedule, turn to Figure 11 (Planning Use of Daily Time) on the next page and review it. Use "Planning Use of Daily Time" as your study schedule (feel free to make enlarged copies of Figure 11).

The best way to begin to develop your study schedule is to fill in all the times you *cannot* study. Do this by following the steps below:

Step 1   Fill in all your classes by putting code C (C = class) in the correct time spaces. For example, if you have an 8:00-9:30 class, draw a line through the center of the 9:00 a.m. box on the study schedule.

Step 2   Fill in the time you work with code W (W = work). This may be difficult, since some students' work schedules may change during the week. The best way to predict work time is to base it on the time you worked the previous week unless you are on a rotating shift. Indicate your approximate work times on the study schedule. As your work hours change, revise the study schedule.

! **Remember:** The study schedule is structured around the number of hours a **!** week you plan to study. Realize that while your work times might change every week, your *total* weekly work hours usually remain the same.

Step 3   Decide the amount of time it takes to eat (E = eat) breakfast, lunch and dinner; this time slot should include both food preparation and clean up. Keep in mind that the amount of time it takes to eat may fluctuate. Eating time also includes time spent in the student cafeteria. If you have an 11:00-12:00 or 1:00-2:00 lunch break, you might not eat during the entire time; you could be there both socializing and eating.

Still put code E in the study schedule, since the main use of your time is for eating.

Step 4　Include your grooming time (G = grooming). Some grooming activities include taking a bath, washing your hair or other activities that you do to get ready for school, dates or work. Grooming varies from minutes to hours per day for college students. Mark your study schedule with code G for the usual amount of time spent on grooming. Remember that more time might be spent on grooming during weekends.

Step 5　Include your tutor time (T = tutor). This is *not* considered study time. Tutor time is the time during which you ask the tutor questions about the previous homework assignment. If you have a tutor scheduled or meet weekly with your instructor, mark these times with code T in the study schedule.

Include time for your grooming.

Step 6　Reserve time for family responsibilities on the study schedule (F = family responsibilities). Some family responsibilities include taking your child on errands, mowing the lawn, grocery shopping and taking out the garbage. Also, if you have arranged to take your children some place every Saturday morning, then put it on the study schedule using code F.

Step 7　Figure out how much time is spent on cleaning each week (CN = cleaning). This time can include cleaning your room, house, car, and clothes. Cleaning time usually takes several hours a week. Indicate with code CN that you have cleaning time on the study schedule, and make sure it is adequate for the entire week.

Step 8　Review your sleep patterns for the week (SL = sleep). Your sleep time will probably be the same from Monday through Friday. On the weekend, you might sleep later during the day and stay up later at night. Be realistic when scheduling your sleep time. If you have been sleeping on Saturday mornings until 10:00 a.m. for the last two or three years, do not plan time at 8:00 a.m. to study.

Plan time to do your chores.

Step 9　Figure the amount of weekly social time (SC = social time). Social time includes being with other people, watching TV or going to church. It can be doing nothing at all or going out and having a good time. You need to have some social time during the week or you will burn out, and you will probably drop out of school. You may last only one semester. If you study and work too hard without some relaxation, you will not last the entire school year. Some daily social time is needed, but do not overdo it.

Step 10　Figure the amount of travel time to and from work (TR= travel time). Travel time could be driving to and from college or riding the subway. If possible, use travel

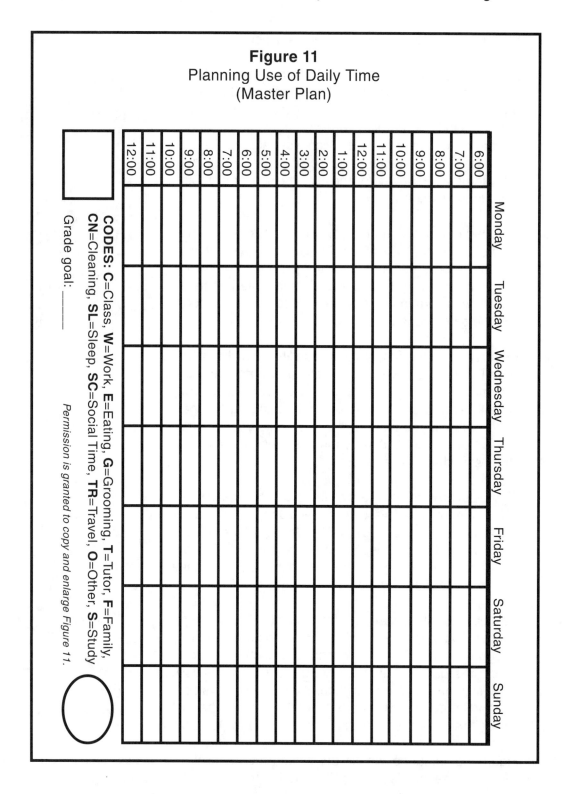

Figure 11
Planning Use of Daily Time
(Master Plan)

CODES: **C**=Class, **W**=Work, **E**=Eating, **G**=Grooming, **T**=Tutor, **F**=Family,
CN=Cleaning, **SL**=Sleep, **SC**=Social Time, **TR**=Travel, **O**=Other, **S**=Study

Grade goal: _____

Permission is granted to copy and enlarge Figure 11.

time to listen to audiotapes of your class or to review notes. Travel time may vary during different times of the year.

Step 11   Recall other time obligations that have not been previously mentioned (O = other). Other time obligations may be aspects of your life, which you do not want to share with other people. Review the study schedule for any other time obligations and mark them.

Now, count up all the blank spaces. Each blank space represents one hour.

Remember: You might have several half-blank spaces which each represent one-half hour. Add together the number of blank spaces left and write the total in the oval (lower right-hand corner of the study schedule).

Next, figure how many hours you have to study during the week. The rule of thumb is to study approximately two hours per week for each class hour. If you have 12 real class hours (not counting physical education) per week, you should be studying 20-24 hours per week to make A's and B's. Write the amount of time you *want* to study per week in the square, located in the lower left-hand corner of your study schedule. This is a study "contract" you are making with yourself.

If the number of contracted (square) study hours is less than the number in the oval, then fill in the times you want to study (S = study). First, fill in the best times to study. If there are any unmarked spaces, use them as backup study time. Now you have a schedule of the best times to study.

On the other hand, if you want to study 15 hours a week and have only 10 hours of space, then you have to make a decision. Go back over your study-schedule codes and locate where you can change some times. If you have a problem locating additional study time, make a priority time list. Take the hours away from the items with the least priority. Complete the study schedule by putting in your best study times.

How to Choose the Grade You Would Like to Make in Math

Determine what grade you want to make in the math course and write the grade on the study schedule. The grade should be an A, a B or a C. Do not write an N, W, X or F because these grades mean you will not successfully complete the course. Do not write D because you may not get credit for the course or be allowed to take the next course. In fact, it is not wise to write C, either, because most students who make a C usually fail the next math course. A grade of C is only for your last math class. Your selected grade is now your goal.

Some developmental math courses are graded on a pass-or-fail basis. Do not take the attitude that all you need to do is pass the course. A passing score for these courses translates into a C. This means that you have only an average foundation that might not be strong enough to pass the next math course in the sequence. Set your goals to make an average high enough that would be equal to an A or a B.

Currently, you have a study schedule representing the number of hours of study per week. You also have a course grade goal. After you have been in the course for several weeks and get back the results of your first tests, you will know if you are accomplishing your goal. Should you not meet your goal, improve the quality and quantity of your studying or lower your course grade goal.

Choosing a GPA (Grade Point Average) Goal for the Semester

After figuring out what grade you want in the math course, write down on your study schedule the grade point average you want for the semester. Do you want a 4.0 average, (all A's), a 3.0 average (all B's), a 2.5 average (B's and C's), or a 2.00 average (all C's)? Do not choose any average below 2.00; you will not graduate with a lower average. Be realistic when deciding upon an overall grade point average.

How to Create a Weekly Study Plan

Schedule study time to avoid getting frustrated.

By using the information from your completed copy of Figure 11 (Planning Use of Daily Time), you will know which time slots are available for study. You can use this information to both develop an effective study plan for the next week and establish weekly study goals.

Each Sunday, use an enlarged copy of Figure 12 (Weekly Study-Goal Sheet) on the next page to plan the best use for your study time during the next week. The first priority, when completing Figure 12, is to establish *the best time to study math*. Math should be studied as soon as possible after each class session. Therefore you should choose study times that are as close to class time as possible.

Be sure to indicate *where* you will study math. Are you going to the math lab to review videotapes or use the software, study in a group at someone's home or work with your tutor in your apartment?

Once you have indicated in the "Weekly Study-Goal Sheet" your math study times and locations, you may then fill in your study goals for your other subjects.

This plan becomes especially important and helpful during the weeks of midterm and final exams.

Example: You have determined from completing Figure 11 (Planning Use of Daily Time) that you have study time available from 3:00 until 6:00 on Monday, Tuesday, Wednesday and Thursday, and from 1:00 until 6 p.m. on Sunday. You will schedule your math study time before scheduling the study time of other classes.

If your math class is the last class of the day, you should schedule your math study time in the first study-time slot for that day. Therefore, you would choose to begin studying your daily math (what you learned that day) at 3:00 on Monday, Tuesday, Wednesday and Thursday. You will mark the box on the math line for Monday, Tuesday, Wednesday and Thursday with: 3 p.m., daily work, home.

Figure 12
Weekly Study-Goal Sheet

Subjects	Monday	Tuesday	Wednesday	Thursday	Friday	Saturday	Sunday
MATH							

Permission is granted to copy and enlarge Figure 12.

You have a math midterm exam on the following Monday, so you should schedule your Sunday math study time last. This way, it will be more "fresh" in your mind during the test on Monday. You have chosen to study for this test for two hours in the library with a group of other students.

You will mark the box on the math line for Sunday with: 4 p.m., midterm, library, group.

Now that your math study goals have been set, you may schedule the study time for your other subjects.

How to Manage Working and Studying

Work/study time management is crucial.

Most college students work and attend college at the same time. Some college students even try to be full-time students and employees. This can be dangerous because many full-time college students who attempt to work full time become dropouts. Students who work and attend college at the same time must manage their time very carefully and balance their work and study schedules. The suggestions below can help you best manage work and study.

Students can be successful in college while working; however, it takes effective time management along with excellent reading and study techniques. Make sure you are not setting yourself up to be successful at work while failing college. If necessary, drop to part-time work while in college and work overtime to obtain enough money to attend college. Also, it is better to "stop out" of college for a term and work instead of juggling both. This is especially true if your work is causing you to fail classes. However, you should only "stop out" for one semester because many students who stay out of college more than one semester usually don't come back.

Suggestions for Students Who Must Work

- Try to find a job that allows you some opportunity to study.
- Try to arrange to go to work right after class.
- Study as much as you can at school, then go to work. Do not go home first. Take work clothes with you to school if needed.
- Study during your lunch time or during breaks.

- Try to review your notes during work if the job allows.

- Record class lectures and play them during your travel to and from work.

- Take only 12 semester hours, which will qualify you as full time for financial aid but will not overburden your time.

- Take one easy course each semester.

- Do not wait until the weekend to do your homework.

- Increase your reading rate and become an efficient studier.

Summary

- A positive study environment can improve your math grades.

- Establishing several appropriate study places can increase your learning potential.

- Using distributive learning and studying new and old material at the appropriate times can improve your learning skills.

- Studying at the most efficient time, which is right after math class, can improve your learning.

- Being an effective collaborative learner will not only help you in math, it will help you in your future career.

- Learning how to use the math lab/LRC resources, which match your learning modality, enhances learning. Therefore, make sure you try each resource at least once to see how it helps you.

- Study skills and math lab/LRC resources can compensate for a mismatch of teaching and learning styles through tutoring.

- The main reason freshman students give for making poor grades is lack of study time.

- You have now completed a study schedule and a Weekly Study-Goal Sheet indicating both the times to study and the number of study hours per week.

- The number of study hours you contracted with yourself can change based on the grades you want.

- If you do not receive the grade you want in math, or your desired overall average during the semester, then increase the quality and quantity of study time.

- Taking control of your study time can greatly improve your grades.

- If you are working, have a family and are attending college full time, your time management is extremely important.

- Full time parents who are also students need to be creative in developing a workable study time.

Remember: Every little bit of studying helps.

Remember: The more you use the appropriate math lab/LRC resources, the better math grades you will make.

<u>Chapter 4 Notes</u>

Name: _____ Date: _____

<u>Assignment for Chapter 4</u>

1. List three ways to improve your study environment:

   Way one: _____

   _____

   Way two: _____

   _____

   Way three: _____

   _____

2. In what order do you need to study your courses? _____

   _____

   _____

   _____

3. When should you learn new material? _____

   _____

   _____

4. What should you do when you cannot study? _____

   _____

   _____

5. What are your best math lab/LRC resources? _____

   _____

   _____

   _____

6. What is the main reason freshman college students give for making poor grades?

_____

_____

_____

7. When is the best time to study math?

_____

_____

8. What are two reasons for developing a study schedule?

Reason one: _____

_____

Reason two: _____

_____

9. Complete Figure 11 (Planning Use of Daily Time), select your math course grade, select your overall GPA for the semester and complete Figure 12 (Weekly Study-Goal Sheet).

10. List five creative ways to study.

Way one: _____

_____

Way two: _____

_____

Way three: _____

_____

Way four: _____

_____

Way five: _____

_____

Understanding and Improving the Memory Process

5

In Chapter 5
you will learn these concepts:

- To improve learning, students must improve the memory process by understanding the following concepts
    - ✓ Information must be processed through each stage of memory: sensory input, sensory register, short-term memory, working memory, abstract reasoning, long-term memory, and memory output.
- Learning styles and modalities are particular ways that students best move information through the memory process.
    - ✓ Modalities include visual, auditory and kinesthetic ways of putting information into the brain.
    - ✓ This chapter explores the learning styles that focus on whether individuals learn best alone or with others.
- Based on learning styles and modalities, students can design a system of strategies that help improve their learning experiences.

Introduction

To understand the learning process, you must understand how memory works. You learn by conditioning and thinking, but memorization is different from learning. For memorization, the brain must perform several tasks including receiving, storing and recalling the information.

By understanding how memory works, you will be able to learn at which point your memory is failing you. Most students usually experience memory trouble between the time the brain receives the information and the time it is stored. There are many techniques for learning information that can help you receive and store information without losing it in the process. Some of these techniques may be more successful than others, based on your skills and how you best learn.

How You Learn

Educators tell us that learning is the process of "achieving competency." More simply put, it is how you become good at something. The three ways of learning are by conditioning, thinking and a combination of conditioning and thinking.

Learning by Conditioning and Thinking

Conditioning is learning things with a maximum of physical and emotional reaction and a minimum of thinking.

> **Example:** Repeating the word "pi" to yourself and practicing where the symbol is found on a calculator are two forms of conditioned learning. You are learning, using your voice and your eye-hand coordination (physical activities), and you are doing very little thinking.

Thinking is defined as learning with a maximum of thought and a minimum of emotional and physical reaction.

> **Example:** Learning about "pi" by thinking is different than learning about it by conditioning. To learn "pi" by thinking, you would have to do the calculations necessary to result in the numeric value which the word "pi" represents. You are learning, *using your mind* (thought activities), and you are using very little emotional or physical energy to learn "pi" in this way.

The most successful way to combine thinking and conditioning is to learn by thinking first and conditioning second. Learning by thinking means that you learn by

- *Observing*,
- *Processing*, and
- *Understanding* the information.

How Memory Works

Memory is an important part of learning

Memory is different from learning; it requires reception, storage and retrieval of information. This memory process is still being explored, but the presented model will best represent how students learn mathematics. The memory process starts with the sensory input, proceeds through the sensory register into short-term memory, and then into working memory where it goes directly into long-term memory, abstract reasoning or memory output (see Figure 13, Stages of Memory). Information can also go through long-term memory and/or abstract reasoning and then into memory output. The double arrows in Figure 13 illustrate how working memory can go both ways.

The *reception* of information is through the sensory input. The *storage* is through the sensory register, short-term memory, working memory, long-term memory and abstract reasoning. The retrieval of this information is usually through doing homework and taking tests. It is important to understand that information can be lost through each stage.

Understanding the Stages of Memory

Memory requires receiving, retaining and recalling information. As we discuss each stage of memory try to locate memory strengths and where your memory may be breaking down. Understanding how the stages of memory affect your learning can be an important tool to improving your learning and making better math grades.

How Sensory Input Affects What You Remember

Learning to focus improves sensory input and sensory register

The way you receive information is accomplished through your five senses (known as the sensory input): what you see, feel, hear, smell and taste.

Examples: In math classes, you will use your sense of *vision* to both watch the instructor demonstrate problems on the chalkboard and to read printed materials. You will use your sense of *hearing* to listen to the instructor and other students discuss the problems. Your sense of *touch* will be used to operate your calculator and to appreciate geometric shapes. In chemistry and other classes, however, you may additionally use your senses of *smell* and *taste* to identify substances.

How Sensory Register Affects What You Remember

The sensory register briefly holds an exact image or sound of each sensory experience until it can be processed. If the information is not processed immediately, it is forgotten. The sensory register helps us go from one situation to the next without cluttering up our minds with trivial information. Processing the information involves placing it into short-term memory. Students who don't attend class do not ever reach this stage of memory and lose valuable information.

If students have visual or auditory impairments, then information must be processed differently or through another sense. For example, deaf students may need interpreters or real time captioning while visually impaired students may need large print, books on tape, tape recorded lectures or Braille texts.

How Short-Term Memory Affects What You Remember

Information that passes through the sensory register is stored in short-term memory. Short-term memory can be in the form of visual information or auditory information. Remembering something for a short time is not hard to do for most students. By conscious effort, you can remember math laws, facts and formulas received by the sensory register (your five senses) and put them in short-term memory. You can recognize them and register them in your mind as something to remember for a short time.

Example: When you are studying math, you can tell yourself the distributive property is illustrated by $a(b+c)=ab+ac$. By deliberately telling yourself to remember that fact (by using conditioning — repeating or writing it again and again), you can remember it, at least for a while, because you have put it in short-term memory.

Taking notes requires good short-term memory skills

Psychologists have found that short-term memory cannot hold an unlimited amount of information. You may be able to use short-term memory to remember one phone number or a few formulas but not five phone numbers or ten formulas. Items placed into short-term memory usually fade fast, as the name suggests.

Figure 13
Stages of Memory

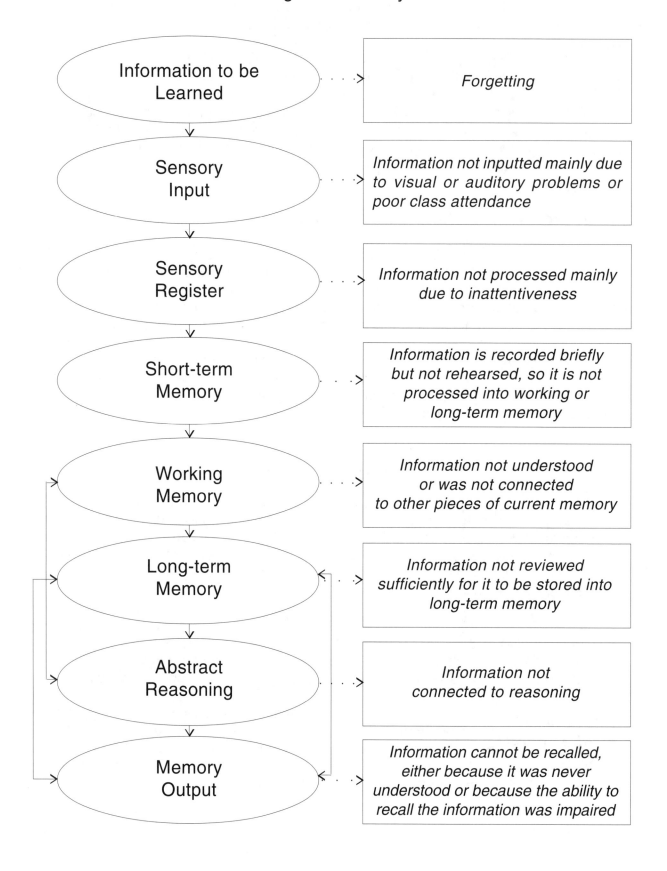

Examples: Looking up a telephone number in the directory, remembering it long enough to dial, then forgetting it immediately. Learning the name of a person at a large party or in a class but forgetting it completely within a few seconds. Cramming for a test and forgetting most of it before taking the test.

In many math classes, information is processed so quickly that no time is allowed for practicing and understanding the math. Instructors are required to cover an immense amount of information and students are lucky if they capture all of it and understand it for a brief moment. The memory process, for the most part, stops at short term in the classroom. That's why students need to have good note-taking skills to record the information, so it can be reviewed later on for better understanding.

How Working Memory Affects What You Remember

Working memory (or long-term retrieval) is that process in the brain that works on problems for a longer period of time than short-term memory. Working memory, then, offers an increase in the amount of *time* information is held in memory. (An increase in the *volume* of information that can be held requires long-term memory.)

Working memory is like the amount of RAM in a computer. Working memory uses the information (such as multiplication tables) recalled from long-term memory, along with new information to learn new concepts. It is the ability to think about and use many pieces of infor-

Using working memory leads to long-term memory.

mation at the same time. For instance, when you solve a linear equation you must use all the math that you learned in elementary school like addition, subtraction, and multiplication. You then have to add this to the new rules for linear equations.

Working memory can be compared to a mental workspace or an internal chalkboard. Just like a chalkboard, working memory has limited space, which can cause a "bottleneck" in learning. It involves the ability to recall information after learning has been consistently interrupted over a period of several minutes. Students with working memory problems may listen to a math lecture and understand each step as it is explained. When the instructor goes back to a previous step discussed several minutes prior, however, the student has difficulty explaining or remembering the reasons for the steps. These students have difficulty remembering series of steps long enough to understand the concept.

Overlearning math facts by storing them in long-term memory can free up working memory to solve problems. Studying every night helps put information into long term memory which makes it easier when it is time to use working memory to learn new information.

Working memory can go both ways in the memory process. First, it can go into long-term memory and abstract reasoning. Second, working memory can bring information out from

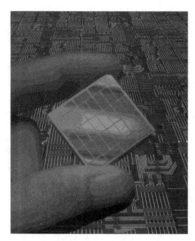

Working memory is like RAM in computers.

long-term memory and abstract memory to use in learning new concepts. When learning a mathematical concept, working memory goes into abstract memory. When learning just facts such as the multiplication tables or definition of words, information goes directly into long-term memory. When solving math problems, in most cases, information is brought in from abstract reasoning and long-term memory into working memory. Students use their working memory to do their homework and when answering test questions. The amount of space in working memory is critical to answering test questions just like the amount of RAM is critical to running computer programs.

Recent research has indicated that working memory is affected by test anxiety. Many students who have test anxiety indicate that during tests they recognize the problem but cannot remember how to work the problem. The problem is that the anxiety is taking up working memory space, leaving less working memory to be used to solve the problems. When the anxiety level goes down, such as right after the test is over, some students remember how to solve the problems because their working memory is freed up. It is the " I knew I knew it" syndrome.

Anxiety slows down working memory when you take a test

> **Example:** In calculating 26 x 32, you would put the intermediate products 52 (*from 2 x 26*) and 780 (*from 30 x 26* — remember 3 is in the 10's place, so make it 30) into working memory and add them together. The more automatic the multiplication, the less working memory you use. If you cannot remember your multiplication, you use up working memory trying to solve the multiplication problem. This leaves you with less working memory to calculate the resulting addition problem.

How Long-Term Memory Affects What You Remember

Information must be reviewed many times to remember it in the long term

Long-term memory is a storehouse of material that is retained for long periods of time. Working memory places information in long-term memory and long-term memory is recalled into working memory to solve problems. It is *not* a matter of trying harder and harder to remember more and more unrelated facts or ideas; it is a matter of organizing your short-term memories and working memories into meaningful information.

In most cases long-term memory is immeasurable. Students have so much room in their long-term memory that no one has measured its total capacity. Long-term memory also relates more to language skills rather than abstract skills. Students with good long-term memory and poor abstract skills can sometimes do well in every subject except math and the physical sciences. These students can use their long-term memory language skills by learning the vocabulary. By understanding the language of mathematics they can put into words how to solve math problems and recall these words during the test instead of depending mainly on their abstract memory. This information must be reviewed many times for it to get into long-term memory. This concept will be explored more in later chapters.

How Reasoning Affects What You Remember

Reasoning or abstract memory is thinking about memories, comprehending their meanings and understanding their concepts. Abstract reasoning involves learning how the rules and laws apply to solving math problems. Students who understand the principals of a certain mathematical concept can use these principles to solve any similar problem. That is why the focus in mathematics is learning how to solve the problem based on concepts instead of just memorizing how to do a problem. In most cases you cannot memorize enough problems and hope they appear on the test. Without understanding the concept, the information cannot be transferred into abstract reasoning. Many students with excellent abstract reasoning major in math related careers.

The main problem most students face is converting information from working memory to long-term and/or abstract reasoning – and understanding it. To place information into long-term memory students must understand math vocabulary and practice problems. To place information into abstract reasoning students must understand the concept and remember it. In most cases student must use part of the long-term memory and abstract reasoning to solve math problems. It will depend on the skills in each area as to which one they use the best to solve math problems.

! **Remember:** Securing math information into abstract reasoning is not accomplished by just doing the homework — you must also understand it. **!**

The Role of "Memory Output" in Testing

Improving memory output allows you to show what you really know

Memory output is what educators call a "retrieving process." It is necessary for verbal or written examinations. The retrieving process is used when answering questions in class, doing math homework or doing math tests. It is the method by which you recall information stored into long-term memory and by using abstract reasoning are able to place it into words or on paper. This retrieval process can come directly from long-term memory. For example, "What are whole numbers?" This is a fact question that comes from long-term memory. The retrieval process can also come from abstract reasoning. For example, "Write down the distributive property and substitute numbers to prove that it works." However, most math problems are solved through working memory by using information from both long-term memory and abstract reasoning. For example, solve: $3y -10 = 9y + 21$. For this problem you are pulling in your number facts from long-term memory and the rules for solving equations from abstract reasoning.

Three things can block memory output:

1. *Insufficient processing* of information into long-term memory or reasoning,

2. *Test anxiety*, or

3. *Poor test-taking skills*.

If you did not completely place all of the information you learned into long-term memory and abstract reasoning, you may not be able to give complete answers on tests.

Test anxiety can decrease your ability to recall important information, or it can cause you to block out information totally. During exams test anxiety mainly affects working memory by decreasing how much information it can process at one time. Ways to decrease test anxiety were discussed in Chapter 3 (How to Reduce Math Anxiety and Math Test Anxiety). Students who work on their test-taking skills can improve their memory output. Techniques to improve both your memory output and test-taking skills will be explained in the chapter on test-taking.

Assessing your Memory Strengths and Weakness

Understanding the stages of memory will help you answer this common question about learning math: "Why do I understand the procedures to solve a math problem one day and forget how to solve a similar problem two days later?"

There are three good answers to this question. First, after initially learning how to solve the problem, you did not *rehearse* the solving process enough for it to enter your long-term memory. Second, you did get the information into long-term memory, but the information was not *reviewed* frequently enough and was forgotten. Third, you memorized how to work the problem but did not *understand* the concept.

There are other areas where your memory process can break down. Your memory could have a partial or full break down in several areas. The following are some common problems students may have in learning, followed by what stages of memory each problem affects:

Learning Problems	Stages of Memory Affected
Having a visual or hearing impairment Dyslexia	*Sensory Input*
Being in a noisy classroom Sitting in the back of the room Being distracted Not knowing what information is important	*Sensory Register*
Being a poor note-taker Not being able to write down the steps of problems	*Short-Term Memory*
Not doing homework problems Having a poor homework system Not reading the text	*Working Memory*
Not reviewing your homework problems Not reviewing your notes Not knowing the meaning to math vocabulary	*Long-Term Memory*
Not understanding properties, rules and key concepts Not applying the properties, rules and key concepts Not understanding how to work the formulas	*Abstract Reasoning*
Breakdown in one or more stages of memory Inadequate test-taking skills Test anxiety	*Memory Output*

Now that you have a better understanding of the stages of memory do a self-assessment to discover where your memory strengths are, and which memory areas need to be improved. Use the stages of memory in Figure 13 and write in each stage if it is strong (S), average (A) or weak (W). What weak area(s) did you have in the Stages of Memory and how can you improve them?

_____

_____

_____

In what area(s) are you average, according to the Stages of Memory, and how can you improve them?

_____

_____

_____

What were your strong areas in the Stages of Memory about which you can be proud?

_____

_____

_____

As you read the rest of this book look for behaviors that will improve your "A's" and "W's" and congratulate yourself for your "S's."

How to Use Your Learning Styles to Improve Memory

Learning styles are the different ways people learn and move through the learning process

There are many different technique which can help you store information in your long-term memory and reasoning. Using your learning sense or learning style and decreasing distraction while studying are very efficient ways to learn. Using your best *learning sense* (what educators call your "predominate learning modality") can improve how well you learn and enhance the transfer of knowledge into long-term memory/ reasoning. Your learning senses are vision, hearing, touching, etc. Ask yourself if you learn best by watching (vision), listening (hearing), or touching (feeling).

Another helpful tool is the Learning Styles Inventory. It is the only inventory that has separate math learning style information. You can go to www.AcademicSuccess.com to learn more about the Learning Styles Inventory. You can also use the results from the Learning Modality Inventory for Math Students (Appendix C). Based on your preferred learning style practice those learning suggestions first.

Remember: Learning styles are neither good nor bad and are based on genetics and environment. Knowing your best learning styles and using them effectively can dramatically improve your math learning and grades.

Visual (watching) Learner

Visual learners learn best by seeing math

Knowing that you are a visual math learner can help you select the memory technique that will work best for you. Repeatedly reading and writing down math materials being studied is the best way for a visual learner to study.

Based on the Learning Styles Inventory students who learn math best by seeing it written are Visual Numerical Learners. If you are a visual numerical learner you will learn best by following the 12 suggestions in Figure 14 on the next page. Try as many of these suggestions as possible and then select and practice those that are most helpful.

A visual way to decrease distractions is by using the "my mind is full" concept. Imagine that your mind is completely filled with thoughts of learning math, and other distracting thoughts cannot enter. Your mind has one-way input and output, which only responds to thinking about math when you are doing homework or studying.

Auditory (hearing) Learner

Auditory learners learn best by hearing information

If you are an *auditory learner* (one who learns best by hearing the information) then learning formulas is best accomplished by repeating them back to yourself, or recording them on a tape recorder and listening to them. Reading out loud is one of the best auditory ways to get important information into long-term memory. Stating facts and ideas out loud improves your ability to think and remember. If you cannot recite out loud, recite the material to yourself, emphasizing the key words.

Based on the Learning Styles Inventory students who learn math best by hearing it are Auditory Numerical Learners. If you are an auditory numerical learner you will learn best by following the 12 suggestions in Figure 15. Try as many of these suggestions as possible and then select and practice those that are most helpful.

An auditory way to improve your concentration is by becoming aware of your distractions and telling yourself to concentrate. If you are in a location where talking out loud will cause a disturbance, mouth the words "start concentrating" as you say them in your mind. Your concentration periods should increase.

Figure 14 — Visual Numerical Learners

These students learn math best by seeing it written. If you are a visual numerical learner, you may learn best by following these suggestions:

1. Use worksheets, workbooks, handouts, additional math texts and any other additional written materials

2. Play games with, and get involved in activities with, visual printed materials such as multiplication or algebra flash cards.

3. Use visually orientated computer programs, CD's, DVD's, homework programs and math websites like those mentioned in this text.

4. Check out videocassette tapes from the math lab or learning resource center.

5. Rework your notes using the suggestions in this text.

6. Make "3 x 5" note or flash cards putting the variables and numbers in different colors.

7. Use Study Stacks to develop your own virtual flash cards or use the virtual flash cards already developed (www. academicsucess.com – Student Math Practice and Learning Sites)

8. Use video websites from your text or www.academicsuccess.com – Student Math Practice and Learning Sites.

9. Use different colors of ink to emphasize different parts of each math formula.

10. Visualize numbers and formulas in detail.

11. Ask your tutor to *show* you how to do the problems instead of *telling* you how to do the problems.

12. Write down each problem step the tutor tells you to. Highlight the important steps or concepts that cause you difficulty.

Figure 15 — Auditory Numerical Learners

If you are an auditory numerical learner, you may learn best by following these suggestions:

1. Say the numbers to yourself or move your lips as you read the problems.

2. Record your class and play it back while reading your notes.

3. Read aloud any written explanations.

4. Make sure all important facts are spoken aloud with auditory repetition.

5. Read math problems aloud and try solutions verbally as you talk yourself through the problems.

6. Record directions to difficult math problems and refer to them when solving those specific types of problems.

7. Record math laws and rules in your own words, by chapters, and listen to them every other day (auditory highlighting).

8. Have the tutor explain how to work problems instead of just showing you how to solve them.

9. Explain to the tutor how to work the math problems.

10. Explain to group members how to solve math problems.

11. During the test, sub-vocally talk yourself through the problems.

12. Take the test in a private room and talk to yourself out loud to solve the problem.

Tactile/Concrete (touching) Learner

Tactile/ concrete learners need to feel and touch the material to learn

A tactile/concrete (kinesthetic) learner needs to feel and touch the material to learn it. Tactile concrete learners, who are also called *kinesthetic* learners, tend to learn best when they can concretely manipulate the information to be learned. Unfortunately, most math instructors do not use this learning sense. As a result, students who depend heavily upon feeling and touching for learning will usually have the most difficulty developing effective math learning techniques. This learning style creates a problem with math learning because math is more abstract than concrete. Also, most math instructors are visual abstract learners and have difficulty teaching math tactilely. Ask for the math instructors and tutors who give the most practical examples and who may even "act out" the math problems.

As mentioned before a tactile concrete learner will probably learn most efficiently by hands-on learning. For example, if you want to learn the FOIL method, you would take your fingers and trace the "face" to remember the steps. See Figure 16 (The FOIL Method). Also, learning is most effective when physical involvement with manipulation is combined with sight and sound. For example, as you trace the face you also say the words out loud.

Based on the Learning Styles Inventory, Tactile Concrete Learners best learn math by manipulating the information that is to be taught. If you are a tactile concrete learner, you may learn best by following the 12 suggestions in Figure 17, on the next page. Try as many of these suggestions as possible and then select and practice the best suggestions that help. If you do not have these manipulatives or don't know how to use them, ask the math lab supervisor or instructor if they have any manipulative materials or models. If the math lab does not have any manipulative materials, you may have to ask for help to develop your own.

Tactile/concrete learners can also use graphing calculators to improve their learning. By entering the keystrokes it is easier to remember how to solve the problems. This practice is also an excellent way to remember how to solve the problem when using a calculator while taking a test.

Another way tactile/concrete learners can learn is to trace the graph with their fingers when it appears on the calculator. They should say out loud and trace every equation to "feel" how the graph changes when using different equations. For example, if you add 2 to one side of the equation, move your finger to where the graph changes and say out loud how much it moved.

A tactile/concrete way to improve your study concentration is by counting the number of distractions for each

---

Figure 16
The FOIL Method

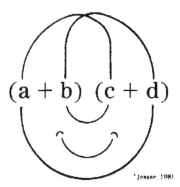

F (a) (c)
O (a) (d)
I (b) (c)
L (b) (d)

(a + b) (c + d)

Jensen, 1985

FOIL is used to remember the procedure to multiply two binomials. The letters in FOIL stand for First, Outside, Inside and Last. To use FOIL, multiply the following

- the First terms ((a) (c)),
- the Outside terms ((a) (d)),
- the Inside terms ((b) (c)),
- the Last terms ((b) (d)).

To learn FOIL, trace your finger along the FOIL route.

study session. Place a sheet of paper by your book when doing homework. When you catch yourself not concentrating put the letter "C" on the sheet of paper. This will remind you to concentrate and get back to work. After each study period, count up the number of "C's" and watch the number decrease.

Figure 17 — Tactile Concrete Learners

These students learn math best by hands on learning. If you are a tactile concrete learner, then you may learn best by following these suggestions:

1. Cut up a paper plate to represent a fraction of a whole.

2. Fold up a piece of paper several times and cut along the fold marks to represent a fraction of a whole.

3. In order to understand math concepts, ask to be shown how to use Cuesinaire rods or algebra tiles as manipulatives.

4. Try to use your hands and body to "act out" a solution. For example, you may "become" the car in a rate-and-distance word problem.

5. Obtain diagrams, objects or manipulatives and incorporate activities such as drawing and writing into your study time. You may also enhance your learning by doing some type of physical activity such as walking.

6. Try to get involved with at least one other student, tutor or instructor that uses manipulatives to help you learn math.

7. Ask to use the Hands-on Equations Learning System using manipulatives to learn basic algebra. You can go to their Web site (www.Borenson.com) to learn more about this system and other systems to help you learn math.

8. Go to one of the "learning stores," usually in your local mall, to see if they have manipulatives.

9. Go to a K–12 learning resource store to see if they have manipulatives, such as magnetic boards, that you can put letters and numbers on and move around.

10. Talk to the coordinator of students with disabilities to see if they use manipulatives when tutoring their students with learning disabilities.

11. Tear up a piece of paper into several pieces and put an x on some of the pieces. Mark the other pieces with numbers 0 to 9. The pieces with the x can represent the variable and the other pieces can represent the numbers. You can now use the pieces of paper to set up and solve equations.

12. Use the virtual manipulative websites at www.academicsuccess.com — Student Resource website or Google "college math manipulative".

Social Individual Learner

If you are a social individual learner, learning math may best be done individually. You may learn best by yourself, working with computer programs and being individually tutored. In some cases, social individuals may have to meet in groups to develop practice tests but leave socializing to a minimum. If you are a social individual learner and visual learner, using the computer may be one of the best learning tools available. If you are a social individual learner based on the Learning Styles Inventory you may learn best by following the 10 suggestions in Figure 18, on the

I am happy learning by myself.

next page. Try as many of these suggestions as possible and then select those that are most helpful.

A problem that a social individual learner may encounter is working too long on a problem for which they could have received help. Social individual learners must understand that getting help is okay, especially if it saves study time and makes them more study efficient.

Social Group Learners

If you are a social group learner (one who best learns in a group) then learning math may best be done in study groups and in math classes that have collaborative learning (group learning). Social group learners may learn best by discussing information. They can usually develop their own study groups and discuss how to solve problems over the phone. If you are a social group learner and an auditory learner then you definitely learn best by talking to people. If you are a social group learner based on the Learning Styles Inventory you may learn best by following the 10 suggestions in Figure 19, on the next page. Try as many of these suggestions as possible and then select and practice those that are most helpful.

A learning problem that a social group learner may have is talking too much about other subjects when in a study group. This is called being off task. You may want to have a student serve as a discussion monitor to let the students know when they need to get back on task. Also, social group learners need to know that they still must study math individually to be successful. During this individual study session prepare questions for the group.

Some students learn better in groups.

Multiple Senses

If you have difficulty learning material from one sense (learning style), you might want to try learning material through two or three senses. Involving two or more senses in learning improves your learning and remembering. Review the figures in this section on using your learning styles and whenever possible combine the learning styles.

If your primary sense is visual and your secondary sense is auditory, you may want to write down equations while saying them out loud to yourself. Writing and reciting the material at the same time combines visual, auditory, and some tactile/concrete styles of learning.

Using two or three senses improves learning

Studying with a pen or highlighter is a visual as well as a tactile/concrete way to improve your concentration. Placing the pen or highlighter in your hand and using it will force you to concentrate more on what you are reading. After you write and recite the material back to yourself, do it five or ten more times to over learn it.

Figure 18

Social Individual Learners

These students learn math best individually. If you are a social individual learner, you may learn best by following these suggestions:

1. Study math, English or other subjects alone.
2. Utilize videocassette tapes or auditory tapes to learn by yourself.
3. Prepare individual questions for your tutor or instructor.
4. Obtain individual help from the math lab or hire your own tutor.
5. Set up a study schedule and study area so other people will not bother you.
6. Study in the library or in some other private, quiet place.
7. Use group study times only as a way to ask questions, obtain information and take pretests on your subject material.
8. Use math learning websites such as the ones at www.academicsuccess.com — Student Math Practice and Learning Sites.
9. Use the math homework sites listed in your text.
10. Set up virtual tutoring as needed.

Figure 19

Social Group Learners

These students best learn math in groups. If you are a social group learner, you may learn best by following these suggestions:

1. Study math, English or your other subjects in a study group.
2. Sign up for math course sections which use cooperative learning (learning in small groups).
3. Review your notes with someone in a group.
4. Obtain help in the math lab or other labs where you can work in group situations.
5. Watch math videocassette tapes with a group and discuss the subject matter.
6. Listen to audiocassette tapes on the lecture and discuss them with the group.
7. Obtain several "study buddies" so you can discuss with them the steps to solving math problems.
8. Form a study group. Each member should bring ten test questions with explanations on the back of the page. The group should complete all the test questions and share the answers.
9. Arrange a meeting with your instructor and several other students to go over math problems.
10. Develop an online chat group to help each other solve math problems.

Students who want to use the information from the Learning Styles Inventory to determine how to study other subjects besides math can refer to the Winning at Math Student Resource Website.

How to Use Memory Techniques

There are many different techniques which can help you store information in your long-term memory. Having a positive attitude about studying, being a selective learner, being organized, using visual imagery, using mnemonic devices and acronyms are techniques that can improve your long-term memory and reasoning.

A Good Study/Math Attitude

Having a positive attitude about studying will help you concentrate and improve your retention. This means you need to have at least a neutral math attitude (you neither like nor dislike it), and you should reserve the right to actually learn to *like* math. View studying as an opportunity to learn rather than as an unpleasant task. Tell yourself that you *can* learn the material and that *learning it will help you pass the course and graduate*.

Be a Selective Learner

Being selective in your math learning will improve your memory. Prioritize the materials you are studying. Decide which facts you need to know and which ones you can ignore. Narrow down information into laws and principles that can be generalized. Learn the laws and principles 100 percent. Also, you must learn the math vocabulary in each chapter to continue to understand the instructor and math material.

> **Example:** If you have been given a list of math principles and laws to learn for a test, put each one on an index card. As you go through them, create two piles: an "I already know this" pile and an "I don't know this" pile. Then, study *only* the "I don't know this" pile until it is completely memorized and understood.

Become an Organizer

Organizing your math material into idea/fact clusters will help you learn and memorize it. Grouping similar material in a problem log or calculator log are examples of categorizing information. Do not learn isolated facts; always try to connect them to other similar material.

Use Visual Imagery

Using mental pictures or diagrams to help you learn is especially helpful for visual learners and those who are right-hemisphere dominant (who tend to learn best by visual and spatial methods). Mental pictures and actual diagrams involve 100 percent of your brainpower. Picture the steps to solve difficult math problems in your mind.

> **Example:** Use the Foil Method (see Figure 16) to visually learn how to multiply binomials. Memorize the face until you can sketch it from memory. If you need to use it during a test, you can then sketch the face onto your scratch paper and refer to it.

Make Associations

Association learning can help you remember better. Find a link between new facts and some well-established old facts and study them together. The recalling of old facts will help you remember the new ones and strengthen a mental connection between the two. Make up your own associations to remember math properties and laws.

❗ Remember: The more ridiculous the association, the more likely you are to ❗ remember it.

> **Examples:** When learning the *commutative property*, remember that the word "commutative" sounds like the word "community." A community is made up of different types of people who could be labeled as an "a" group and a "b" group. However, in a community of "a" people and "b" people, it does not matter if we count the "a" people first or the "b" people first; we still have the same total number of people in the community. Thus, a+b=b+a.
>
> When learning the *distributive law of multiplication over addition,* such as a(b+c), remember that "distributive" sounds like "distributor," which is associated with giving out a product. The distributor "a" is giving its products to "b" and "c."

Use Mnemonic Devices

The use of mnemonic devices is another way to help you remember. Mnemonic devices are easily remembered words, phrases or rhymes associated with difficult-to-remember principles or facts.

> **Example:** Many students become confused when using the *Order of Operations.* These students mix up the order of the steps in solving a problem, such as dividing instead of first adding the numbers in the parentheses. A mnemonic device to remember the *Order of Operations* is "Please Excuse My Dear Aunt Sally." The first letter in each of the words represents the math function to be completed from the first to the last. Thus, the *Order of Operations* is **P**arentheses (*Please*), **E**xponents (*Excuse*), **M**ultiplication (*My*), **D**ivision (*Dear*), **A**ddition (*Aunt*), and **S**ubtraction (*Sally*). Remember to multiply and/or divide whatever comes first, from left to right. Also, add or subtract whatever comes first, from left to right.

Using mnemonic devices can improve a student's mathematics learning. Students making up their own mnemonic devices can remember them better than the ones given to them. Try to make up your own mnemonic device, but if you have difficulty, use the mathematic mnemonic devices on the Winning at Math Student Resource website.

Use Acronyms

Acronyms are another memory device to help you learn math. Acronyms are word forms created from the first letters of a series of words.

> **Example:** FOIL is a common math acronym. FOIL is used to remember the procedure to multiply two binomials. Each letter in the word FOIL represents a math operation. **FOIL** stands for **F**irst, **O**utside, **I**nside and **L**ast, as it applies to multiplying two binomials such as $(2x+3)(x+7)$. The **F**irst product is $2x$ (in the first expression) and x (in the second expression). The **O**utside product is $2x$ (in the first expression) and 7 (in the second expression). The **I**nside product is 3 (in the first expression) and x (in the second expression). The **L**ast product is 3 (in the first expression) and 7 (in the second expression). This results in **F** $((2x)(x))$ + **O** $((2x)(7))$ + **I** $((3)(x))$ + **L** $((3)(7))$. Do the multiplication to get $2x^2 + 14x + 3x + 21$, which adds up to $2x^2 + 17x + 21$. See Figure 16 (The FOIL Method).

Using acronyms can improve a student's mathematics learning. Making up your own acronym devices is the best way to remember them. If you are having difficulty making up acronyms then use the Winning at Math Student Resource website.

How to Develop Practice Tests

Developing a practice test is one of the best ways to evaluate your memory and math skills before taking the real test. You want to find out what you do not know *before* the real test instead of *during* the test. Practice tests should be as real as possible and should include the use of time constraints.

You can create a practice test by reworking all the problems that you have recorded in your problem log. Another practice test can be developed using every other problem in the textbook chapter tests. Further, you can use the solutions manual to generate other problems with which to test yourself. You can also use old exams from the previous semester. Check to see if the math lab/LRC has tests on file from previous semesters, or ask your instructor for other tests. For some students, the group method is a better way to prepare for a test.

If group work improves your learning, you may want to hold a study group session at least once a week. Make sure the individual or group test is completed at least three days before the real test.

Completing practice math tests will help you increase testing skills. It will also reveal your test problem weaknesses in enough time for you to learn how to solve the problem before the real test. If you have difficulty with any of the problems during class or after taking the practice test, be sure to see your tutor or instructor.

After taking the practice test(s), you should know what parts you do not understand (and need to study) and what is likely to be on the test. Put this valuable information on one sheet of paper. This information needs to be understood and memorized. It may include formulas, rules or steps to solving a problem.

Use the learning strategies discussed in this chapter to remember this information. A good example of how this information should look is what students might call a mental "cheat sheet." Obviously, you cannot use the written form of this sheet during the real test.

If you cannot take a practice test, put down on your mental cheat sheet the valuable information you will need for the test. Work to understand and memorize your mental cheat sheet. Chapter 8 (How to Improve Your Math Test-Taking Skills) will discuss how to use the information on the mental cheat sheet — *without cheating*.

How to Use Number Sense

When taking your practice tests, you should use "number sense" or estimations to make sure your answer is reasonable. Number sense is like common sense but it applies to math. It is the ability to see if your answer makes sense without using algorithms. (Algorithms are the sequential math steps used to solve problems.) These following two examples demonstrate solving two math problems (from a national math test given to high school students) using algorithms and number sense.

Example One: Solve 3.04 x 5.3. Students use algorithms to calculate this problem by multiplying the number 3.04 by 5.3, in sequence. 72 percent of the students answered the problem correctly using algorithms.

Example Two: Estimate the product of 3.04 x 5.3, and answer given the choices below

A)	1.6	C) 160
B)	16	D) 1600

Only 15 percent of the students chose "B," which is the correct answer. Twenty-eight percent of the students chose "A." Using *estimating* to solve the answer, a whopping 85 percent of the students got the problem wrong.

These students were incorrectly using their "mental black board" instead of using number sense. In using number sense to answer, you would multiply the numbers to the left of the decimal in each number to get an estimate of the answer. To estimate the answer you would multiply 3 (the number to the left of the decimal in 3.04) by 5 (the number to the left of the decimal in 5.3) and expect the answer to be a little larger than 15.

It appears that the students' procedural processing (the use of algorithms) was good, but when asked to solve a non-routine problem using estimating (which is easier than using algorithms), the results were disappointing.

Example: Solve 48 + 48 by rounding off. Rounding off means mentally changing the number (up or down) to make it more manageable to you, without using algorithms. By rounding off, 48 becomes 50 (easier to work with). 50 + 50 = 100. If the choices for answers were 104, 100, 98 and 96, you would then subtract four from the 100 (since each number was rounded up by 2) and you get 96.

Another example of using number sense or estimating is in "rounding off." Taking the time to estimate the answer to a math problem is a good way to check your answer.

Another way to use number sense is to check your answer to see if it is reasonable. Many students forget this important step and get the answer wrong. This is especially true of word or story problems.

Examples: When solving a rate-and-distance problem, use your common sense to realize that one car cannot go 500 miles per hour to catch the other car. However, the car could go 50 miles per hour.

The same common-sense rule applies to age-word problems where the age of a person cannot be 150 years, but it could be 15 years.

Further, in solving equations, *x* is *usually* a number that is less than 20. When you

> solve a problem for *x* and get 50, then this isn't reasonable, and you should recheck your calculations.

Also remember, when dealing with an equation, to make sure that you put the answer back into the equation to see if one side of the equation equals the other. If the two sides are not equal, you have the wrong answer. If you have extra time left over after you have completed a test, you should check answers using this method.

> **Example:** In solving the equation $x + 3 = 9$, you calculated that $x = 5$. To check your answer, substitute *x* with 5 and see if the problem works out correctly. $5 + 3$ does not equal 9, so you know you have made a mistake and need to recalculate the problem. The correct answer, by the way, is $x = 6$.

❗ Remember: Number sense is a way to get more math problems correct by estimating your answer to determine if it is reasonable. ❗

Metacognition — Putting It All Together

Metacognition is a new concept in mathematics that looks at what students are thinking when solving math problems. Using your memory process to learn how to solve math problems is the first step, but you must also be able to apply concepts to solve homework or test problems. The key to your success is the self-monitoring of problem solving, not memorizing how to do the problems. Memorization of steps instead of understanding the rules and principles leads to passive learning and unsuccessful problem solving. You need a model to follow when solving math problems.

Joy (1991) in her article, "Ideas in Practice: Metacognition and Mathematical Problem Solving", suggests a math solving model based on metacognition. This model of **plan, monitor and evaluate** is a framework for solving math problems also supported by other researchers.

Planning consists of understanding what the problem wants, the strategies to solve the problem and potential obstacles. It also includes understanding what information is required, doing the calculations and predicting the outcome. Monitoring is putting the steps in order, keeping one's place, identifying and finding errors, understanding when additional information is needed, knowing when to use another strategy and knowing when you have part of the answer. Evaluating includes knowing if the answer seems right (number sense), putting the answer back into the equation, doing the opposite of the function to see if the answer is correct, and measuring the efficiency of the plan and monitoring.

Joy (1991) continues to make suggestions on how students can use the model. In the plan students can make a list of questions to ask themselves while solving the problems. This will be further discussed in Chapter 7 (How to Improve Your Reading and Homework Techniques).

They can also make a list of things they need to know to solve the problem. Monitoring can be accomplished by having students rewrite problems in their own words, sometimes leaving out the numbers until they understand the question. Students need to ask themselves what they are solving before starting the problem. Improving self-monitoring can also be enhanced by examining previous errors and making sure that students don't repeat the same mistakes. This is accomplished by using the Six Types of Test-taking Errors discussed in Chapter 8, "How to Improve Your Math Test-Taking Skills."

Monitoring improvement can also be improved in small groups or using a study buddy. You can use the "think out loud" method by taking turns, having each student state what they are thinking while solving the problem. The other student (s) can listen and correct the incorrect problems solving steps. You can also learn from the other student's new ways to solve the problems. The evaluation process can speed up by having students practice checking their homework problems. This practice will pay off during the limited test-taking time.

Using metacognition to solve math problems will increase your homework and test-taking success. At this time it is not expected that you will be able to totally use metacognitive techniques to solve homework and test problems. However, as mentioned previously, the next chapters in this book will help you develop that model so you can use it effectively.

 Remember: The goal of learning math is to understand the underlying concept, so you can solve any related problem. It is not memorizing how to do certain problems. Memorization will lead to math failure.

Summary

- Remembering what you learn begins with understanding the relationship between receiving (sensing), storing (processing) and retrieving (recalling) information.

- Having enough working memory to recall information from long-term memory to solve a problem is important.

- Transforming working memory into long-term memory is the major memory problem for most students.

- While studying, many students do not complete this memory-shifting process.

- Understanding the stages of memory and using memory techniques can help you store information in long-term memory.

- Understanding your best learning style and how to use it will dramatically improve your grades.

- Common memory techniques include maintaining a good math/study attitude, becoming a selective learner, becoming an organizer, using visual imagery, making associations, using mnemonic devices and using acronyms.

- Developing practice tests can also help you learn where your memory is failing you, and creating practice tests helps you increase your test-taking skills.

- Memory output skills (or recalling long-term memory or reasoning into working memory) can be improved.

- Use your imagination to adapt these learning techniques to the math material you need to understand and learn.

- One way to improve these skills is to become more automatic with your mental processing of numbers and using number sense.

- These two techniques, plus the use of a calculator, can free up more working memory to help you solve the problem.

- Using the metacognition model of planning, monitoring and evaluating will improve your math success.

Remember: Locating where your memory breaks down and compensating for those weaknesses will improve your math learning.

<u>Chapter 5 Notes</u>

Name: _____ Date: _____

Assignment for Chapter 5

1. List and describe the stages of memory. _____

   _____

   _____

   _____

   _____

   _____

   _____

   _____

2. Explain the difference between short-term and working memory. _____

   _____

   _____

3. What are your best math learning styles and how can you use them to learn math?

   _____

   _____

   _____

4. Go to the Winning at Math Student Resource website and review the recommendations for Visual Language Learners and Auditory Language Learners.

5. Describe your three best memory techniques. _____

   _____

   _____

   _____

6. Give an example of how you can use association to learn a math principle. _____

_____

_____

_____

7. Give an example of a mnemonic device and an acronym that could be used to improve your learning of math principles.

_____

_____

_____

_____

8. How are you going to develop your practice test? _____

_____

_____

_____

9. Give two applications of number sense examples. _____

_____

_____

10. Define metacognition in your own words and how you plan on using this skill to learn math.

_____

_____

_____

_____

How to Improve Listening and Note-Taking Skills

6

In Chapter 6
you will learn these concepts:

- The first key step to improving how you learn math is to turn classroom time with the instructor into a productive learning experience. Two skills needed for this are listening and note-taking.
  - ✓ Learn how to listen effectively and identify the important information in the instructor's lecture
  - ✓ Develop listening and recording habits that improve the content of your notes
  - ✓ Design a system of note-taking, like the "Seven Steps to Math Note-Taking"
  - ✓ Increase the use of language to learn math
  - ✓ Improve the way you use the calculator in class

Introduction

Listening and note-taking skills in a math class are very important, since most students do not read the math text or have difficulty understanding it. In most of your other classes, if you do not understand the lecture you can read the book and get almost all the information. In the math class, however, the instructor can usually explain the textbook better than the students can read and understand it.

Students who do not have good listening skills or note-taking skills will be at a disadvantage in learning math. Most math understanding takes place in the classroom. Students must learn how to take advantage of learning math in the classroom by becoming effective listeners, calculator users and note-takers.

How to Listen Effectively

Becoming an effective listener is the foundation for good note-taking. You can become an effective listener using a set of skills, which you can learn and practice. To become an effective listener, you must prepare both physically and mentally.

Sitting in the Golden Triangle

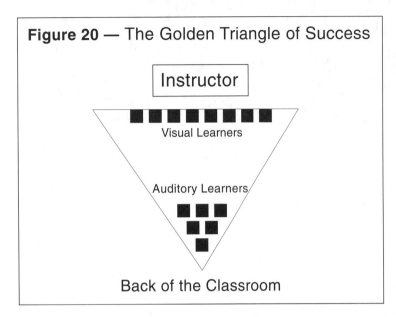

Figure 20 — The Golden Triangle of Success

Instructor

Visual Learners

Auditory Learners

Back of the Classroom

The physical preparation for becoming an effective listener involves *where you sit* in the classroom. Sit in the best area to obtain high grades, "The Golden Triangle of Success." See Figure 20 (The Golden Triangle of Success). Students seated in this area (especially on the front row) directly face the teacher and will most likely pay attention to the lecture. This is a great seating location for visual learners. There are also fewer tendencies for distraction by activities outside the classroom or by students making noise or movement in the classroom.

Examples: Watching the speaker, listening for main ideas and nodding your head or saying to yourself, "I understand," when agreeing with the instructor can maintain your attention.

Where you sit can affect how well you learn.

The middle seat in the back row is another point in "The Golden Triangle" for students to sit, especially those who are auditory (hearing) learners. You can hear the instructor better because the instructor's voice is projected to that point. This means that there is less chance of misunderstanding the instructor, and you can hear well enough to ask appropriate questions.

Sitting in "The Golden Triangle of Success" forces you to pay more attention during class and be less distracted by other students. This is very important for math students because math instructors usually go over a point once. If you miss that point in the lesson, then you could be lost for the remainder of the class.

Warming Up for Math Class

The first step of mental preparation for note-taking involves "warming up" before class begins. Just as an athlete must "warm up" before a game begins, you must "warm up" before taking notes. "Warm up" by reviewing the previous day's notes, reviewing the reading material, reviewing the homework, preparing questions, and working one or two unassigned homework problems.

This mental "warm up" before the lecture refreshes your memory, making it easier to learn the new material. Students who "warm up" are "ready to go" as soon as the instructor starts lecturing, and they keep up with what is discussed in class.

❗ **Remember**: The first information the instructor tells you is very important. Be ❗ ready to listen and copy it down.

How to Become an Active Listener and Learner

The other step of mental preparation for note-taking is to listen actively. Active listening means integrating the thinking and learning process with listening and recording information. First, it involves learning the instructor's lecture style, how he or she indicates when information is important. What information do they tend to leave out? Is it best to keep the book open during lecture? How parallel is the lecture with the book? The pace of the instructor's lecture is important. If it is too slow, you must think of ways to remain focused like finding sample problems in the book. If it is too fast, you must find a way to make short cuts in recording information while still getting the details.

Second, you must be a participant in the class, asking questions, listening to other students' questions. Be willing to ask questions for clarification when confused because if you are confused, so is someone else. Questions are another way to force an instructor to repeat information or provide more details. Sometimes it is easy to fall into the frame of mind where you just go to class, get the notes down, planning to learn it later. That is passive listening.   No more sitting in the back, slouched in the desk, waiting to write whatever the instructor puts on the board.

Active listeners learn the concepts while they are listening.

Class is like a race:

1. On your mark — sit in your desk

2. Get set — be focused and ready to take notes as soon as the instructor begins.

What do you think about while in the math class? First, listen for the instructor to discuss what you learned when you previewed the chapter as a "warm up." Sometimes it helps to have the book opened to the chapter the instructor is talking about. You can compare the information from the lecture with the book. Second, if the instructor is speeding on, ask a question to help you understand what is being discussed. This also gives a mental break for everyone. Just don't ask too many questions that are irrelevant. Classmates do not appreciate those questions. Third, as the instructor is explaining how to do something, listen for the explanation of why particular steps are completed. If you do not hear the "why," be brave and ask the instructor. Usually the answer will include

3. Go — keep a steady pace with note-taking.

4. Last lap — stay focused, even though tired.

5. Finish line — class is over. You have good notes. Time to practice for your next race.

the rules, properties or laws that explain why certain steps are taken. This will help you and many of your classmates understand what is going on. Make sure you record this information in your notes.

There will be times when the instructor has to present so much information at a fast pace, all that you can do is make sure you get it down. One trick is to sit next to someone who is trying to listen as intently as you. Then, when one of you spaces out, the other one will still be focused in and getting the notes down. At the end of class you can compare notes and fill in each other's gaps. If you can, sit close enough to each other to be able to look at each other's notes in order to fill in the gaps. This is particularly helpful in a class that meets for a long time. The catch is that in these situations, you must review the notes as soon as possible because you didn't have as much time to think about the information in class.

Class time should be considered a valuable study period where you can listen, take notes and learn at the same time. Some students think listening to the instructor and taking notes is a waste of valuable time. Too often, students sit in class and use only a fraction of their learning ability. One way to learn more in class is to memorize important facts when the instructor is talking about material you already know. Another technique is to repeat back to yourself the important concepts right after the instructor says them in class. Using class time to learn math is an efficient learning system.

! **Remember:** Class time is an intense study period that should **!** not be wasted.

How to Become a Good Note-Taker

Becoming a good note-taker requires two basic strategies. One strategy is to be specific in detail. In other words, *copy* the problems down, step by step. The second strategy is to listen for the general principles, general concepts and general ideas and record them in your notes.

Copying from the Board

While taking math notes, you need to copy each and every step of each problem on the board, even though you may already know them. While in the classroom, you might understand each step, but a week later you might not remember unless all the steps were written down. In addition, as you write down each step, you are memorizing it. The major reason for recording every step of a problem is to understand how to do the problems while the instructor is explaining them instead of trying to remember unwritten steps when you are studying on your own. It may seem time consuming; however, it pays off during homework and test time.

There will be times when you will get lost while listening to the lecture. Nevertheless, you should keep taking notes even though you do not understand the problem. This will provide you with a reference point for further study. Put a question mark (?) by those steps you do not understand. As you take notes on confusing problem steps, skip lines; then go back and fill in information that clarifies your misunderstanding of the steps in question at some later point. Ask your tutor or instructor for help with the uncompleted problem steps and write down the reasons for each step in the space provided.

Remember, the goal is to get all the details without writing an essay. A procedure to save time while taking notes from the board is to stop writing complete sentences. Write your main thoughts in phrases. Phrases are easier to jot down and easier to memorize. Another strategy to streamline taking notes off the board is to develop an abbreviation system. An abbreviation system is your way to reduce long words to shorter versions, which you still can understand. By writing less, you can listen more and have a better understanding of the material.

Example: When the instructor starts explaining the commutative property, you need to write it out the first time. After that, use "Comm." You should develop abbreviations for all the most commonly used words in math.

Figure 21 (Abbreviations), below, provides a list of abbreviations. Add your own abbreviations to this list. By using abbreviations as much as possible, you can obtain the same meaning from your notes and have more time to listen to the instructor.

Figure 21 — Abbreviations

E.G.	(for example)	1, 2, 3, 4	(to indicate a series of facts)
CF.	(compare, remember in context)	D	(shows disagreement with statement or passage)
N.B.	(note well, this is important)		
$\therefore$	(therefore)	REF	(reference)
$\because$	(because)	et al	(and others)
$\supset$	(implies, it follows from this)	bk	(book)
$>$	(greater than)	p	(page)
$<$	(less than)	etc.	(and so forth)
$=$	(equals, is the same)	V	(see)
$\neq$	(does not equal, is not the same)	VS	(see above)
		SC	(namely)
( )	(parentheses in the margin, around a sentence or group of sentences indicates an important idea)	SQ	(the following)
		Comm.	(Commutative)
		Dis.	(Distributive)
?	(used to indicate you do not understand the material)	A.P.A.	(Associative Property of Addition)
O	(a circle around a word may indicate that you are not familiar with it; look it up)	A.I.	(Additive Inverse)
		I.P.M.	(Identity Property of Multiplication)
TQ	(marks important materials likely to be used in an exam)		

Taking Notes

The goal of note-taking is to take the least amount of notes and get the greatest amount of information on your paper

The goal of note-taking is to take the least amount of notes and get the greatest amount of information on your paper. This could be the opposite of what most instructors have told you. Some instructors tell you to take down everything. This is not necessarily a good note-taking system, since it is very difficult to take precise, specific notes while at the same time understanding the instructor. On the other hand, some instructors during the lecture ask you to stop taking notes and just listen. These instructors know that when explaining a major point you need to listen and not write. If you are doing both you may not understand the important concept. Let these instructors explain the major point and then record your notes. If you didn't have enough time to take the notes, see the instructor during his/her office hours or get the notes from a friend.

Getting notes from another student instead of doing your own notes is not a good idea. Notes from other students are their thoughts that pertain to their math knowledge to remind them how to do problems that they don't know how to solve. You might not have the same knowledge as they do so the notes may not help you. It is best to take your own notes and then compare them to a classmate's notes to gain additional information.

What you need to develop is a note-taking system in which you write the least amount possible and get the most information down while still understanding what the instructor is saying. The first step to this system is to know when to take notes.

When to Take Notes

To become a better note-taker you must know when to take notes. The instructor will give cues that indicate what material is important. Some cues include:

- Presenting usual facts or ideas
- Writing on the board
- Summarizing
- Pausing
- Repeating statements
- Enumerating, such as, "1, 2, 3" or "A, B, C"
- Working several examples of the same type of problem on the blackboard
- Saying, "This is a tricky problem. Most students will miss it."

- Saying, "This is the most difficult step in the problem.
- Saying these types of problems will be on the test, such as coin- or age-word problems
- Explaining bold-print words
- Saying, "This will be on the test."

You must learn the cues your instructor gives indicating important material. If you are in doubt about the importance of the class material, do not hesitate to ask the instructor about its importance. If you are not sure if something is important in the lecture, write it down just in case it is important.

While taking notes you may become confused about math material. At that point, take as many notes as possible, and do not give up on note-taking.

When important cues indicate that this information may be on the test make sure to put TQ in the margin of your notes. These TQs could be the instructor indicating that this information will be on the test. If an instructor does the same type of problem several times and told you that you must know how to work these types of problems, it is TQ. These TQs need to be reviewed and learned before each test. You should list these TQ's on a separate page in the back of your notebook to review for the test and final exam.

The Seven Steps to Math Note-Taking

Since most students are not court reporters, the key to effective note-taking is to record the fewest words while retaining the greatest information. As you know, it is very difficult to record notes and, at the same time, fully understand the instructor. The "seven steps to math note-taking" system was developed to decrease the amount of note-taking while at the same time improving math learning.

The seven steps to math note-taking system consists of three major components. Steps One through Three focus on *recording* your notes. Steps Four through Six focus on *checking* yourself to see how much information is retained. This is done by recalling key words and concepts and putting a check mark by misunderstood information. Recalling information is one of the best learning techniques. Step Seven, the third component, is a math glossary.

Note-Taking Memory Cues

One of the best math note-taking methods is demonstrated in Figure 22 (Modified Three-Column Note-Taking Sample) on the next page. To set up this system, do the following on regular notebook paper:

1. Label the top space between the notebook ring and the red line, "Key Words."
2. Label the other side of the red line, "Examples."
3. Next, label "Explanations/ Rules" about four inches from the red line.
4. Draw a vertical line between the "Examples" and "Explanations/Rules" sections.
5. Record the same information on the next 10 pages. After using this system for 10 pages, you may not need to label each page.

Figure 22 — Modified Three-Column Note-Taking System		
Key Words/Rules	**Examples**	**Explanations**
Solve a linear equation	$5(x + 4) + 3(x - 4) = 2(x - 2)$	Have to get x on one side of the $=$ and numbers on the other side of the $=$.
Distributive Property	$5x + 20 + 3x - 12 = 2x - 4$	Multiply numbers to the left of the ( ) by each variable and number in the ( ).
Commutative Property	$5x + 3x + 20 - 12 = 2x - 4$	Regroup numbers and variables.
Combine like terms	$8x + 8 = 2x - 4$	Add x's together and numbers together.
Additive Inverse Property	$8x - 2x + 8 = 2x - 2x - 4$ $6x + 8 = -4$	Subtract $2x$ from both sides to get variables all on the left side of the $=$.
Additive Inverse Property	$6x + 8 - 8 = -4 - 8$ $6x = -12$	Subtract 8 from both sides to get numbers all on the right side of the $=$.
Multiplicative Inverse Property	$\dfrac{6x}{6} = \dfrac{-12}{6}$	Divide both sides by 6 to get x by itself on the left side of the $=$.
Simplify	$x = -2$	Solution. Now, check your answer.
	Insert new problem	

Follow these seven steps to improve your note-taking:

Step One   Record each problem step in the "Examples" section.

Step Two   Record the reasons for each step in the "Explanation/Rules" section by using:
- Abbreviations;
- Short phrases, not sentences; and
- Key words, properties, principles or formulas.

Step Three   Record key words/concepts in the left two-inch margin either during or immediately after lecture by reworking your notes.

Step Four   Cover up the "Example and Explanation" sections and recite out loud the meaning of the key words or concepts.

Step Five   Place a check mark by the key words/concepts that you *did not* know.

Step Six   Review the information that you checked until it is understood.

Step Seven   Develop a math glossary for difficult-to-remember key words and concepts.

After practicing this note-taking system, you may want to modify it to meet your personal note-taking needs. Some students wait and convert their notes into a three column system after class. They also put information from the math book into the three columns. Other students use graph paper and turn it landscape in order to make the columns wider. The graphing lines help keep everything straight. One group of calculus students created a "group" three column system on large poster paper because the problems were so complicated. They kept it on the wall in the tutoring center. The key is to organize all the details in your notes into a system that helps you see how everything connects.

In some cases student may be auditory abstract learners and not take many notes. I have seen these students take a few notes down and spend most of their working memory understanding the abstract concepts. If you are this type of student then at least take a few notes down to remind you of the concepts and still develop a math glossary. This is very important for you to remember the vocabulary that connects to the abstract learning.

Use a system while taking notes.

A Math Glossary

Since math is a foreign language, vocabulary is important

The third component in the seven steps to math note-taking is devoted to developing a math glossary. A math glossary for each chapter dramatically improves learning and remembering the math. It can be a combination of lecture notes, text readings or text notes (the latter two are discussed in the next chapter). Since math is considered a foreign language, understanding the math vocabulary becomes a key to comprehending math.

A good glossary can be the key to success for students who have good language skills but have difficulty learning math. Even though math is an abstract subject, it is still learned through using language to recall how to work the problems. In fact, some students talk their way through solving the equations by using their math vocabulary. Use your language skills to improve your math by understanding the math vocabulary.

A math glossary should be created for each chapter to define math vocabulary words and concepts. Label a section in the back of your notebook "Math Vocabulary for Chapter One." Your glossary should include all words printed in bold print in your text, words emphasized by your instructor and any other words you do not understand. The glossary can be divided into three areas which include the book definition, your definition in your own words and if appropriate an example. It can look similar to the note-taking system. If you cannot explain the math vocabulary in your own words, ask your instructor or tutor for help. If your instructor or tutor cannot help you then go to www.academicsuccess.com and click on Student Math Practice and Learning. Go to Other Support Sites and click on the sites with a math glossary or math vocabulary. Look up the definitions of the words and then try to put the definitions in your own words. Review your math glossary every week.

Some students put the vocabulary words and definitions on tape.

Some students put the vocabulary words and definitions on tape. If you are using a tape recorder, leave a few seconds between the word and definition. The definition should be in your own words. These words are usually the words that you could not remember from your glossary. To practice your vocabulary words, play the tape when you have a few minutes between classes by using a recorder and headphones. You can also listen to the tape in your car. Once you listen to the vocabulary word, put the tape on pause and repeat the definition back. Then take the pause button off and listen to the definition. If you did not repeat it back correctly, then continue repeating until you do. Keep practicing until you can correctly repeat back all the definitions. This is an excellent way for auditory math learners to memorize and learn vocabulary. Other types of learners can also use this learning system.

Students who are visual or kinesthetic (hands on) learners may be able to learn math vocabulary more effectively by developing a virtual web-based math glossary. StudyStack is a free website that is designed to help people memorize and learn information. Using the StudyStack website, you can use your computer to develop and display a stack of "virtual cards" of information that you want to learn. Just like flashcards, you can review the cards at any time, at your own pace, and you can discard the cards that you already know. The site is set up to find information on any subject, to develop your own flashcards, to play games such as hangman and matching, and also to help you study anytime/anywhere, 24/7. You can also print out the cards and export the flashcards to your cell phone, PDA or iPod.

StudyStack already has math sites developed by other students featuring algebra definitions, math definitions and math vocabulary. However, by developing your own site you will learn the vocabulary more effectively and customize the site to your course. Also you may want some of your classmates to develop math vocabulary or other math sites so that you can share them with each other.

! **Remember**: once you develop the site it can be shared with anyone. !

To learn how to use StudyStack go to www.academicsuccess.com and click on Student Math Practice and Learning Site. Go to the Other Support Sites and click on StudyStack. As stated before, using StudyStack is an excellent way for visual and kinesthetic learners to improve their math learning.

Visual math learners can also learn vocabulary the old fashion way — by putting the vocabulary word on one side of the flash card and the definition on the other side. Auditory math learners can also develop flash cards, making sure to say the information out loud while learning the information. It is also helpful to write the vocabulary words next to homework problems they are associated with. The examples in Figure 23, on the next page, are 3x5 cards that show only words. These memory devices can be more effective if you include pictures or other diagrams that you have created for yourself.

How to Rework Your Notes

The note-taking system does not stop when you leave the classroom. As soon as possible after class, rework your notes to decrease the amount of forgetting. This is an excellent procedure to transfer math information from short-term to long-term memory and abstract reasoning.

 Remember: Most forgetting occurs right after learning the material. You need to rework the notes as soon as possible. The longer you wait , the more you forget and have to relearn.

The following are important steps in reworking your notes:

Step 1   *Rewrite the material you cannot read or will not be able to understand a few weeks later.* If you do not rework your notes you will be frustrated when studying for a test if you come across notes you cannot read. Another benefit of rewriting the notes is that you immediately learn the new material. Waiting means it will take more time to learn the material.

Step 2   *Fill in the gaps.* Most of the time, when you are listening to the lecture, you cannot write down everything. Locate the portions of your notes, which are incomplete. Fill in the concepts that were left out. In the future, skip two or three lines in your notebook page for anticipated lecture gaps.

Step 3   *Add additional key words and ideas in the left-hand column.* These key words or ideas were the ones not recorded during the lecture.

> **Example:** You did not know you should add the *opposite* of 18 to solve a particular problem, and you incorrectly added 18. Put additional important key words and ideas (such as "opposite" and "negative of") in the notes; these are the words that will improve your understanding of math.

Step 4   Add *to your problem log the problems which the teacher worked in class.* The problem log is a separate section of your notebook that contains a listing of the problems (without explanations — just problems) your teacher worked in class. If your teacher chose those problems to work in class, you can bet that they are considered important. The problems in this log can be used as a practice test for the next exam. Your regular class notes will not only contain the solutions but also all the steps involved in arriving at those solutions and can be used as a reference when you take your practice test

Figure 23
Example 3x5 Vocabulary Cards

Front	**Back**
Card 1 Multiplicative identity Additive Identity	Identity property a times 1 = a Additive identity a + 0 = a
Card 2 Five steps for solving rational equations	1. Determine LCD of all rational expressions in the equation. 2. Multiply both sides of the equation by the LCD (every term is multiplied by the LCD separately) 3. Remove any parentheses and combine like terms on each side of the equation 4. Solve the equation. 5. Check the solution you find by substituting it into the original equation.
Card 3 Order of polynomials	Place the terms in descending order of exponents. Highest on the left to lowest on the right. *x* cubed, next *x* squared, *x* to the first, constant (number).
Card 4 Decimals — rational numbers and irrational numbers	Rational numbers have terminating or repeating decimal equivalents. e.g. ¾ = .75, 5/7 = .714285714285… Continuing but non-repeating or nonterminating decimals are called irrational numbers (e.g. the square root of 2 and *pi*).

Step 5 *Add calculator keystroke sequences to your calculator handbook.* The calculator handbook can be a spiral-bound set of note cards or a separate section of your notebook that holds only calculator-related information. Your handbook should also include an explanation of when that particular set of keystrokes is to be used.

Step 6 *Reflection and synthesis.* Once you have finished going over your notes, review the major points in your mind. Combine your new notes with your previous knowledge to have a better understanding of what you have learned today.

Use a Tape Recorder

If you have problems recording all the information in your math class, ask your instructor about using a tape recorder. To ensure success, the tape recorder must have a tape counter and must be voice activated.

The tape counter displays a number indicating the amount of tape to which you have listened. When you find you are in an area of confusing information while you are recording the lecture, write the beginning and ending tape counter numbers in the left margin of your notes. When reviewing your notes, the tape counter number will be a reference point for obtaining information to work the problem. You can also reduce the time it takes to listen to the tape by using the pause button to stop the recording of unnecessary material during the lecture.

Ask Questions

To obtain the most from a lecture, you must ask questions in class. By asking questions, you improve your understanding of the material and decrease your homework time. By *not* asking questions, you create unnecessary confusion during the remainder of the class period. Also, it is much easier to ask questions in class about potential homework problems than it is to spend hours trying to figure out the problems on your own at a later time.

If you are shy about asking questions in class, write down the questions and read them to your instructor. If the instructor seems confused about the questions, tell him/her you will discuss the problem after class. To encourage yourself to ask questions, remember:

- You have paid for the instructor's help.
- Five other students probably have the same question.
- The instructor needs feedback on his/her teaching to help the class learn the material.
- Not asking a question can stop your learning.
- There is no such thing as a "stupid" question.

There is no such thing as a dumb question.

How to Correctly Use
a Calculator in Class

In math, you are not only expected to learn the course material, you must also learn how to use a calculator. This adds another dimension to note-taking in a math class that you will not encounter in humanities or other classes.

Do Not Stop Taking Notes

When a calculator is being used and demonstrated by an instructor while solving a problem, most students stop taking notes and attempt to duplicate the steps on their own calculators. *This is one of the biggest mistakes that a student can make.*

Unless you are very familiar with your calculator and know the location of important keys and functions, you will very likely get lost in the process of following along with the instructor. That old adage, "garbage in — garbage out" is universally true when using calculators. If you miss one keystroke, you might as well quit. You will not get the right answer.

Further, most students cannot take notes and manipulate the calculator at the same time. As a result, vast holes appear in your notebook where the explanations of the math involved and the interpretation of the answers for the problems should appear. And, finally, when you do your homework, you will probably find that you do not remember the exact sequence of keystrokes used to arrive at a particular answer.

Take Notes on Keystrokes

Write down every keystroke in your notes

You can see how calculators can tremendously complicate the note-taking process. However, the solution to taking effective notes *and* becoming a proficient calculator user is quite simple. Instead of manipulating your calculator while the teacher is explaining, *write every keystroke down in your notes.*

Whenever possible, also write *why* a particular key was used to arrive at the answer and especially be sure to record the interpretation of the answer given by the calculator. (What does that number mean in the context of the problem being solved?)

Add Keystrokes to the Abbreviations List

You will certainly want to expand your own abbreviation list to include calculator keystrokes. In most cases, what is printed on the key can be used; however, you might consider using some of the following, especially if you are using a graphing calculator:

E for **[ENTER]**

G for **[GRAPH]**

AL for **[ALPHA]**

You can see that recording keystrokes, rather than executing them while the teacher is explaining, solves the note-taking problems listed earlier. You do not miss steps or get behind. You can continue to take notes the whole time, and when you do your homework, the step sequence is in your notes.

Summary

- Effective listening is the first step to excellent note-taking.

- The effective listener knows where to sit in the classroom (The Golden Triangle of Success) and practices good listening techniques.

- The goal of note-taking is to write the least amount possible to record the most information.

- This allows you to enhance your ability to listen to the lecture and increase your learning potential in the classroom.

- Figure 22 (Modified Three-Column Note-Taking Sample) is an excellent example to use for both taking notes and testing yourself on the information. Make sure you practice covering up the left side of the note page and recalling the information. Do not waste your time studying information you already know.

- Making a math glossary can especially help students with good language skills understand mathematics.

- Use the StudyStack website to develop your own virtual flash cards and review them any time you want by using your computer, cell phone, PDA or iPOD.

- Rework your notes as soon as possible after class. When reworking your notes, make sure you complete your problem log; it will become very important when preparing for tests.

- If you wait too long to review your notes, you might not understand them and it will be more difficult to learn them.

- Reworking your notes will improve not only your understanding of math but also your grades in the course.

- Calculator usage in the classroom has become a very effective learning tool; however, it is difficult to take notes and use your calculator at the same time.

- With complicated calculator usage, it is more important to write down the keystrokes rather than try to learn them in the classroom.

- Record these difficult calculator steps in your notes and rewrite them in your calculator log; then, practice the calculator steps until you know them.

Remember: The better note-taking skills you have, the more math you can learn in the classroom.

Chapter 6 Notes

Name: _____ Date: _____

Assignment for Chapter 6

1. Review and use Figure 22 (Modified Three-Column Note-Taking Sample) as a model for your notes. List and define the key words that were discussed while using this system.

   _____

   _____

   _____

   _____

2. List three ways you can become a more effective/active listener.

   Way one: _____

   _____

   Way two: _____

   _____

   Way three: _____

   _____

3. Why do you need to copy down each step of the math homework?_____

   _____

   _____

4. How does the use of a calculator complicate note-taking, and how can you solve this problem?

   _____

   _____

5. List five abbreviations you use in your math notes. _____

   _____

   _____

6. List and describe the seven steps to math note-taking.

   1 _____

   2 _____

   3 _____

   4 _____

   5 _____

   6 _____

   7 _____

7. Attach either a copy of your glossary or examples of your StudyStack flashcards when turning in this assignment.

8. How does asking questions in math class decrease the time you will spend on homework?

   _____

   _____

   _____

9. Who is the classmate with whom you can compare math notes? _____

10. Write down two problems from your problem log.

   _____

   _____

   _____

   _____

   _____

   _____

   _____

   _____

How to Improve Your Reading and Homework Techniques

7

In Chapter 7
you will learn these concepts:

- The textbook is a resource for students to use to understand their homework and to use along with the instructor's lecture notes to prepare for tests.
  - ✓ Selecting the best time for reading the textbook
  - ✓ Reading a textbook effectively
  - ✓ Recording information from a textbook
  - ✓ Using the textbook in distance learning courses
- Homework is a learning experience, not busy work.
  - ✓ Purpose of homework
  - ✓ Ways to do homework effectively
  - ✓ Tips for solving word problems
  - ✓ Ways to use a calculator
  - ✓ Studying with other classmates
  - ✓ Ways to recall what you have learned
  - ✓ Using online homework in distance learning courses

Introduction

How many times have you thought, "Why do I have to do all the problems when I understand how to do it after finishing five?" Or, perhaps this thought has run through your mind, "I'm not going to read the book. It's too confusing."

Math students are expected to know how to do their homework. In truth, however, most math students do not have a homework system. They begin their homework by going directly to the problems and trying to work them. When they get stuck, they usually quit. This is not a good homework system. A good system will improve success in homework, as well as help your overall understanding of math. Two key components to a good math study system deal with using the textbook as a resource of information and completing homework to learn the math well enough to perform well within a timed test.

This chapter will help you design a system to learn from completing homework and to use the math textbook as a resource for information. Special suggestions will be given to distance learning students. To get started, you need to read and understand the course syllabus to know when to read the text and complete the homework.

When Should You Read the Textbook?

Reading ahead prepares you for what you will hear in the lecture.

Most students don't read the math textbook because in the past the textbooks were poorly written. These books were difficult to understand, composed mostly of example problems, and written for the instructor instead of the student. Now math textbooks are more student friendly with more support materials. When we are discussing reading a math textbook, we are also focusing on the additional products that come with the textbook such as a solution manual, videotapes, CD ROMS, support web sites and tutor sites. Review all these materials to see which work best for your learning style.

Math instructors and students often debate over the best time to read a math textbook. Some instructors prefer that students read the textbook before coming to class while other instructors prefer that students read the textbook after class. If students read the textbook before going to class, they become familiar with the vocabulary and concepts. Students don't need to understand all the material when they read the book before the class. Yet, understanding even just a third of the material will free up the mind to understand more material during the lecture. Read ahead two or three sections and put question marks (in pencil) by the material you don't understand. Make a list of the vocabulary words that will most likely appear in the lecture.

When the instructor starts discussing the material, have your questions ready and take good notes. When the instructor starts discussing a topic with the question marks by them, pay special attention. If you do not understand the instructor's explanation then you MUST ask questions. If there is not enough time for questions, make an appointment with the instructor to go over the material. Reading the textbook before the lecture will help you better understand it and know when to ask questions.

Reading the textbook after the lecture can reinforce the material and further explain misunderstood information. Instructors who believe in this format think that they can explain the mathematical concepts better than the textbook or don't want you to get confused by its explanations. Reading the textbook after the lecture helps students to remember the notes taken during class. The textbook may also explain the mathematical concept in a different way so you can better understand it. In addition, the textbook might cover material that was not discussed in the lecture that will help clarify a concept. Sometimes math instructors are so familiar with the math, they accidentally exclude important steps.

Reading the mathematics textbook before or after the lecture may depend on how well the book is written. It also may depend on your cognitive learning style. Try both ways of reading the textbook and see which one works best. However, we all agree that students should review the math textbook before doing their homework. Now let's look at how to read the math textbook.

How to Read the Syllabus

The syllabus will tell you what to do and when it should be done. You need to read and study the syllabus. It should be a week-by-week description of the course. The syllabus can contain course title, course number, instructor's name, reading assignments, dates to complete chapter section, which homework problems to complete, absence policy, drop date, withdraw date, test dates, test make-up policy, grading scale and how the course is graded. Students need to use this valuable syllabus information to their advantage.

Some students know how to use the syllabus to their advantage, checking it before and after every class period. I have worked with hundreds of students who after adding two or three classes figured out they were in the wrong math course after examining the syllabus. The course level was too high for them and, based on the syllabus, they dropped down to the next math level during the first week without penalty. Other students come to me while failing a course, knowing the date they can still get a W (withdraw) without getting an F. They usually take the W, and we start to prepare to take the course again the next semester. Some students who know the test dates, make sure they are

A syllabus is like a road map to success in a math course.

off from work the day before the test to allow for more study time. In addition many students, knowing the grading system for their particular course, figure out what their overall grade is in the class after each test. They use this information to adjust their schedule for reading the text and doing their homework. Knowing, understanding and using the syllabus to your advantage can help in your learning and also improve your math grades.

I have some students that come to me who do not understand the syllabus and figure it out too late to use it to their advantage. For example, a student came to me during the last two weeks of a semester wanting to withdraw from a math course. I asked her if she was failing the course and she said no. The student said that she was in the wrong course because she took this course two years ago and made a B. She learned about being in the wrong course when being "blocked" from registering for the next course. I asked her if she reviewed her course syllabus to make sure she was in the correct course. She indicated that she never read the syllabus.

Another student came to me in the last part of a semester indicating he was failing the course and wanted to withdraw. Receiving an F in the course would eliminate his financial aid next semester. I asked him if he read the syllabus to see when that last day to drop the course with a W (instead of an F) was. He said no. He did not have his syllabus and I informed him that it was the previous week.

A third student indicated that his instructor was not fair to him because she would not let him make up a missed test. He indicated that he made up one missed test before. I asked the student about the instructor's test make up policy on the syllabus. The student indicated that he did not know what it was and had lost his syllabus. We found out that the instructor had a "one make-up test" policy and then there were no more make-ups. The student then admitted that he volunteered to work overtime instead of taking the test, and that if he had known about the policy he wouldn't have come to that decision. Make sure you understand the syllabus to avoid these problems.

Students taking distance learning courses MUST know and understand the syllabus. If you are in a distance learning course, the syllabus is your BOSS.

Read the Syllabus for Distance Learning

The syllabus for distance learning courses is very important and will tell you what to do and when it should be done. You MUST read and study the syllabus. It should be a week-by-week description of the course. The syllabus should be lengthy and in great detail. If possible read the syllabus before you sign up for the course. Ask the department secretary or instructor if the syllabus is online or if they can fax or email it to you. Looking at the syllabus will give you an idea on how the course is designed and if the instructor is experienced in teaching distance-learning courses. Read it thoroughly because the instructor is not there to tell you the important parts and you do not want any surprises. Highlight the important dates of assignments, tests, and projects. If the course does not have a syllabus, or if it is a very short syllabus, then consider not taking the course. It is a warning sign that the instructor might be relatively new to the learning environment or not detailed in presentation of material.

Remember: There is no eye contact with the instructor reading the syllabus. The instructor cannot tell if you are confused and may not remind you of important dates.

The first section on the syllabus to look at is the computer and software requirements: minimum computer speed, RAM, email, software and internet connection. Even if you meet the minimum requirements, it may take a long time to download the files and send them. If you don't meet the minimum requirement, obtain another computer or don't take the course. I know several students who learned this lesson the hard way. They signed up for their distance-learning class and when downloading the files their computers crashed.

Look at the course requirement and the grading system. You must completely understand what you are expected to learn and how you will be graded. You need to know how the text will be used. In some cases your grades will come from tests, papers and outside projects. You need to know what percent each one will count and when they are due. Write down these dates and put them where you can easily refer to them. Just like in regular classes, instructors expect papers to be emailed on time and tests taken at the correct time.

Remember: The syllabus is your contract with the institution. You must abide by it and follow it to the letter.

How to Read a Math Textbook

As mentioned previously in other chapters, reading a math textbook is more difficult than reading other textbooks. They are written differently than English or social science textbooks. Math textbooks are condensed material, which takes longer to read. Mathematicians can reduce a page of writing to one paragraph, using math formulas and symbols. To make sure you understand that same information, an English instructor might take that original page of writing and expand it into two pages. Mathematicians pride themselves on how little they can write and still cover the concept. This is one reason why it may take two to three times as long to read a math book as it might any other book.

The way you read a math textbook is different from the traditional way students are taught to read textbooks in high school or college. Students are taught to read quickly or skim the material. If you do not understand a word, you are supposed to keep on reading. Instructors of other courses want students to continue to read so they can pick up the unknown words and their meanings from context. This reading technique may work with your other classes, but using it in your math course will be totally confusing. By skipping some major concept words or bold-print words, you will not understand what you are reading and therefore will not be able to do the homework. Reading a math textbook takes more time and concentration than reading your other textbooks.

It may take two to three times as long to read a math textbook as it might any other book.

If you have a reading problem, it would be wise to take a developmental reading course before taking math. This is especially true with math reform delivery, where reading and writing are more emphasized. Reform math classes deal more with word problems than do traditional math courses. If you cannot take the developmental reading course before taking math, then take it during the same semester as the math course.

Now that you know the *importance* of reading the math text, the next step is reviewing *how* you read the text. To start the evaluation, check the appropriate area that best describes your usual textbook reading tactics (continue to the next statements):

_____ I read all the text.

_____ I read a few pages of the text.

_____ I don't read the text.

Does reading the math text help improve your mathematics learning?

Yes _____ A little _____ Not at all _____ Don't read the text _____

If reading the text does not help you then explain why: _____

_____

Describe how you read the text: _____

_____

_____

This short self-assessment will help you understand how you approach reading the math text. Most students don't read the text because they believe it doesn't help them. Even some students who read the text don't do it effectively. The next section will describe a proven math reading technique that will help you.

! **Remember:** Reading a math textbook will take longer than reading other text- **!** books.

Ten Steps to Understanding Reading Materials

Before practicing the ten steps to understanding reading materials, you need to get to know your textbook. Each textbook has its own organizational pattern for presenting the information. It is important to understand how the book works.

- Are there learning objectives at the beginning of the chapter that can be used as a checklist to make sure you are learning everything important?

- How are the vocabulary words highlighted? Are they just bold print? Are they in highlighted boxes?

- How are the mathematical rules highlighted?

- Does each section of the chapter have learning objectives?

- Are the homework problems at the end of the chapter arranged according to the chapter sections?

If you can't figure out how your textbook is organized, go to your instructor or a learning center to receive assistance in "figuring the book out." Once you understand how to use your book, then take the following steps and adapt them in a way that they work for you.

There are several appropriate steps in reading a math textbook:

Step 1 *Skim the assigned reading material in order to get a general idea of what the chapter is about.* Skimming is an excellent skill to develop. First, it is an excellent way to get familiar with what will be covered in the next class. Second, as you sit down to study your math after the lecture, it helps you to see how all the "pieces of the puzzle" fit together. Third, after you have learned the material, it is a good strategy to use as a quick ten-minute review so that you do not forget what you learned. Here are the steps we suggest:

- Read the chapter introduction and/or learning objectives and each section summary and/or learning objectives. As you read, try to see the connections between each section. Remember, when you skim, do not try to learn the material; you simply want to get an overview of the assignment.

- As you skim, think about similar math topics that you already know. What do you already know about the chapter objectives?

- As you skim the chapter, circle (using pencil) the new words that you do not understand.

You can also skim after learning the material, pretending you are a tutor explaining how each objective connects with one another. You can even explain in your own words what each vocabulary word means as if you were tutoring. This skimming also helps you remember what you have spent so much time learning.

> **Example:** Skimming will allow you to see if problems presented in one chapter section are further explained in the next chapter sections.

Step 2   *Put all your concentration into reading.* While reading the textbook, highlight the material that is important to you. However, do not highlight more than 50 percent of a page because the material is not being narrowed down enough for future study. If you are reading the textbook after the lecture, highlight the material that was discussed in the class. Material discussed both in the textbook and lecture usually appears on the test. The purpose for highlighting is to emphasize the important material for future study.

Don't let yourself get distracted.

 Remember: Reading a math textbook is very difficult. It might take you half an hour to read and understand just *one* page. Do not skip reading assignments. Always read with paper and pencil handy to take notes or solve problems

Step 3   *When you get to the examples, go through each step.* If the example skips any steps, make sure you write down each one of those skipped steps in the textbook for better understanding. Later on, when you go back and review, the steps are already filled in. You will understand how each step was completed. Also, by filling in the extra steps, you are starting to over learn the material for better recall on future tests.

Step 4   *Mark the concepts and words that you do not know.* Maybe you marked them the first time while skimming. If you understand them now, erase the marks. If you do not understand the words or concepts, then reread the page or look them up in the glossary. Try not to read any further until you understand all the words and concepts. This might be a good time to call your classmate.

Step 5   Take *notes from your math textbook on principles, properties and rules.* Taking meaningful notes after reading the math textbook helps students remember what they have read. These notes also serve as a review sheet for preparing for the test. This note-taking system is different from taking notes in the classroom. These notes become a quicker resource for information while completing homework and are beneficial in learning math vocabulary. The steps are as follows:

   • Before reading the math book, label the top of your notebook page with the chapter and section numbers. For example, at the top of the note page put Chapter 2.3 to 2.6.

   • Divide the page into three columns. Label the left one "Terms," the middle one

"Examples" and the third one "Definitions and Explanations."

- As you read about principles, properties or rules, write down their names, define them, give one or two examples, and explain the process.

Terms	Example	Definitions/Explanation
Multiplication principle	$1/3x = -15$ $3(1/3x) = 3\,(-15)$ $x = -45$	Def. = for real numbers a, b, c, with c not = to 0, if a=b then ca=cb. Multiply each side of the equation by 3 (this isolates the x). Multiply the other side by 3.

Step 6 *Now we can look at how to learn math vocabulary words. If you do not clearly understand some words, add these words to the note-taking glossary in the back of your notebook.* Your glossary will contain the bold print words that you do not understand. You should have the book definition and the definition in your own words. If you have difficulty understanding the bold-print words, ask the instructor for a better explanation. You should know all the words and concepts in your notebook glossary before taking the test.

Step 7 *If you do not understand the material, follow these eight points, one after the other, until you are comfortable with it.*

Point 1   Go back to the previous page and reread the information to maintain a train of thought. Make sure you have learned the previous information correctly.

Point 2   Read ahead to the next page to discover if any additional information better explains the misunderstood material.

Point 3   Locate and review any diagrams, examples or rules that explain the misunderstood material.

Point 4   Read the misunderstood paragraph(s) several times aloud to better understand its meaning.

Point 5   Refer to your math notes for a better explanation of the misunderstood material.

Point 6   Refer to another math textbook, computer software program or videotape that expands the explanation of the misunderstood material.

Point 7   Define exactly what you do not understand and call your study buddy for help.

Point 8   Contact your math tutor or math instructor for help in understanding the material.

Step 8 *Reflect on what you have read.* Combine what you already know with the new information that you just read. Think about how this new information enhances your math knowledge. Prepare questions for your instructor on the confusing information. Ask those questions at the next class meeting.

Step 9 *Review your math textbook notes and math glossary several times a week.* Anytime you have a spare five to ten minutes, review your notes or vocabulary words. These short periods of time allow you to study in little chunks and become confident in your understanding of the material. Try reviewing before the math lecture starts, in-between classes, or at lunch. Over a period of several weeks you will be amazed at how much you can learn. This process can ensure that you know the information before taking the test.

Step 10 *Write anticipated test questions.* Research has noted that students have about 80 percent accuracy in predicting test questions. Think about what is the most important concept you just read and what problems the instructor could give you that would test the knowledge of that concept. Make up four or five problems and add them to your problem log (this was part of your note-taking system). Indicate that these questions are from reading the textbook. Review the questions and answers before taking the next test.

! **Remember:** Math is a foreign language and knowing the principles, properties, rules and vocabulary in your own words can lead you to success. This is especially true of students who have better language skills than abstract skills. **!**

By using this reading technique, you have:

- Narrowed down the important material to be learned,
- Skimmed the textbook to get an overview of the assignment,
- Carefully read the material and highlighted the important parts,
- Recorded important information into a three column note-taking system, and
- Added to your note-taking glossary unknown words or concepts.

The highlighted material and your textbook notes should be reviewed before doing the homework problems, and the glossary has to be learned 100 percent before taking the test.

How to Establish Study-Period Goals

Before beginning your homework, establish goals for the study period. Do not just grab a coke and chips, sit down and turn to the homework problems.

Ask yourself this question: "What am I going to do tonight to become more successful in math?" By setting up short-term homework goals and reaching them, you will feel more confident about math. This also improves your self-esteem and helps you become a more internally motivated student. Set up homework tasks, which you can complete. Be realistic.

Study-period goals are set up either on a time-line basis or an item-line basis. Studying on a time-line basis is studying math for a certain amount of time.

Example: You may want to study math for an hour, then switch to another subject. You will study by time-line basis.

Studying by item-line basis means you will study your math until you have completed a certain number of homework problems.

> **Example:** You might set a goal to study math until you have completed all the odd problems in the chapter review. The odd problems are the most important problems to work. These, in most texts, are answered in the answer section in the back of the book. Such problems provide the opportunity to recheck your work if you do not get the answer correct. Once you have completed these problems, do the even-numbered problems.

No matter what homework system you use, remember this important rule: Always finish a homework session by understanding a concept or doing a homework problem correctly. Do not end a homework session with a problem you cannot complete. You will lose confidence since all you will think about is the last problem you could not solve instead of the 50 problems you correctly solved. If you did quit on a problem you could not solve, return and rework problems you have done correctly.

! **Remember:** Do not end your study period with a problem you could not complete. **!**

Why Do Instructors Assign Homework?

Talking to the instructor improves grades and can decrease homework time.

That is a good question. I have asked this question to students, math instructors and math department chairs. Some of them knew the answer, but I was surprised when some of them, including the instructors, did not know the answer. Again, let me ask you the question, "Why do instructors assign math homework?"

Yes, you are correct. Homework is given not just to waste time but to have you practice the math problems often enough to understand the mathematical concept that can be put into your abstract reasoning or long-term memory. In other words, you do math homework to remember how to do the problems during the test. However, just memorizing how to do the problems will create difficulty recalling how to do them on the test. Doing your homework is an excellent time to practice doing problems as if on a test and to understand the mathematical concepts. Completing homework needs to be a learning experience. Now that you know the reasons to do your homework, I have another question. "Has anyone taught you the best way to do your homework?" Probably not. The next section will answer that question.

How to Do Your Homework

Doing your homework can be frustrating or rewarding. Most students jump right into their homework, become frustrated and stop studying. These students usually go directly to the math problems and start working them without any preparation. When they get stuck on one problem, they flip to the back of the textbook for the answer. Then, they either try to work the problem backwards to understand the problem steps, or they just copy down the answer.

Other students go to the solution guide and just copy the steps. After getting stuck several times, these students will inevitably quit doing their homework assignment. Their homework becomes a frustrating experience, and they may even quit doing their math homework altogether. Now that you know how some students do their homework, the next step is reviewing how you do your homework. To start the evaluation check the appropriate area that best describes your usual homework process (continue to the next statements):

_____ I do all the homework.

_____ I do some of the homework.

_____ I don't do the homework.

Doing the math homework helps improve your mathematics learning:

Yes _____   A little _____   Not at all _____   Don't do homework _____

If doing the homework does not help you, then explain why: _____

_____

Describe your homework process: _____

_____

_____

This short self-assessment will help you understand how you approach homework. Many students don't do all their homework because they believe doing every problem doesn't help them. Even students who do all the homework sometimes don't do it effectively. To improve your homework success and learning, refer to the following 10 steps:

10 Steps to Doing Your Homework

Step 1   *Review the textbook material that relates to the homework.* You can also use your glossary and textbook notes in your notebook. A proper review will increase the chances of successfully completing your homework. If you get stuck on a problem, you will have a better chance of remembering the location of similar problems. If you do not review prior to doing your homework, you could get stuck and not know where to find help in the textbook.

! **Remember:** To be successful in learning the material and in completing homework assignments, you must first review your textbook. **!**

Step 2   *Review your lecture notes that relate to the homework.* If you could not understand the explanation in the textbook on how to complete the homework assignment, then review your class notes.

! **Remember:** Reviewing your notes will give you a better idea about how to **!** complete your homework assignment.

Step 3   *Do your homework as neatly as possible.* Doing your homework — organized and neatly — has several benefits. When approaching your instructor about problems with your homework, he or she will be able to understand your previous attempts to solve the problem. The instructor will easily locate the mistakes and show you how to correct the steps without having to decipher your handwriting. Another benefit is that, when you review for midterm or final exams, you can quickly relearn the homework material without having to decipher your own writing.

! **Remember:** Neatly prepared homework can help you immediately and in the **!** future.

Step 4   *When doing your homework, write down every step of the problem.* Even if you can do the step in your head, write it down anyway. This will increase the amount of homework time, but you are over learning how to solve problems, which improves your memory. Doing every step is an easy way to memorize and understand the material. Another advantage is that when you rework the problems you did wrong, it is easy to review each step to find the mistake.

! **Remember:** In the long run, doing every step of the homework will save you **!** time and frustration.

Step 5   *Understand the reasons for each problem step and check your answers.* Do not get into the bad habit of memorizing how to do problems without knowing the reasons for each step. Many students are smart enough to memorize procedures required to complete a set of homework problems. However, when slightly different problems are presented on a test, they cannot solve the problems. To avoid this dilemma, keep reminding yourself about the rules, laws, or properties used to solve problems. A good idea is to write each name of the rule, law or property by several of the homework problems. Then, the homework becomes a test review.

> **Example:** *Problem:* $2(a + 5) = 0$. What property allows you to write the equation as $2a + 10 = 0$? *Answer:* The distributive property.

Once you know the correct reason for going from one step to another in solving a math problem, you can answer any problem requiring that property. Students who simply memorize how to do problems instead of understanding the reasons for correctly working the steps will eventually fail their math course.

! **Remember:** Understanding "why" you are doing "what" you are doing helps **!** you remember what to do on the test. Approach doing homework as studying for a test.

Checking your homework answers should be a part of your homework process because it improves your learning and helps you prepare for tests. Check the answers of the problems for which you do not have the solutions. This may be the even-numbered or odd-numbered problems or the problems not answered in the solutions manual.

First, check your answer by estimating the correct answer. You can also check your answers by substituting the answer back into the equation or doing the opposite function required to answer the question. The more answers you check, the faster you will become. This is very important because increasing your answer checking speed can help you catch more careless errors on future tests.

> **Example**: Solve this equation: $6x + 5 = 4x + 1$. The answer is $x = -2$. Now put this back into the equation: $6(-2) + 5 = 4(-2) + 1$. Reduces to $-12 + 5 = -7$ which is $-7 = -7$. If one side of the equation equals the other you have the correct answer. If not rework the problem.

Step 6   *If you do not understand how to do a problem, refer to these points:*

Point 1   Review the textbook material that relates to the problem.

Point 2   Review the lecture notes that relate to the problem.

Point 3   Review any similar problems, diagrams, examples or rules that explain the misunderstood material.

Point 4   Refer to another math textbook, solutions guide, math computer program software or videotape to obtain a better understanding of the material.

Point 5   Call your study buddy.

Point 6   Skip the problem and contact your tutor or math instructor as soon as possible for help.

Step 7   *Always finish your homework by successfully completing problems.* Even if you get stuck, go back and successfully complete previous problems before quitting. You want to end your homework assignment with feelings of success.

Step 8   *After finishing your homework assignment, recall to yourself or write down the most important learned concepts.* Recalling this information will increase your ability to learn these new concepts. This information can be placed in your textbook notes, glossary, or lecture notes, which ever you choose.

Step 9   *Make up note cards containing hard-to-remember problems or concepts.* Note cards are an excellent way to review material for a test. More information on the use of note cards as learning tools is presented later in this chapter.

Step 10   *Getting behind in math homework is academic suicide.* As mentioned in Chapter 1, math is a sequential learning process. If you get behind, it is difficult to catch up because each topic builds on the next. It would be like going to Spanish class without learning the last set of vocabulary words. The teacher would be talking to you using the new vocabulary, but you would not understand what was being said.

Do Not Fall Behind

To keep up with your homework, it is necessary to complete the homework every school day and even on weekends. Doing your homework one-half hour each day for two days in a row is better than one hour every other day.

If you have to get behind in one of your courses, *make sure it is not math.* Fall behind in a course that does not have a sequential learning process, such as psychology or history. After using the 10 Steps to Doing Your Homework, you may be able to combine two steps into one. Find your best combination of homework steps and use them.

> **Remember:** Getting behind in math homework is the fastest way to fail the course.

Before moving on, take a breath. This study process seems very involved. However, if you adapt this process to work for you, this is what could happen:

- You will actually learn the math. This will help not only immediately but also in your future math courses.

- You will work with the math so much that it will land in your long-term memory, and you will not have to cram the night before the test.

- Imagine knowing how to do everything on the test the night before. Very little stress. A good night's sleep.

Watch out for Shortcuts

When doing your math homework you may get help from a friend or tutor. This friend or tutor wants to help you and should show you *every* step in working the problem. However, if you ever hear the statement "*Let me show you a shortcut to solving this problem,*" BEWARE! Many students have told me that they were shown shortcuts to working problems and followed the steps. However, later on, they could not use the shortcuts to solve homework problems or test problems. Learning shortcuts can lead to over confidence and poorer grades. Some major problems with shortcuts are:

a. Shortcuts may require math knowledge above your math level

b. Shortcuts may not be able to be used on similar problems

c. Instructors may not want the shortcuts used on the test

d. Shortcuts may not have a reference in the text to "fall back on"

e. Shortcuts are usually shown once and not remembered

f. Shortcuts may be used by tutors or friends because they do not know how to work the problem step-by-step, and neither will you.

Not all shortcuts are bad, but you need to know the reasoning behind a shortcut. If a friend or tutor wants to show you a shortcut for solving a math problem, ask them for the rules or properties that support the shortcut. Once you understand the rule or property you can then apply the shortcut. Shortcuts are not bad when you understand the reasons behind them.

Distance Learning and Online Homework

Community colleges and universities are now offering more distance learning math courses and requiring online homework for their classroom math courses. Distance learning students have difficulty in communicating with their instructors and classmates. These students have told me that they did not know how or when to communicate with their instructor. Also these students did not know that they could communicate with other students for support and help. As a result of this lack of communication they withdrew from the course or made a lower grade. Distance learning students need to know the protocol for talking to their instructor and other students in their class.

Students in math classroom courses and distance learning math courses are having difficulty developing strategies for completing their required online homework assignments and learning the material. Students are used to doing homework with paper and pencil, not on the computer. Many of these students have told me that they completed the online homework and submitted it, only to realize later on that they have no homework to review for tests. Also they had no homework to compare with other students or use as a basis for in class questions. In short, they did not know how to use online homework to improve their grades and learning. These students need a system for doing online homework.

Communicating with the Instructor and Classmates

Communicating with your instructor and classmates from a distance can be a challenge. The syllabus should have the email address and telephone number of your instructor. The first chance you get, send a "test" email to your instructor to make sure your email systems are compatible. If you get an error message, then call the instructor to see if the email system is down or if the trouble is on your end.

Some students feel that it is an inconvenience to email their instructors questions. This is not so. The instructor expects your emails and will answer them. However, it is best not to start your email with, "I hate to bother you but...."or "I know this sounds like a stupid question but...". These types of introductions show that you are a novice distance learner and sometimes irritate the instructor. Start your email off with a direct question and you will get a direct answer. Don't do what you *think* is the correct assignment. Rather, ask first so you don't waste time doing something you did not have to do or take the risk of doing an incorrect assignment.

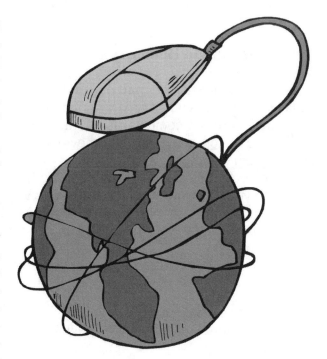

Online communication has its own set of rules.

Other students expect that their instructors will be on the computer 24 hours a day, seven days a week. This is not true. These students expect the instructors to answer their questions immediately even if it is 1:00 am. Usually your instructors have set times of day that they answer email questions. You may want to email your instructor and ask when he/she usually answers the questions and how long it usually takes for a return response.

Don't forget about the phone. If you have some detailed questions, it might be better to have them answered over the phone. You can email your instructor and set up a time when it would be best to call. Make sure you have the questions ready and can record the answers. Remember: Your time and the instructor's time is valuable.

Even with the best time management you may not be able to finish the course on time. How do you communicate to your instructor that you may not finish the course on time? DON'T WAIT! Instructors hate to see an email the last week of class saying that you will not finish. As soon as you know you may not finish, let the instructor know about your difficulties. Ask the instructor, "What do I need to do to complete the course," but also deal with the situation that has occurred. The instructor may be able to make suggestions and can give you the consequences of not finishing before it becomes a crisis. The later you wait, the less flexible the instructor will be.

Many distance-learning courses have group chat rooms. These chat rooms are live or the messages can be posted. The instant message capability of many email systems can set the stage for study groups. Ask your instructor if a time is set up for a group chat or study group. Also ask if your instructor will join the chat group and at what times. You may also get the email address of some of the other students so you can keep up with assignments and help each other with difficult problems.

Communicating with your instructor can solve many problems students face in distance-learning classes. Just don't wait too long to start the process.

How to do Online Homework

In some courses, all or part of your homework may be assigned to be done online. This is usually the case if you are taking a distance-learning course, a hybrid or blended course, or a course where the computer is an integral part of the learning process. In addition, some lecture instructors may assign homework to be done online as an alternative to homework done from the textbook. Whatever the case may be, you will need to develop study skills that can help you improve your online homework success and learning.

Doing your homework online can be a rewarding and enriching experience, but it can also be frustrating if you run into technical problems. Before you take a course that requires you to do homework online, you should ask yourself these questions:

1. Do I have easy access to computer equipment and software, including high-speed internet access, to run the homework program?

2. Do I have the necessary computer skills to use the computer and software?

3. Am I comfortable doing my homework on the computer?

If you answered yes to all the questions, then you are ready to begin doing homework online! The 10 Steps to Doing your Homework are still valid, but we will adapt the steps to online homework.

10 Steps to Doing Online Homework

Step 1   *Review the textbook material that relates to the homework.* This step is still essential when doing online homework. However, the software you are using may have an online textbook that has additional resources that you can access to help you learn the concepts. Some programs, such as MyMathLab, provide you with lecture videos, animations, audio clips, and interactive exercises that you can practice working as you read through the examples in the multimedia textbook. Take advantage of these resources to help you be successful in learning the material.

Step 2   *Review your lecture notes that relate to the homework.* If you are taking a course where the instructor does not lecture, you will have to develop your own set of notes. Many software programs will provide you with lecture videos. You should watch these lectures and create your own notes as the presenter goes through the material. One big advantage of watching a video lecture is the ability to pause the video at crucial points, and to watch a segment over again if you need further review. In a live lecture, this is obviously not possible, and some students find it difficult to take good notes when the instructor moves too fast.

Step 3   *Do your homework as neatly as possible.* Although you will be doing your homework online, it is still important to do your work on paper and keep it in a notebook. Then, if you have a question about the homework, or if you disagree with the answer given by the program, you will be able to refer to your notes when discussing the homework with your instructor. You will also be able to refer to your notebook when studying for the exams.

Step 4   *When doing your homework, write down every step of the problem.* First, write down the problem statement. This is especially important when doing online homework, since many programs such as MyMathLab will generate different problems for each student. If you do not write down the problem, it can be difficult for you or your instructor to figure out what the original problem was. Next, solve the problem and show all the steps. Finally, enter the answer into the program. It is essential that you enter the answer in the correct format. For example, if the program asks you to enter the answer as a fraction and you entered the answer as a decimal, your answer may be marked incorrect even if it is equivalent to the correct answer.

Step 5   *Understand the reasons for each problem step and check your answers.* Many software programs will check your answer and give you immediate feedback. This is one of the major advantages of doing homework online, and can make a huge difference in your understanding of the concepts. If you get an answer incorrect, use the feedback along with your notes to try and figure out where you made the mistake. The program may also give you another opportunity to work the problem, perhaps with different numbers, and you should take advantage of this option to redo the problem.

Step 6   *If you do not understand how to work the problem, use the resources provided by the software to learn how to do the problem correctly.* For example, in the MyMathLab program, you can ask the program to guide you through the solution one step at a time. Use this approach to learn how to solve the problem. You may also be able to view an example that is similar to the problem you are trying to solve. You may also want to review the video lectures, multimedia textbook, or other online resources to help you understand the concepts. Once you understand how to solve the problem, you can ask the program to generate a new problem for you to solve.

Step 7   *Always finish your homework by successfully completing problems.* With online homework, it's easier to end your homework session with feelings of success, since you can usually redo problems until you get the correct solution. Many students find that online homework not only helps them understand the concepts more readily, but it also gives them a boost in morale because of the immediate and positive feedback.

Step 8 *After finishing your homework assignment, recall to yourself or write down the most important learned concepts.* This is still an important step when doing online homework, so resist the temptation to skip this step.

Step 9 *Make up note cards containing hard-to-remember problems or concepts.* Some programs will provide students with ready-made note cards, and you can print these out and use them as starting points for your own note cards.

Step 10 *Getting behind in math homework is academic suicide.* In a distance-learning, hybrid, or computer-aided course, there may not be fixed deadlines for each homework assignment, and students may be allowed to work at a flexible pace. However, if the course must be completed by the end of the term, it is better to pace yourself and complete the work in a timely manner rather than rushing to complete the bulk of the work just before the end of the term. Be sure to complete the online homework assignments in order. Math is still a sequential learning process regardless of how you do your homework!

Now that you have read the Ten Steps for Doing Online Homework practice these steps to improve your homework learning. Remember, effectively completing your homework is one of the best ways to have information transferred from working memory to long-term memory and abstract reasoning.

! Remember: Doing homework correctly can pay off in better grades! **!**

Samples of Metacognitive Techniques to Solve Homework Problems

Metacognition was discussed in the Understanding and Improving the Memory Process chapter and can be applied to textbook and online homework. It is what students are thinking about when solving math problems. This is a self-monitoring process used to develop problem solving steps to find the solution to the problem. Memorization of problem steps instead of understanding the rules and principles to solve the problems leads to passive learning and unsuccessful problem solving. You need a model to follow when solving math problems.

The model of **plan, monitor and evaluate** is the framework for solving math problems. This model involves asking yourself questions when solving problems. *Planning* consists of understanding what the problem wants, the strategies to solve the problem, potential obstacles, understanding what information is required, doing the calculations and predicting the outcome. *Monitoring* is putting the steps in order, keeping one's place, identifying and finding errors, understanding when additional information is needed, knowing when to use another strategy and knowing when you have part of the answer. *Evaluating* includes knowing if the answer seems right (number sense), putting the answer back into the equation or doing the opposite of the function to see if the answer is correct and measuring the efficiency of the plan and monitoring.

Now that we know the theory about metacognition, let's apply it to solving some math problems. Let's look at the process for solving linear equations.

Solve: $-3(x-6) + 2 = 2(4x-1)$

The first step is making a plan by asking yourself questions about solving linear equations. Some example questions to solve this equation are:

1. Question: What is a linear equation?

   Answer: *It must have at least one variable and some numerals or variables and an = sign but no exponents greater than one.*

   Example: $-3(x-6) + 2 = 2(4x-1)$

2. Question: Are there any ( ) ?

   Answer: *Yes. Then multiply the number or variable in front times everything inside the ().*

   Example:
   $$-3(x-6) + 2 = 2(4x-1)$$
   $$-3x + 18 + 2 = 8x - 2$$

3. Question: Are there like terms on the same side of the equation?

   Answer: *Yes. Then combine the like terms on the same side only.*

   Example:
   $$-3x + 18 + 2 = 8x - 2$$
   $$-3x + 20 = 8x - 2$$

4. Question: Are there letters and/or numbers on both sides of the = ?

   Answer: *Yes. Then put the letters on one side and the numbers on the other side.*

   Example:
   $$-3x + 20 = 8x - 2$$
   $$-3x + 20 + 2 = 8x - 2 + 2$$
   $$-3x + 22 = 8x$$
   $$3x - 3x + 22 = 8x + 3x$$
   $$22 = 11x$$

5. Question: Is there a number attached to x?

   Answer: *Yes. Then divide both sides by the number that is attached to x.*

   Example:
   $$\frac{22}{11} = \frac{11x}{11}$$

   $$2 = x$$

6. Question: Does this seem to be the right answer?

   Answer: *Yes. The answer is about right. It is not too large.*

Question: How can you find out if it is right?

Answer: *Substitute the answer back into the equations and see if one side equals the other side.*

Example: $-3 (x - 6) + 2 = 2 (4x - 1)$ substitute 2 for x
$-3 (2 - 6) + 2 = 2 (4 (2) - 1)$
$12 + 2 = 2 (7)$
$14 = 14$

Question: Is this the right answer?

Answer: *Yes. One side equals the other side.*

The metacongnitive process involves planing, monitoring and evaluating. Step one is part of the plan, steps two through five involve a combination of planning and monitoring and step six is the evaluation. You can use this as a model of asking yourself questions while solving linear equations. You can ask your instructor about exceptions to these problems.

Now let's look at the steps for solving quadratic equations. What are some of the questions you need to ask yourself to solve $x^2 + 6x = 16$. The first step to planning is to ask yourself questions about quadratic equations. Some example questions to solve this equation are:

1. Question: What is a quadratic equation?

   Answer: *It has a square term and has an = sign.*

   Example: $x^2 + 6x = 16$

2. Question: Does one side of the equation equal to 0?

   Answer: *No. Then move the term from the right side to the left side by using the opposite sign.*

   Example: $x^2 + 6x = 16$
   $x^2 + 6x - 16 = 16 - 16$
   $x^2 + 6x - 16 = 0$

3. Question: Can you factor the left side of the equation

   Answer: *Yes.*

   Example: $(x + 8) (x - 2) = 0$

4. Question: Do we have two factors?

   Answer: *Yes.*

Question: What are the factors?

Answer: *(x + 8) and (x - 2)*

5. Question: Can we make each factor individually equal to 0?

   Answer: *Yes.*

   Example: $x + 8 = 0$ and $x - 2 = 0$

6. Question: Can you solve each equation?

   Answer: *Yes.*

   Example:

$$x + 8 = 0 \qquad\qquad x - 2 = 0$$
$$x + 8 - 8 = 0 - 8 \qquad x - 2 + 2 = 0 + 2$$
$$x = -8 \qquad\qquad x = 2$$

7. Question: You should have two solutions. Do you?

   Answer: *Yes. They are -8 and 2.*

8. Question: Does this seem to be the right answer?

   Answer: *Yes. They are two answers and they are not too large.*

   Question: How can you find out if it is right?

   Answer: *Put the answers back into the equation and see if one side equals the other side.*

   Example: $x^2 + 6x = 16$; Solution one is $x = -8$

$$64 - 48 = 16$$
$$16 \ \ = 16$$

   or

   $x^2 + 6x = 16$; Solution two is $x = 2$

$$4 + 12 = 16$$
$$16 = 16$$

   Question: Are these the right answers?

   Answer: *Yes. One side equals the other side.*

Like the previous problem, step one is part of the plan, steps two and three are a combination of planning and monitoring while step four is monitoring. Steps five and six are a combination of planning and monitoring. Step seven is monitoring again while step eight is evaluating. This is a model you can use to help ask yourself questions while solving problems. You can ask your instructor about exceptions to these problems.

Using metacognition to solve math problems will increase your homework and test-taking success. You may ask yourself different questions based on the different types of problems. These questions may come slowly at first, but they will speed up and become almost automatic, just like your basic multiplication tables. Your math instructors have already achieved this goal and can solve linear and quadratic equations almost at the speed of light. Don't be intimidated. It has taken them many years to accomplish these skills. With practice, some day you can be just as effective.

Additional Learning Resources:
In Class and Distance Learning

For many students, additional outside resources are a necessity for doing well in the course. These outside resources supplement the online instruction and in some cases may become the primary instruction. The learning resources can be in the traditional sense and in the nontraditional sense. Traditional learning resources include the textbook, private tutoring, tutor centers, adult education centers, libraries, study skills training, video tapes, and commercial math computer programs. Non-traditional resources include textbook CD ROMs, call-in tutor centers, online tutor centers (comes with some textbooks), commercial online tutor centers and self help web sites. These resources can enhance your learning.

Learning resources can also be categorized based on location. There are campus based, community based and personal resources. Campus based resources are becoming very important because of the unexpected number of students who take both distance-learning courses and regular classroom courses. Students who are distance learners and cannot visit the campus look for local community resources to support their learning. The personal resources such as the computer have tremendously expanded because of the need to support distance-learning students. Taking advantage of these resources, especially early in the term can increase your learning and grades. Try to find out what academic resources are available before enrolling in a distance-learning course in math. It doesn't have to be just you and the course. You can always get additional help.

Distance-learning students who have access to their campus resources may want to go to the college or university web page. This web page should give you the resource information you need to make further contacts. You may want to contact the math lab, learning center, assessment center, library, returning adult center or any other place that may be able to assist in your learning. You want to ask them the following questions:

1. Is tutoring by appointment or is it drop-in?

2. When is the best time to get tutoring?

3. Do you have evening hours for tutoring?

4. Do you have any computer programs to assess my study skills and learning styles?

5. Can math videotapes, resource books or computer programs be checked out?

6. Do you have a homework hot line?

7. What other learning resources do you have?

8. Do you have any locations that have these resources in my area?

Asking these questions will give you a good idea of the additional support that you can use on your campus.

In many cases it is too far to visit the campus to obtain this additional help. Look in your community to see if there are resources. Some of the places you can look are:

1. The local community, junior or technical college
2. The adult high school center
3. Goodwill learning centers
4. County libraries
5. Commercial tutor centers such as Sylvan Learning Center or Hunting Learning Center
6. Private tutoring

Once a resource is located you can ask them some of the same questions that you would ask the on campus resources.

Personal resources are accessible from your home and can supplement your learning. Personal resources have greatly expanded over the last several years to include all sorts of help aids and materials. Some of the personal resources include:

1. Private in home tutoring
2. Educational TV
3. Live telephone tutoring
4. Online book ordering
5. CD ROMs
6. Online mini-lessons, algebra models and worksheets
7. Online automated algebra problem solving
8. Live online tutoring.

Tutoring with trained tutors can be a great benefit to your learning. Some of these tutors will come to your home. You can find tutors in the phone book by calling high school and college math departments or by asking your online instructor. Make sure that the tutors are trained or they have references that you can call. Tutors can be a great help in improving your learning, but most students wait too long to use them. As soon as you are in difficulty, or if you anticipate the need for assistance, find it immediately. Don't wait until you are failing.

There are many educational programs on television. Your local PBS station may have programs on mathematics. Also, some other colleges may have broadcast shows on how to do algebra, statistics or even calculus. Call your local cable company or PBS station to see if they have any programs on mathematics. It does not matter when the shows are broadcast because you can video tape and play them back at your own convenience.

The college/university where you are taking the course may have live telephone tutoring. Also, some college textbook companies offer limited live tutoring if your college/university is using their text. Some high schools or community service groups may also have telephone tutoring. Contact these sources to see if live telephone tutoring is an option for you. If tutoring exists, then call with specific questions about a problem. Don't just tell them, "I don't know how to do the problem." Give them the problems and tell them where you got stuck.

Sometimes your book does not give a good description on how to work certain problems. Math instructors know that some books give better explanations on how to work certain problems than other books. It would be a good idea to obtain another book on how to solve the problems. Some of the self help books or high school books may have a better explanation on how to work the problems. Now if you are in college taking a developmental pre-algebra course, then the text you want is a combination of arithmetic and beginning algebra. If you are in college in a developmental algebra course you would want an algebra I book. If you are in college taking an intermediate algebra course you may want algebra II and algebra III books. If you are in college algebra then you want a college algebra book. You can get these books at your local bookstore, or you can go online at Amazon.com and order the books. One extra book may make the difference in a letter grade in your course.

Many math books now come with CD ROMs attached to the back cover. See if your book has a CD ROM with supplemental homework problems and solutions. If your text does not have a CD ROM then you should purchase a commercial CD ROM that supports your area of study. Ask the instructor or the math lab/learning support center director for the names of some good software such as Algeblaster. Make sure this software is for adults instead of children and matches the area that you need to study.

Web Resources

Online mini-lessons, algebra models, worksheets, virtual algebra solutions, and sites that solve math problems are on certain websites. Some websites are free, while others require a registration fee. Some of these sites have advertisement that pays for the site. You might want to review the websites under Student Math Practice and Learning Sites at www.academicsuccess.com. The websites are arranged by math course name with supplemental learning in calculator skills, virtual flash cards and video lessons. Using these Internet sources can improve your math learning and skills. Distance learning students can also find free sites that will solve their submitted math problems.

Additional learning resources can make the difference in being successful in a distance-learning course. Explore the different resources to see which ones meet your learning style and time constraints. If you are not sure which learning resource meets your needs, then try several of the different learning resources to discover which one best improves your learning.

How to Solve Word Problems

The most difficult homework assignment for most math students is working story/word problems. Solving word problems requires excellent reading comprehension and translating skills. Students often have difficulty substituting English terms for algebraic symbols and equations, but once an equation is written, it is usually easy to solve. To help you solve word problems follow these 10 steps:

Step 1   *Read the problem three times.* Read the problem quickly the *first time* as a scanning procedure. As you are reading the problem the *second time*, answer these three questions:

1. *What is the problem asking me?* (Usually at the end of the problem.)

2. *What is the problem telling me that is useful?* (Cross out unneeded information).

3. *What is the problem implying?* (Usually something you have been told to remember).

Read the problem a *third time* to check that you fully understand its meaning.

Step 2   *Draw a simple picture of the problem to make it more real to you* (e.g., a circle with an arrow can represent travel in any form — by train, by boat, by plane, by car, or by foot).

Step 3   *Make a table of information and leave a blank space for the information you are not told.*

Word problems are like mini-mysteries.

Step 4   *Use as few unknowns in your table as possible.* If you can represent all the unknown information in terms of a single letter, do so! When using more than one unknown, use a letter that reminds you of that unknown. Then write down what your unknowns represent. This eliminates the problem of assigning the right answer to the wrong unknown. Remember you have to create as many separate equations as you have unknowns.

Step 5   *Translate the English terms into an algebraic equation using the list of terms in Figure 24 (Translating English Terms into Algebraic Symbols) and Figure 25 (Translating English Words into Algebraic Expressions).* Remember the English terms are sometimes stated in a different order than the algebraic terms.

Step 6   *Immediately retranslate the equation, as you now have it, back into English.* The translation will not sound like a normal English phrase, but the meaning should be the same as the original problem. If the meaning is not the same, the equation is incorrect and needs to be rewritten. Rewrite the equation until it means the same as the English phrase.

Step 7   *Review the equation to see if it is similar to equations from your homework and if it makes sense.* Some formulas dealing with specific word problems may need to be rewritten. Distance problems, for example, may need to be written solving for each of the other variables in the formula. Distance = Rate x Time; therefore, Time = Distance/Rate, and Rate = Distance/Time. Usually, a distance problem will identify the specific variable to be solved.

Step 8   *Solve the equation using the rules of algebra.*

Remember: Whatever is done to one side of the equation must be done to the other side of the equation. The unknown must end up on one side of the equation, by itself. If you have more than one unknown, then use the substitution or elimination method to solve the system of equations.

Figure 24
Translating English Terms Into Algebraic Symbols

Sum	+
Add	+
In addition	+
More than	+
Increased	+
In excess	+
Greater	+
Decreased by	-
Less than	-
Subtract	-
Difference	-
Diminished	-
Reduce	-
Remainder	-
Times as much	x
Percent of	x
Product	x
Interest on	x
Per	/
Divide	/
Quotient	/
Quantity	( )
Is	=
Was	=
Equal	=
Will be	=
Results	=
Greater than	>
Greater than or equal to	≥
Less than	<
Less than or equal to	≤

Figure 25
Translating English Words Into Algebraic Expressions

English Words	Algebraic Expressions
Ten more than x	$x + 10$
A number added to 5	$5 + x$
A number increased by 13	$x + 13$
5 less than 10	$10 - 5$
A number decreased by 7	$x - 7$
Difference between x and 3	$x - 3$
Difference between 3 and x	$3 - x$
3 less than a number	$x - 3$
Twice a number	$2x$
Ten percent of x	$.10x$
Ten times x	$10x$
Quotient of x and 3	$x/3$
Quotient of 3 and x	$3/x$
Five is three more than a number	$5 = x + 3$
The product of 2 times a number is 10	$2x = 10$
One half a number is 10	$x/2 = 10$
Five times the sum of x and 2	$5(x + 2)$
Seven is greater than x	$7 > x$
Five times the difference of a number and 4	$5(x - 4)$
Ten subtracted from 10 times a number is that number plus 5	$10x - 10 = x + 5$
The sum of 5x and 10 is equal to the product of x and 15	$5x + 10 = 15x$
The sum of two consecutive integers	$(x) + (x + 1)$
The sum of two consecutive even integers	$(x) + (x + 2)$
The sum of two consecutive odd integers	$(x) + (x + 2)$

Step 9   *Look at your answer to see if it makes common sense.*

Step 10   *Put your answer back into the original equation to see if it is correct.* If one side of the equation equals the other side of the equation, then you have the correct answer. If you do not have the correct answer, go back to Step 5.

The most difficult part of solving word problems is translating part of a sentence into algebraic symbols and then into algebraic expressions. Review Figure 24 (Translating English Terms into Algebraic Expressions) and Figure 25 (Translating English Words into Algebraic Expressions), on the next two pages.

How to Recall What You Have Learned

After completing your homework problems, a good visual learning technique is to make note cards. Note cards are 3x5 index cards on which you place information that is difficult to learn or material you think will be on the test.

On the front of the note card write a math problem or information that you need to know. Color-code the important information in red or blue. On the back of the note card write how to work the problem or give an explanation of important information.

Make note cards on important information you might forget. Every time you have five spare minutes, pull out your note cards and review them. You can glance at the front of the card, repeat to yourself the answer and check yourself with the back of the card. If you are correct and know the information on a card, do not put it back in the deck. Mix up the cards you do not know and pick another card to test yourself on the information. Keep doing this until there are no cards left that you do not know.

If you are an auditory learner, then use the tape recorder like the note cards. Record the important information just like you would on the front of the note card. Then leave a blank space on the recording. Record the answer. Play the tape back. When you hear the silence, put the tape on pause. Then say the answer out loud to yourself. Take the tape player off pause and see if you were correct. You can use this technique in the car while driving to college or work.

Review What You Have Learned

After finishing your homework, close the textbook and try to remember what you have learned. Ask yourself these questions, "What major concepts did I learn tonight?" or "What test questions might the instructor ask on this material?"

Recall for about three to four minutes the major points of the assignment, especially the areas you had difficulty understanding. Write down questions for the instructor or tutor. Since most forgetting occurs right after learning the material, this short review will help you retain the new material.

! **Remember:** The skimming strategy for reading the textbook? This is a good **!** time to skim all that you have worked on.

How to Work with a Study Buddy

You need to have a study buddy in case you miss class or have questions when doing your homework. Group learners can especially benefit from a study buddy. A study buddy is a friend or classmate who is taking the same course. You can find a study buddy by talking to your classmates or making friends in the math lab.

Try to find a study buddy who knows more about math than you do. Tell the class instructor that you are trying to find a study buddy and ask which students might work well with you. Meet with your study buddy several times a week to work on problems and to discuss math. If you miss class, get the notes from your study buddy, so you will not get behind.

Studying together helps us make sure we are learning everything we need to.

Call your study buddy when you get stuck on your homework. You can solve math problems over the phone. Do not sit for half an hour or an hour trying to work one problem; that will destroy your confidence, waste valuable time and possibly alienate your study buddy. Think how much you could have learned by trying the problem for 15 minutes and then calling your study buddy for help. Spend, at the maximum, 15 minutes on one problem before going on to the next problem or calling your study buddy.

Remember that you are part of the study buddy team. If you adapt the study system that you are reading about to meet your needs, you will be an excellent study buddy.

 Remember: A study buddy can improve your learning while helping you complete the homework assignment. You can return the favor. Just do not overuse your study buddy or expect that person to do your homework for you.

Summary

- Reading a math textbook is more difficult than reading texts for other courses.

- Students who learn how to correctly read a math text will be able to improve their math learning and understanding of the lecture material.

- Using the "Ten Steps to Understanding Reading Material" is an excellent way to comprehend your math text.

- After using and understanding these steps, you may be able to customize your own reading steps to make reading easier and more efficient.

- Establishing study period goals is an excellent way to successfully manage homework time.

- Make sure to set a goal of either completing a given number of problems or working on problems for a set amount of time.

- Setting up short-term goals and accomplishing them is one of the best ways to gain control over math.

- Make sure you finish every homework session by working problems you can do.

- Using the "10 Steps for Doing Your Homework" is a way to do your homework and learn math at the same time.

- These steps will decrease the chances of doing the homework one day and two days later forgetting how to work the problems.

- Follow these 10 steps until you are comfortable using them and until they become a part of your normal study routine. Then you may want to adjust the 10 steps to make your own efficient homework system.

- Applying the "10 Steps for Doing Online Homework" to distance learning courses or required online homework can increase your math learning.

- Now, and even more so in the future, students who are graphing- calculator literate will have a learning and testing advantage over other students.

- You must learn how to effectively use a graphing calculator or graphing/programmable calculator to be at least equal with your fellow students.

- Taking a calculator course or attending calculator workshops, along with understanding your calculator manual, will improve your calculator knowledge.

! **Remember:** You need to know how to use your calculator efficiently prior to **!**
the test instead of learning how to use it during the test.

Assignment for Chapter 7

1. List and describe three reasons you need to read and understand your course syllabus.

   Reason one: _____

   Reason two: _____

   Reason three: _____

2. How is reading a math textbook different from reading other textbooks?

   _____

   _____

   _____

3. List and describe the ten steps to reading a math textbook.

   Step one: _____

   Step two: _____

   Step three: _____

   Step four: _____

   Step five: _____

   Step six: _____

   Step seven: _____

   Step eight: _____

   Step nine: _____

   Step ten: _____

4. Explain how taking notes while reading your textbook and developing a math glossary can help you learn math.

   _____

   _____

5. What do you need to do before starting your math homework?

   _____

   _____

6. What are the reasons for writing down every problem step while doing the homework?

   _____

   _____

Assignment for Chapter 7

7. List and describe the 10 Steps for Doing Your Homework or Online Homework.

   Step one: _____

   Step two: _____

   Step three: _____

   Step four: _____

   Step five: _____

   Step six: _____

   Step seven: _____

   Step eight: _____

   Step nine: _____

   Step ten: _____

8. List five additional resources that you use to improve your learning.

   Resource one: _____

   Resource two: _____

   Resource three: _____

   Resource four: _____

   Resource five: _____

9. List and describe the 10 steps to solving word problems.

   Step one: _____

   Step two: _____

   Step three: _____

   Step four: _____

   Step five: _____

   Step six: _____

   Step seven: _____

   Step eight: _____

   Step nine: _____

   Step ten: _____

10. List and describe three strategies to help you recall what you have learned.

    Strategy one: _____

    Strategy two: _____

    Strategy three: _____

How to Improve Your Math Test-Taking Skills

8

In Chapter 8
you will learn these concepts:

- Many times students do not demonstrate how much they know on a test because they do not have a plan for taking the test. Students often think doing their homework and going to class is sufficient preparation, but it isn't.

  ✓ Reasons why just attending class may not be enough to pass tests.

  ✓ Reasons why just completing homework may not be enough to pass tests.

  ✓ Students have been taught how to take multiple choice tests, but not math tests. Also students do not know how to analyze math test results. Both can lead to poor test grades.

  ✓ The general rules to follow before the test

  ✓ Ten steps to better test-taking

  ✓ Six types of test-taking errors

  ✓ Ways to prepare for the final exam

  ✓ Ways to take distance-learning tests

Introduction

Taking a math test is different from taking tests in other subjects. First, math tests not only require you to recall the information but apply it as well. Multiple-choice tests, for example, usually test you on recall, and if you do not know the answer, you can guess. Second, math tests build on each other where history tests often do not test you on previous material. Third, most math tests are speed tests where the faster you are the better grade you can receive, while most social science tests are designed for everyone to finish.

Subsequently, math test preparation and test-taking skills are different from preparation and skills needed for other tests. You need to have a test-taking plan to demonstrate your total knowledge on math and a test-analysis plan to discover ways to improve your test-taking strategies. Students with these plans make better grades compared to students without them. Math instructors want to measure your math knowledge, not your poor test-taking skills.

Why Attending Class and Doing Your Homework May Not Be Enough to Pass

Most students and some instructors believe that attending class and doing all the homework ensures an "A" or "B" on tests. This is far from true. Listening in class and understanding how to solve the problems is very different from actually solving the problems on a test. Here are the reasons why:

1. While in class, instructors can ask you questions to lead you to the next step.
2. While in class, instructors can give you a hint to solving the problem.
3. While in class, you can ask questions about solving the problems.
4. While in class, instructors can do all the problem steps for you and get the correct answer.
5. You can refer to the math text or solution manual during class.
6. In small groups, other students can help you solve the problems.
7. There is less anxiety solving the problems in class than during a test.
8. If you do not learn how to solve the problem in class, you can go to the instructor or tutor after class.

Many students get a false sense of security because they know how to do the math problems while in class. Then, when the test comes around, they have difficulty solving the same problems. Don't let this happen to you! This false sense of security can also happen when doing your homework. Doing all the homework and getting the correct answers is very different in many ways from taking tests:

1. While doing homework there is little anxiety. A test situation is just the opposite.
2. You are not under a time constraint while doing your homework; you may have to complete a test in 55 minutes or less.
3. If you get stuck on a homework problem, your textbook and notes are there to assist you. This is not true for most tests.
4. Once you learn how to do several problems in a homework assignment, the rest are similar. In a test the problems are all in random order.
5. In doing homework, you have the answers to at least half the problems in the back of the text and answers to all the problems in the solutions guide. This is not true for tests.
6. While doing homework, you have time to figure out how to correctly use your calculator. During the test, you can waste valuable time figuring out how to use your calculator.
7. When doing homework, you can call your study buddy or ask the tutor for help, something that you cannot do on the test.
8. When doing your homework, you can go to the web and do online tutoring.

Do not develop a false sense of security by believing you can make an "A" or "B" by just doing your homework. Tests measure more than just your math knowledge.

The General Pretest Rules

General rules are important when taking any type of test:

1. *Get a good night's sleep before taking a test.* This is true for the ACT, the SAT and your math tests. If you are going to cram all night and imagine you will perform well on your test with three to four hours of sleep, you are wrong. It would be better to get seven or eight hours sleep and be fresh enough to use your memory to recall information needed to answer the questions.

2. *Start studying for the test at least three days ahead of time.* Make sure you take a practice test to find out what you do not know. Review and work the problems in your problem log. If you did not do a problem log, then use the chapter review test to find out what you don't know. However, a better way is to work with some classmates to make up test questions to make sure you know the material. Review the concept errors you made on the last test. (How to identify and correct your concept errors will be discussed later on in this chapter.) Meet with the instructor or tutor for help on those questions you cannot solve.

3. *Only review already-learned material the night before a test.*

4. *Make sure you know all the information on your mental cheat sheet.* Review your notebook and glossary to make sure you understand the concepts. Work a few problems and recall the information on your mental cheat sheet right before you go to bed. Go directly to bed; do not watch television, listen to the radio or party. While you are asleep, your mind will work on and remember the last thing you did before going to sleep.

5. *Get up in the morning at your usual time and review your notes and problem log.* Do not do any new problems. Make sure your calculator is working.

The 10 Steps to Better Test-Taking

Taking a math test is different than taking other tests. Most students know how to take a multiple choice test but have no clue about the best way to take a math test. When taking any test you are being measured in two areas: The content of the material, and how well you take a test. To take a math test you need a plan. This plan will make you more efficient, confident and lowers test anxiety. The plan needs to be developed before you take the test and needs to be followed during the test. I have known hundreds of students who have lost tests points because they did not have a test plan and did not practice that plan before taking the test. Make sure you develop and memorize your mental cheat sheet so you can write down the information on the test (don't use the sheet during the test) and practice the test-taking steps below before taking the tests.

By reviewing how you took your last math test we can determine what changes you can make to improve your test-taking skills. In the space below list your test-taking steps and explain them:

Step 1: _____

_____

Step 2: _____

_____

Step 3: _____

_____

Step 4: _____

_____

Step 5: _____

_____

Other steps: _____

_____

As you are reading the 10 Steps to Better Test-taking compare them to your steps. Once you begin a test, follow the 10 steps to better test-taking, below:

Step 1   *Use a memory data dump.* When you get your test, turn it over and write down the information that you put on your mental cheat sheet. Your mental cheat sheet has now turned into a mental list and writing down this information is not cheating. Do not put your name on the test, do not skim it, just turn it over and write down those facts, figures and formulas from your mental cheat sheet or other information you might not remember during the test. This is called your *first memory data dump*. The data dump provides memory cues for test questions.

You must have a game plan

> **Example:** It might take you a while to remember how to do a coin-word problem. However, if you had immediately turned your test over and written down different ways of solving coin-word problems, it would be easier to solve the coin-word problem.

Step 2   *Preview the test.* Put your name on the test and start previewing. Look through the entire test to find different types of problems and their point values. Put a mark by the questions that you can do without thinking. These are the questions that you will solve first.

Step 3   *Do a second memory data dump.* The second data dump is for writing down material that was jarred from your memory while previewing the test. Write this information on the back of the test.

Step 4   *Develop a test progress schedule.* When you begin setting up a test schedule, determine the point value for each question. You might have some test questions that are worth

Make sure you do your memory dump first.

more points than others. In some tests, word problems are worth five points and other questions might be worth two or three points. Just like in a video game, you must decide the best way to get the most points in the least amount of time. This might mean working the questions worth two to three points first and leaving the more difficult word problems for last. Decide how many problems should be completed halfway through the test. You should have more than half the problems completed by that time.

Step 5   *Answer the easiest problems first.* Solve, in order, the problems you marked while previewing the test. Then, review the answers to see if they make sense. Start working through the test as fast as you can while being accurate. Answers should be reasonable.

> **Example:** The answer to a problem of trying to find the area of a rectangle cannot be negative, and the answer to a land-rate-distance problem cannot be 1,000 miles per hour.
>
> Clearly write down each step to get partial credit, even if you end up missing the problem. In most math tests, the easier problems are near the beginning of the first page; you need to answer them efficiently and quickly. This will give you both more time for the harder problems and time to review.

Step 6   *Do the difficult problems you know how to do.* These are the problems that have quite a few steps and take some time to complete, but are also problems you can complete without any real trouble. These problems are usually worth more points than the rest of the test, so it is important to finish them before you attempt problems that you don't know how to do. By finishing these problems early on in your test time, you can relax, knowing that you already have quite a few points in the bag. This will boost your confidence as you head into the problems you might not know how to do.

Step 7   *Tackle the toughest problems.* These are the problems that you might remember a few things about, but you don't know enough to complete them. You might remember the first step, but then draw a blank on what to do next. It is important to begin the problem, even if you know that you cannot complete it. By starting the problem and writing down what you know, you are warming up your brain, which might trigger the "Ah ha!" response. The "Ah ha!" response is when your brain suddenly remembers how to complete a problem. A memory from your homework or a lecture sometimes will pop back into your head right when you need it most. Take some time on these problems, but move on if you are completely stuck.

Step 8   *Guess at the remaining problems.* Do as much work as you can on each problem, even if it is just writing down the first step. If you cannot write down the first step, rewrite the problem. Also remember that the way you learned how to solve a problem was by writing not just looking at the problem.

Sometimes rewriting the problem can jar your memory enough to do the first step or the entire problem. If you leave the problem blank, you will get a zero. Do not waste too much time on guessing or trying to work the problems you cannot do.

Step 9   *Review the test.* Look for careless errors or other errors you may have made. Students usually lose two to five test points on errors that could have been caught in review. Do not talk yourself out of an answer just because it may not look right. This often happens when an answer does not come out even. It is possible for the answer to be a fraction or a decimal.

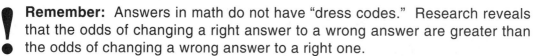

Remember: Answers in math do not have "dress codes." Research reveals that the odds of changing a right answer to a wrong answer are greater than the odds of changing a wrong answer to a right one.

Step 10 *Use all the allowed test time.* Review each problem by substituting the answer back into the equation or doing the opposite function required to answer the question. If you cannot check the problem in these ways, rework the problem on a separate sheet of paper and compare the answers. Do not leave the classroom unless you have reviewed each problem two times or until the bell rings.

Even though we encourage students to work until the end of the test period most students leave the classroom before the end of the period. These students state that even though they know they should use all the test time, they cannot stay in the room until the end of the test time. These students also know that their grades would probably improve if they kept checking their answers or kept working the problems they are having difficulty with. After talking to hundreds of these students, I discovered two different themes for leaving the classroom early. First, test anxiety gets so overwhelming that they cannot stay in the room. The relief from the test anxiety (leaving the room) is worth more than getting a better grade. If you are one of these students, you must learn how to decrease your test anxiety by following the suggestions in Chapter 3 or by using the *How to Reduce Test Anxiety* CD. Don't let the anxiety control your grades!

The other reason for leaving the test early is that they do not want to be the last or one of the last few students to turn in their tests. They still believe that students who turn their tests in last are "dumb and stupid." These students also believe that students who turn their tests in first make "A's" and "B's" and those students who turn their tests in last make "D's" and "F's." If you are one of these students, you don't need to care about what other students think about you (it's usually wrong anyway). YOU need to fight the urge to leave early and use all the test time. Remember, passing mathematics is the best way to get a high paying job and support yourself or your family. DO IT NOW!

Remember: There is no prize for handing your test in first, and students who turn their papers in last do make "A's."

Stapling your scratch paper to the math test when handing it in has several advantages:

• If you miscopied the answer from the scratch paper, you will probably get credit for the answers.

• If you get the answer incorrect due to a careless error, your work on the scratch paper could give you a few points.

• If you do get the problem wrong, it will be easier to locate the errors when the instructor reviews the test. This will prevent you from making the same mistakes on the next math test.

Remember: Handing in your scratch paper may get you extra points or improve your next test score.

You can go to the Winning at Math Student Resource Website for a condensed version of the "Ten Test-Taking Steps" that may make it easier to memorize.

Test-Taking Skills for Distance Learning Courses

Each instructor in a distance-learning class may set up the testing process differently. It is important that you understand how this process works the first week to avoid any surprises. It is possible that you may not be able to take the tests in the way that they are set up. Math tests in distance-learning classes have been particularly problematic. Review the syllabus to see how and where you will be tested. In most cases, you may take practice tests and quizzes online, but the major tests will probably be in a secure test center, usually on a college campus. In some cases you may have to go to the local community college or university and pay to take the test in their testing centers. Make sure you are able to do this if it is the way the test administration is set up. If you can't, talk to the instructor immediately during the first week of classes. This way, if there are no alternative ways to take the tests, you are still allowed to drop or change sections of the math class.

Taking tests in a distance-learning course can be different. The same test-taking strategies will work, but you must concentrate more on developing and taking practice tests under real conditions. Using the web based practice tests is a good idea; however, if you are getting your friends to help you, or you are using outside resources during the tests, you may be building a false sense of security. The best preparation is to practice taking the tests under the same conditions that are indicated in the syllabus.

> **Remember:** Students in regular classrooms get to practice taking several tests before taking the midterm or final. Distance-learning students may take only one or two tests to determine their grades.

Getting ready to take the test also involves knowing what aids you can use on the test. Check the syllabus to see if any test aids, such as calculators or index cards, can be used. If you are not sure about what you can use on the test, email or call your instructor and ask. If you are allowed to use a calculator, make sure you know what type is permitted. When you practice taking a test, practice using the aids you are allowed to use.

Sometimes students feel a little more stressed when they have to go to a new testing center that they have never visited. First, some people get nervous about even finding the testing center. It is wise to call the testing center and get directions. If you think you are one of these people, do like some students and practice getting there on a day before the test. You will know how much time to allow for travel. Second, some students just get nervous in new environments, so when you make the "practice run" to the test center, stop in and talk to the staff just to say hi. Then if you need to call them for some reason, you can ask for particular staff who will remember who you are. Ask to see the room where you will be taking the test. Your early visit might also make the staff double check to see if they are ready for your class to come. Third, if you are used to taking tests with others around you, it might be that the testing administration is set up for students to come in within certain time limitations that could be certain hours on one day or over a period of several days. You may be taking the test by yourself. Just be mentally prepared. Finally, unless you have met with several students in a study group, it will be easy to get distracted with meeting all the students with whom you have conversed over the internet or during video conferences. Stay focused and visit after the test.

The Six Types of Test-Taking Errors

When students get their tests back they usually don't look at them. Some throw them away or stick them in their books and forget about them. In most cases it does not matter if the students make a good grade on the test or a poor grade. They do not like reviewing the tests. Some instructors make the students review the tests by going over them in class, but rarely do the students analyze the tests. This leads to repeating mistakes. As a comparison, imagine what would happen if your doctor gave you a blood test to see why you were sick and you decided to just throw away the results and just pick some medicine off the shelf to see if it would cure you. The doctor would be sued for malpractice, and you may pick the wrong medicine and die. Perhaps the analogy exaggerates, but it makes the point.

Mom always said, "Learn from your mistakes."

The real question is, "Why do instructors return math tests?" Instructors return math tests to give you feedback on your progress in the course and to allow you to correct your mistakes. As mentioned several times in this text, MATH IS SEQUENTIAL. This means what you learn in class today is used in the next class. This is why students need to review their returned tests, so that they can correct and understand their mistakes. This process will enhance learning.

The real question is, "What do you do with your returned tests?" Below put a check by what you do (you can mark more than one):

_____ Throw the test away

_____ Look at the grade and put the test in your book

_____ Review the test without working out the missed problems

_____ Review the test and work out the missed problems

_____ Compare the problems you missed with another student's problems

_____ Work problems that are similar to the ones that you missed

_____ Go over the missed problems with your tutor

_____ Go over the missed problems with your instructor

_____ Use the test review to develop new test-taking strategies

Other: _____

Analyzing your math test will not kill you, but not doing it may kill your grades. Many students make the same mistakes over and over again which could cause them to fail too many tests. Students who analyze their tests are at a great advantage (just like a doctor who reviews your blood test) to determine how to improve on their next tests. These students find out the types of mistakes they made and now can change them. They develop better test-taking strategies for the next test and in most cases make higher scores.

To improve future test scores, you must conduct a test analysis of previous tests. In analyzing your tests, look for the following kinds of errors:

1. Misread-direction errors
2. Careless errors
3. Concept errors
4. Application errors
5. Test-taking errors
6. Study errors

Look at your last test to determine how many points you lost in the six types of test-taking errors. Analyze any previous tests to determine if there is a pattern of test errors. The type of errors is very important to determine how you can improve your studying and test-taking.

Misread-direction errors

Now look at your last test and see how many points you lost to misread-direction errors. Misread-direction errors occur when you skip directions or misunderstand directions and do the prob-

Don't lose points because of carelessness.

lem incorrectly. If you do not understand if a problem you missed was a result of misread directions, ask the instructor for clarification.

> **Examples:** 1. You have this type of problem to solve: (x+1)(x+1). Some students will try to solve for x, but the problem only calls for multiplication. You would solve for x only if you have an equation such as (x+1)(x+1) = 0.
>
> 2. Another common mistake is not reading the directions before doing several word problems or statistical problems. All too often, when a test is returned, you find only three out of the five problems had to be completed. Even if you did get all five of them correct, it costs you valuable time which could have been used obtaining additional test points.

To avoid misread-direction errors, carefully read and interpret all the directions. Look for anything that is unusual, or if the directions have two parts. If you do not understand the directions, ask the instructor for clarification. If you feel uneasy about asking the instructor for interpretation of the question, remember the instructor in most cases does not want to test you on the interpretation of the question but how you answer it. Also, you don't want to make the mistake of assuming that the instructor will not interpret the question. Let the instructor make the decision to interpret the question, not you.

If you have difficulty interpreting test questions, you need to practice this skill to determine what operation or type of answer the instructor wants. Copy the chapter review tests that are for your next test and cut up the problems. Mix up the problems and select one. Don't work the problem but decide what you are supposed to do with it: solve, reduce, factor, etc. Then select another problem and do the same thing. Soon it will become easier to decide what should be done with each problem.

Careless Errors

Careless errors are mistakes made because students lose complete focus on the question. If a student is nervous or in a hurry, little mistakes like switching signs mess up the entire problem. Sometimes simple problems turn into nearly impossible problems if a student makes a careless error. This can really waste precious test time. Careless errors can be caught automatically when reviewing the test. Both good and poor math students make careless errors. Such errors can cost a student the difference of a letter grade on a test.

Examples: 1. *Dropping the sign*: -3(2x) = 6x, instead of -6x, which is the correct answer. 2. *Not simplifying your answer*: Leaving (3x -12)/3 as your answer instead of simplifying it to x - 4. 3. *Adding fractions*: 5/16 + 7/16 = 12/16 instead of 3/4. 4. *Word problems*: X = 15 instead of the "student had 15 tickets."

Many students want all their errors to be careless errors when they analyze their tests because it is easier to admit carelessness than admitting that they just didn't know the material. In such cases, I ask the student to solve the problem immediately while I watch. If the student can solve the problem or point out his/her mistake in a few seconds, it is a careless error. If the student cannot solve the problem immediately, it is not a careless error and is probably a concept error.

When working with students who make careless errors, I ask them two questions: First, "How many points did you lose due to careless errors?" Then I follow with, "How much time was left in the class period after you handed in your test?" Students who lose test points to careless errors are giving away points if they hand in their test papers before the test period ends.

To reduce careless errors, you must realize the types of careless errors made and recognize them when reviewing your test. If you cannot solve the missed problem immediately, it is not a careless error. If your major error is not simplifying the answer, review each answer as if it were a new problem and try to reduce it.

Concept Errors

Concept errors are mistakes made when you do not understand the properties or principles required to work the problem. Concept errors, if not corrected, will follow you from test to test, causing you to lose a lot of points.

Examples: Some common concept errors are not knowing:

$(-)(-)x = x$, *not "-x"*
$-1(2) > x(-1)$ *implies 2<x, not "2>x"*

$5/0$ *is undefined, not "0"*
$(a+x)/x$ *is not simplified to "a"*
The order of operations
$2 + 3 \times 5 = 17$, *not 25*
$1/2 + 1/3 = 5/6$, *not 2/5*

Concept errors must be corrected to improve your next math test score. Students who have numerous concept errors will fail the next test since each chapter builds on the previous ones. Just going back to rework the concept error problems is not good enough. You must go back to the textbook or notes and learn why you missed those types of problems, not just the one problem itself.

The best way to learn how to work those types of problems is to set up a concept-problem error page in the back of your notebook. Label the first page "Test One Concept errors." Write down all your concept errors and how to solve them. Then, work five more problems, which use the same concept. Now, in your own words, write the reasons that you *can* solve these problems.

If you cannot write the concept in your own words, you do not understand it. Get assistance from your instructor if you need help finding similar problems using the same concept or cannot understand the concept. Do this for every test. For example, when preparing for your second test, review the concept errors on the first test. Continue the process all the way into the final. This is a proven system to improve your test scores.

Application Errors

Application errors occur when you know the concept but cannot apply it to the problem. Application errors usually are found in word problems, deducing formulas (such as the quadratic equation) and graphing. Even some better students become frustrated with application errors; they understand the material but cannot apply it to the problem.

To reduce application errors, you must predict the type of application problems that will be on the test. Then think through and practice solving those types of problems using the concepts.

> **Example:** If you must derive the quadratic formula, you should practice doing that backward and forward while telling yourself the concept used to move from one step to the next.

Application errors are common with word problems. When solving word problems, look for the key phrases displayed in Figure 25 (Translating English Words into Algebraic Expressions) to help you set up the problem. After completing the word problem, reread the question to make sure you have applied the answer to the intended question. Application errors can be avoided with appropriate practice and insight. However, if all else fails, then memorize a word problem or a graphing problem and use it as part of your memory data dump. Write it down on your test and use it as an example to solve the problems on the test.

Test-Taking Errors

Test-taking errors apply to the specific way you take tests. Some students consistently make the same types of test-taking errors. Through recognition, these bad test-taking habits can be replaced by good test-taking habits. The result will be higher test scores. The list that follows includes the test-taking errors, which can cause you to lose many points on an exam.

1. *Missing more questions in the first third, second third or last third part of a test* is considered a test-taking error. Divide your test in thirds. For example, if your test had 20 problems, look at the number of points missed from problems 1 through 6. How many points were missed from problems 7 through 13? How many points were missed from problems 14 to 20? Missing more questions in the first third of a test could be caused by carelessness when doing easy problems or from test anxiety. Missing questions in the last part of the test could be due to the fact that the last problems are more difficult than the earlier questions or due to increasing your test speed to finish the test.

   If you consistently miss more questions in a certain part of the test, use your remaining test time to review that section of the test first. This means you may review the last part of your test first.

2. *Not completing a problem to its last step* is another test-taking error. If you have this bad

habit review the last step of the test problem first before doing an in-depth test review.

3. *Changing test answers from correct ones to incorrect ones* is a problem for some students. Look for erased answers on your test. I have seen students erase the correct way to solve the problem and thus the correct answer and then change it to an incorrect answer. I have asked these students why they erased the correct answer. In almost every case the student said that the answer was too easy to solve, so they thought it was wrong. These students need to build their test-taking confidence and know how to check their answers. If this is you, make sure you learn how to check your answers and have confidence in your answers.

Don't change answers just because the answer seems too easy.

Find out if you are a good or bad answer-changer by comparing the number of answers changed to correct and to incorrect answers. If you are a bad answer-changer, write on your test, "Don't change answers." Change answers only if you can prove to yourself or the instructor that the changed answer is correct.

On multiple choice tests most students indicated that they were bad answer changers. That is because they only remembered changing answers from right to wrong. They usually do not remember the times they changed answers from wrong to right. Now let's see if you are a good, bad or neutral answer changer.

On multiple choice problems you can change your answer three ways. From right to wrong, wrong to right and wrong to wrong. Look at the eraser marks on your answer sheet that represent the number of answers that you changed. You may want to do this on several of your tests. Count the number of changes that represent the three categories and change them into percents. If you have a pattern of changing over 50 percent of your answers from wrong to right then keep changing your answers. If over 50 percent of your answers are changed from right to wrong then stop changing answers. If the three categories of changing answers are about the same, then do what makes you feel the best because it is not affecting your grade. If you don't have previous tests to measure the effectiveness of your answer changing, then wait to review several tests before you make your decision. If you are indeed a bad answer changer, then on test day use a pencil without an eraser to mark your multiple choice tests. This should stop you from changing your answers.

4. *Getting stuck on one problem and spending too much time on it* is another test-taking error. You need to set a time limit on each problem before moving to the next problem. Working too long on a problem without success will increase your test anxiety and waste valuable time that could be used in solving other problems or in reviewing your test. For example, if your test has twenty problems that must be completed in one hour, how long should you spend on each problem? You should spend the maximum of three minutes on each problem. Of course this depends on the complexity of the problems. Spending more than three minutes, unless it is the last problem you are working on, can cost you test points.

However, some students will spend five to ten minutes on some problems and still not solve them. I have asked many of these students the reasons for spending so much time on one certain problem. Their answers varied, but the same themes appeared time and time again. These students indicated that they had practiced that type of problem over and over again before the test and told themselves that they must solve the problem. In other words, their ego got the best of them. They said no matter what (even if I failed the test) they were going to get that problem correct. To them solving that problem meant that their study time was not wasted, and that they knew how to solve the math problems. Unfortunately many of these students are not test wise because they could be getting a lot more test points by skipping that problem and working on other ones. Remember: it doesn't matter how you get the test points as long as you get enough points to make the best grade possible. Don't let your ego get the best of you.

5. *Rushing through the easiest part of the test and making careless errors* is a common test-taking error for the better student. If you have the bad habit of getting more points taken off for the easy problems than for the hard problems, first review the easy problems and then the hard ones.

6. *Miscopying an answer from your scratch work to the test* is an uncommon test-taking error, but it does cost some students points. To avoid these kinds of errors, systematically compare your last problem step on scratch paper with the answer written on the test. In addition, always hand in your scratch work with your test.

7. *Leaving answers blank* will get you zero points. If you look at a problem and cannot figure out how to solve it, do not leave it blank. Write down some information about the problem, rewrite the problem or try to do at least the first step.

   ❗ Remember: Writing down the first step of a problem is the key to solving the ❗ problem and obtaining partial credit.

8. *Answering only the first step of a two-step problem* causes problems for some students. These students get so excited when answering the first step of the problem that they forget about the second step. This is especially true on two-step word problems. To correct this test-taking error, write "two" in the margin of the problem. That will remind you that there are two steps or two answers to this problem.

9. *Not understanding all the functions of your calculator* can cause major testing problems. Some students barely learn how to use the critical calculator functions. Then they forget or have to relearn how to use their calculator during the test, which costs test points and time. Do not wait to learn how to use your calculator on the test. Over learn the use of your calculator *before* the test.

10. *Leaving the test early without checking all your answers.* Do not worry about the first person who finishes the test and leaves. Many students start to get nervous when other students start to leave early. This can lead to test anxiety, mental blocks and loss of recall.

    According to research, the first students finishing the test do not always get the best grades. It sometimes is the exact opposite. Ignore the students who leave and use the full time allowed.

    Make sure you follow the 10 steps to better test-taking. Review your test-taking procedures for discrepancies in following the 10 steps. Deviating from these proven 10 steps will cost you points. Taking the time to practice the 10 steps will earn you points.

Study Errors

Study error, the last type of mistake to look for in a test analysis, occurs when you study the wrong type of material or do not spend enough time on pertinent material. Review your test to find out if you missed problems because you did not practice that type of problem or because you did practice it but forgot how to do it during the test. Study errors will take some time to track down, but correcting study errors will help you on future tests.

Most students, after analyzing one or several tests, will recognize at least one major, common test-taking error. Understanding the effects of this test-taking error should change your study techniques or test-taking strategy.

> **Example:** If there are seven minutes left in the test, should you review for careless errors or try to answer those two problems you could not totally solve? This is a trick question. The real question is, "Do you miss more points due to careless errors or concept errors, or are the missed points about even?" The answer to this question should determine how you will spend the last minutes of the test. If you missed more points due to careless errors or missed about the same number of points due to careless/concept errors, review for careless errors.
>
> Careless errors are easier to correct than concept errors. However, if you made very few or no careless errors, you should be working on those last two problems to get the greatest number of test points. Knowing your test-taking errors can add more points to your test by changing your test-taking procedure.
>
> Sometimes math tests have objective test questions. Objective test questions are in the form of true/false, multiple-choice and matching. To better understand the procedures in taking an objective test, visit the Winning at Math Student Resource website to learn how to take an objective test.
>
> Very few math tests have essay questions. However, improving the skills required to take an essay test could give you more time for studying math.

Go to the Winning at Math Student Resource Website to review a condensed version of Six Steps to Test Analysis. Visit the Winning at Math Student Resource website to learn how to take an essay test.

To have some practice identifying some of the Six-Types of Test-Taking Errors, review the test in Figure 26, "Math Test for Prealgebra," on the next page. See if you can identify the test-taking errors and compare your answers with the key.

How to Prepare For the Final Exam

Start preparing for the final exam on the first day of class.

The first day of class is when you start preparing for the final exam. Look at the syllabus or ask the instructor if the final exam is cumulative. A cumulative exam covers everything from the first chapter to the last chapter. Most math final exams are cumulative.

The second question you should ask is if the final exam is a departmental exam or if your instructor makes it up. In most cases, departmental exams are more difficult and need a little different preparation. If you have a departmental final, you need to ask for last year's test and ask other students what their instructors say will be on the test.

The third question is, how much will the final exam count? Does it carry the same weight as a regular test or, as in some cases, will it count a third of your grade? If the latter is true, the final exam

Figure 26
Math Test for Prealgebra

The answers are in boldface. The correct answers to missed questions are shaded.
Identify the type of error based on the Six Types of Test-Taking Errors. The student's test
score is 70. The answer key is on the next page.

1. Write in words: 32.685

    Thirty-two and six hundred eighty-five thousanths

2. Write as a fraction and simplify: 0.078

    $\dfrac{78}{1000}$ $\dfrac{39}{500}$ *-2*

3. Round to the nearest hundredth: 64.8653

    64.865   **64.87**   *-4*

4. Combine like terms:
    $6.78x - 3.21 + 7.23x - 6.19$

    = 6.78x + 7.23x + (-3.21) + (-6.19)
    = 14.01x - 9.4

5. Divide and round to the nearest hundredth: 68.1357 ÷ 2.1

    32.4454 → 32.45

6. Write as a decimal: $\dfrac{5}{16}$

    0.3125

7. Insert < or > to make a true statement.

    $\dfrac{3}{8}$ < $\dfrac{6}{13}$

8. Solve: $\dfrac{3}{x} = \dfrac{9}{12}$

    9x = 3(12)

    $\dfrac{x}{9} = \dfrac{36}{9}$

    x = 5   **x = 4**   *-2*

9. What number is 35% of 60?

    2100   **21.00**   *-4*

10. 20.8 is 40% of what number?

     52   *-8*

11. 567 is what percent of 756?

     $\dfrac{756}{567} = \dfrac{9}{100}$ *-8*

     = 133.3%   **75%**

12. Multiply: *-2*

     (-6.03) (-2.31) = 13.9   **13.9293**

Answer Key for Prealgebra Test (Figure 26)

1. Correct

2. *Misread-directions error*—forgot to simplify by reducing the fraction.

3. *Concept error*—did not know that hundredths is two places to the right of the decimal.

4. Correct

5. Correct

6. Correct

7. Correct

8. *Careless error*—divided incorrectly in the last step.

9. *Test-taking error*—did not follow step 5 in test-taking steps: reviewing answers to see if they make sense. The number that equals 35% of 60 can't be larger than 60.

10. *Test-taking error*—did not follow steps 7 and 8 in test-taking steps: don't leave an answer blank.

11. *Application error*—solved the equation correctly but the equation setup was wrong.

12. *Concept error*—did not know that when you multiply with one number in the hundredths, the answer must include the hundredths column.

---

will usually make a letter grade difference on your final course grade. The final exam could also determine if you pass or fail the course. Knowing this information before the final exam will help you prepare.

The fourth question pertains to a new concept in developmental education called the exit exam. Some states like Florida have an exit exam for developmental math. Ask your instructor if you must pass an exit exam (usually the final exam) to pass the course even if you are making an "A." If this is true then ask if there is a required grade in the course such as a "C" to be eligible to take the exit test. Knowing all this information before taking the final exam will help you prepare.

You can get this grade!

Preparing for the final exam is similar to preparing for each chapter test. You must create a pretest to discover what you have forgotten. You can use questions from the textbook chapter tests or questions from your study group.

Make every minute count for earning points on the test

Review the concept errors that you recorded in the back of your notebook labeled "Test One," "Test Two," etc. Review your problem log for questions you consistently miss. Even review material that you knew for the first and second test but which was not used on any other tests. Students forget how to work some of these problems.

If you do not have a concept error page for each chapter and did not keep a problems log you need to develop a pre-test before taking the final exam. If you are individually preparing for the final, then copy each chapter test and do every fourth problem to see what errors you may

Review your test with your instructor to learn what to do better next time.

make. However, it is better to have a study group where each of the four members brings in ten problems with the answers worked out on a separate page. Then each group member can take the 30-question test to find out what they need to study. You can refer to the answers to help you solve the problems that you miss. Remember you want to find out what you don't know before the test, not during the test. Developing and using these methods before each test will improve your grades.

Make sure to use the 10 steps to better test-taking and the information gained from your test analysis. Use all the time on the final exam because you could improve your final grade by a full letter if you make an "A" on the final.

To learn more about taking tests, go to www.academicsuccess.com and click on Winning at Math Student Resources. Put WAM as the uername and Student as the password to access the site, and click on "Studying for and Taking Exams." Also listen to the CD, *How to Ace Tests*, available at www.academicsuccess.com.

Summary

- Just completing your homework and attending class does not guarantee that you will pass math.

- Do not cram for your math tests.

- Improving your math test-taking skills begins with completing a practice math test several days before the actual exam. This pretest can help you locate math areas that need improvement.

- Follow the general principles of good test-taking before each math test.

- Weakness can be corrected by reviewing homework or obtaining help from your instructor or tutor.

- Follow the 10 steps to better test-taking to obtain the greatest number of test points in the least amount of time.

- Make sure you develop a mental cheat sheet before each test for your memory data dump.

- After your first major test you need to complete a test analysis to learn from your mistakes and to increase test points on the next exam.

- Decide before each test if you are going to spend the last few minutes of each test checking for careless errors or finishing problems you left incomplete.

- Without conducting a test analysis, you will probably continue to make the same old test errors and lose valuable test points.

- You need to start preparing for the final exam the first day of class.

- Ask if the final exam is going to be made up by the instructor or if it is a departmental exam. Find out how much the final exam counts for the final grade and if it is cumulative.

- To be prepared for each test and the final exam, you must keep up with your problem log and concept errors from each test.

- Before each test, make sure you review your problem log, math glossary and the concept errors from your previous tests. This type of review will make it easier when preparing for the final exam.

  When preparing for the final exam, make sure to take a pretest developed by either the instructor or yourself. This pretest must be taken under the same timed conditions as the final exam.

- You must have enough time after taking the pretest to learn how to solve the missed problems before the final exam.

- To learn more about taking tests, go to www.academicsuccess.com and click on Winning at Math Student Resources. Put in *WAM* as the username and *Student* as the password to access the site, and click on "studying for and Taking Exams." Also listen to the CD, *How to Ace Tests*, available at www.academicsuccess.com.

Remember: It may not be fair, but students with good math test-taking skills can score higher on tests compared to students who have more math knowledge.

Assignment for Chapter 8

1. List four reasons how you can understand how to do the math problems in class but can still miss them on the test.

   Reason 1: _____

   _____

   Reason 2: _____

   _____

   Reason 3: _____

   _____

   Reason 4: _____

   _____

2. List four reasons how you can correctly complete all the homework assignments and still not score high on math tests.

   Reason 1: _____

   _____

   Reason 2: _____

   _____

   Reason 3: _____

   _____

   Reason 4: _____

   _____

3. List two ways you can use a study group to prepare for a math test.

   Way 1: _____

   _____

   Way 2: _____

   _____

4. List and discuss two general pretest rules that can help you become more successful in taking your math test.

   Rule 1: _____

   Rule 2: _____

5. List and explain three reasons you make a plan before taking a math test.

   Reason 1: _____

   _____

Reason 2: _____

_____

Reason 3: _____

_____

6. List the Ten Steps for Better Test-Taking.

1_____   6_____

2_____   7_____

3_____   8_____

4_____   9_____

5_____   10_____

7. List the Six Types of Test-Taking Errors

1_____   4_____

2_____   5_____

3_____   6_____

8. Complete a test analysis on your last test. List the type of errors you made and how you can correct them.

Error type 1: _____

Correction: _____

Error type 2: _____

Correction: _____

Error type 3: _____

Correction: _____

9. What are the answers to the three questions you need to ask your instructor about the final exam?

Answer 1: _____

_____

Answer 2: _____

_____

Answer 3: _____

_____

10. From the website, list three test-taking strategies you learn for your other tests:

Strategy 1: _____

Strategy 2: _____

Strategy 3: _____

How to Take Control and Motivate Yourself to Learn Math

9

In Chapter 9
you will learn these concepts:

- Past experiences shape everyone's attitude toward learning math, some students with confident attitudes and others with anxious attitudes. These personal perspectives toward learning math influence the level of success that students experience in their math classes.
  - ✓ Strategies to develop an internal locus of control
  - ✓ Ways to avoid or overcome learned helplessness
  - ✓ Steps to overcome procrastination
  - ✓ Process to improve self-esteem and self-efficacy
  - ✓ How to communicate with your math instructor

Introduction

You can take control and learn math by understanding your learning strengths, by improving your weaknesses, and by making a commitment to change your behaviors.

Many students who have problems with math want to improve their learning, but no one has shown them how to change. It is not your fault that you have not been taught how to study math. Even students taking general study skills courses are often not taught how to study and learn it.

You need to take on the responsibility to improve your math learning skills and to use these new learning strengths. Thousands of students who have taken this responsibility have passed math and gone on to graduate. Taking this responsibility requires an internal locus of control. Students with an internal locus of control take the responsibility to change their learning behaviors and do not blame the teacher or the math department for their poor grades. Such students believe that they can change their lives and become successful math students.

Students with an internal locus of control are also aware that, even without knowing it, some part of them may try to sabotage their math learning. This sabotage often comes in the form of procrastination that is meant to protect their self-esteem. This is one of the leading causes of learned helplessness.

Due to previous math failures, students with learned helplessness have learned to not even *try* to pass math. By better understanding themselves, such students can guard against the effects of procrastination through the use of successful math study skills.

Past experiences with elementary or math teachers may have been positive or negative. To help take control over learning, math students need to communicate with their instructor. However, many students are intimidated by the thought of approaching their teacher, which can cause problems in overall learning as well as poor grades.

Students also may have difficulty talking to their current math teachers. In the past they may have only been called into the math teacher's office when something was wrong. The math instructor probably asked them questions related to their homework, class attendance or motivation. Even though the teacher was trying to help them, it may not have felt that way. It is important for students to know that it is possible to build a communication line with a professor, and that in doing so, they can improve their grades.

How to Develop an Internal
Locus of Control and Self-Efficacy

The ways you can take control over math are by developing an internal locus of control, avoiding learned helplessness, and eliminating (or at least decreasing) procrastination. This is first accomplished by setting short-term goals and accomplishing them, in order to see the relationship between changing learning behavior and mathematics success. Then you can develop long-term goals such as making an "A" or "B" in your math class and graduating.

Defining Locus of Control and Self-Efficacy

Locus of Control

Locus of control has to do with the *locus*, or location, in which a student places the control over his/her life, in other words, who or what the student feels controls his/her behavior and grades. Review your locus of control results from the survey that was in the Assessing and Using Your Math Learning Strengths chapter. Using this chapter can help external students to become internal and also for internal students to remain that way.

Students who feel that conditions beyond their control prevent them from getting good grades have an *external* locus of control. These students blame instructors, home conditions and money problems for their poor grades, and they can do nothing about their problems. In essence, *external* students feel their lives are controlled by *outside forces*, such as fate or the power of other people.

When it comes to your success, you are behind the wheel.

Other students feel they have the power to control their situation, and this power comes from *within*. These *internal* students take responsibility for their success, while most external students reject responsibility. Internal students believe that they can overcome most situations, since results depend on their behavior or personal characteristics.

Internal students accept the responsibility for their behavior and realize that studying today will help them pass the math test scheduled for next week. Internal students can delay immediate rewards; instead of going to a party, they study for tomorrow's test. Internal students also know when to postpone putting in extra hours at their workplace in order to study for a math test.

Generally, locus of control means that students who are internal will work harder to meet their educational goals than will external students. The internal student can relate today's behavior (e.g., studying, textbook reading) to obtaining a college degree and gainful employment. On the other hand, external students cannot connect the behavior of studying today with getting passing grades and obtaining future career opportunities. Thus, internals are more oriented toward making high math grades than are externals.

Self-Efficacy

Self-efficacy is a new term that is being used in colleges and universities. This term is related to locus of control but is more specific to certain tasks. Locus of control is an overall belief that you can be successful. Self-efficacy is more specific to the belief that you have the abilities or skills to complete certain tasks (Bandura, 1982). To determine self-efficacy, ask yourself this question by filling in the blank, "Do I have the skills and ability to succeed at _____." The blank could include tasks such as employment, an English course, history course, math course or graduating from college.

Just like in locus of control, education research has found out that self-efficacy is an important success predictor of student motivation and self-management behavior (Schunk, 1991). Students with high efficacy are more likely than students with low efficacy to complete difficult tasks, to put in more effort, to show persistence, to have used different learning strategies, and to have less fear about completing a task. In short, these students believe they can complete tasks such as taking notes, reading the textbook, completing their homework and managing their time. They persist at these skills until proficient. Before reading this text you may not have had these skills and may have suffered from low self-efficacy. Now, you can use these learning and test-taking skills to improve your self-efficacy in math, which will lead to more motivation to becoming successful in math.

Developing Short- and Long-Term Goals

Goals need to be stated in concrete words and should be measurable

Externals can change into internals by taking more responsibility for their lives and completing their education. You can take more responsibility by developing and accomplishing both short-term and long-term goals. Some of your short-term goals can be using the learning techniques presented in this text.

Short-term goals are goals developed and accomplished within a day or a week. The steps to obtaining your short-term or long-term goals must be thought out *and written down*. Keep the written goals in a place where you will see them many times each day. This will help to frequently remind you of the goals that you have set for yourself.

> **Example:** A short-term goal could be a goal of studying math today between 7:00 p.m. and 9:00 p.m. A long-term goal, for example, could be earning an "A" or "B" in the math course for the semester.

Some students need a more precise process to set up goals. It is more difficult to develop short-term goals than long-term goals. In a previous chapter, you should have developed long-term goals for your GPA and math course grade. By using the following information, it will make it easier to learn how to set up short-term goals and to evaluate your progress.

The effects of goals on successfully completing a task are related to specificity, proximity and difficulty (Schunk, 1991). Goals that can be easily measured and accomplished in a short period of time have a good chance at being met. These specific goals can help you determine how much effort is needed for the goal and how it will feel when accomplished. Now, students can believe they have the ability to do the tasks that lead to goal accomplishment (Dembo, 2000). Doesn't this sound like internal locus of control and self-efficacy? The overall result is improving motivation!

New learning and test taking skills are excellent learning tasks to use for short-term goals. These skills have been proven to increase math success. If you have not done so already it is now time to set up goals to use these skills. Use the **SMART goals** (Smith, 1994) system for goal setting, which stands for: **S**pecific, **M**easurable, **A**ction-oriented, **R**ealistic, and **T**imely.

Specific means that you want to be exact about what you want to complete. You need to describe a certain behavior to be accomplished or an outcome that you can see. Describe the specific outcome to be obtained and avoid general terms such a "satisfied", "good", "understood" and "accomplished".

General statement: I want to do my homework

Specific statement: I will use the "Ten Steps for Doing Your Homework" and complete the 25 assigned problems.

Measurable means that you can easily see if you completed the goal. You need to determine how to measure the results or you will not know if the goal is accomplished. Establish a maximum level of goal attainment, and if need be, a minimum level.

General statement: I am going to read my math text.

Measurable statement: I will read all the pages in sections 2.1 to 2.8.

Action-Oriented means that the goal includes the action that is required to accomplish that task. You need to know what skill or behavior is required to best accomplish that task.

General statement: I am going to read my math text.

Action-Oriented statement: I will use the Ten Steps for Reading a Math Text to read all the pages in sections 2.1 to 2.8.

Realistic means that you can really accomplish the goal during the specified time. Make sure the goal is not too challenging to be accomplished. It is better to set *two* short-term goals that can be accomplished than *one* unrealistic goal.

General statement: I will study Sunday night for Monday's math test so I can make an A.

Realistic statement: I will study Friday afternoon, Saturday afternoon and Sunday night for the Monday math test and want at least a B.

Timely means that you are breaking down a long-term goal into several short-term-goals with a specific date of completion. Breaking down a goal that can be accomplished by shorter goals can improve motivation.

General statement: "I want to make an A in my math class."

Timely statement: "I want to make an A or B on my next math test.

The preceding were examples of each aspect of the SMART goal system. The following are some short-term goals that use the SMART system:

- I will review my math notes the same day as the class using Six Steps to Reworking Your Notes.

- I will practice two short-term relaxation techniques each day for the next two weeks.

- Two days before my next test on March 16, I will develop my "memory data dump" with at least five items.

- For every homework assignment, I will review my textbook and notes before starting the problems.

- I will develop my weekly time management schedule with eight hours a week for studying math.

- I will do all my online homework using the Ten Steps for Doing Online Homework before the next class meeting.

These are some examples of appropriate short-term goals to improve math success. Think about three other short-term goals that will help you in math. Use the SMART system to write them in the space given below:

Goal 1. _____

Goal 2. _____

Goal 3. _____

Now that you have developed your goals, use the information in this text and on the website to help you obtain these goals.

After one week (it may be shorter for some goals) you need to evaluate the progress on obtaining your goals. In some cases you may have to alter or rewrite your goals. Put a check by the correct response for each goal and answer the questions that apply to the goal.

Goal 1. _____

Accomplished _____

Partially accomplished _____

Not accomplished _____

This is a continuous goal _____

What was the evidence of accomplishing the goal_____

The goal needs to be rewritten Yes _____   No _____

Goal 2. _____

Accomplished _____

Partially accomplished _____

Not accomplished _____

This is a continuous goal _____

What was the evidence of accomplishing the goal_____

The goal needs to be rewritten Yes _____   No _____

Goal 3. _____

Accomplished _____

Partially accomplished _____

Not accomplished _____

This is a continuous goal _____

What was the evidence of accomplishing the goal_____

The goal needs to be rewritten Yes _____   No _____

Rewarding yourself after meeting short-term goals increases your internal control by making a strong mental connection between your behavior and the desired reward. Successes in meeting short-term goals lead to greater successes in meeting long-term goals. The ultimate success is passing your math courses and graduating.

How to Avoid Learned Helplessness

I achieved my long-term goal. I graduated!

As students become more external (feeling less in control of their lives and their math grades) they develop *learned helplessness*. Learned helplessness means believing that other people or influences from such things as instructors, poverty or "the system" control what happens to them. Students who have failed math several times may develop learned helplessness. Some students may ultimately adopt the attitude of "Why try?"

A good example of learned helplessness is the total lack of motivation to complete math assignments. In the past, students may have completed the math assignments but did not get the course grade they had hoped for. This led to the attitude of "Why try?" because they tried several times to be successful in math and still failed the course.

The problem with this thinking is the way these students actually "tried" to pass the math course. Their ineffective learning processes, lack of anxiety reduction and poor test-taking techniques proved to be their demise. For them, it was like trying to remove a flat tire with a pair of pliers instead of using a tire iron.

This text is your "tire iron." The question is, are you motivated enough to put forth the effort to *use* the tire iron in order to learn more and make a good grade?

! Remember: Students who develop "learned helplessness" *can break this bad habit*. Take responsibility, and you will be on your way to winning at math. **!**

How to Overcome Procrastination by Defeating Fear of Failure, Fear of Success, Rebellion Against Authority and Perfectionism

Procrastination is not just a personality flaw

Procrastination is no way to take control over math. Students may procrastinate by not reading the textbook or not doing their homework due to fear of failure, fear of success or rebellion against authority.

Fear of Failure

Some students who fear failure procrastinate to avoid any real assessment of their true ability. By waiting too long to begin work on a paper or studying for a test, real ability is never measured — the rushed paper or the lack of preparation for a test does not reflect what you are *really* capable of accomplishing. Thus, you can never learn the degree of "goodness" or "badness" of your academic ability.

Procrastinators always console themselves after failure because it does not feel as bad if you only study for a test for two hours and fail it compared to studying for a test for ten hours and failing.

> **Example:** A math student who was failing the course at midterm decided to drop it and to retake it the next semester. She set a goal to make an "A" when the next semester began. After making a "C" on the first major test, she became frustrated at not reaching her goal, and she started procrastinating in her math studies. She fully *expected* to fail the course. This student believed that it was preferable not to try to pass the course if she could not make an "A."

Fear of Success

Fear of success means not making an all-out effort toward becoming successful. This is due to the student's fear that "someone" might be hurt or offended by the student's success. Some students believe becoming too successful will lose them friends, lovers or spouses. They feel overwhelmingly guilty for being more successful than their family or close friends.

This "fear of success" can be generalized as "fear of competition" in making good grades. These students do not fear the chance of making low grades when competing, but they fear that others will not like them if they make high grades.

> **Example:** A math student may fear that by studying too much she will make the highest test grade and set the grading curve. She has more fear that students will not like her due to her high grades than the fear of just making average grades. Such students need to take pride in their learning ability and let the other students take responsibility for their own grades.

Some of my female students have told me that this is not an unrealistic fear. According to them, if a girl does better than a boy, he often wants nothing to do with her. Sometimes they have to act dumb in order to get dates. This still happens in colleges and universities.

! **Remember:** Set the curve — somebody is going to! Grades are *privileged information* between you and the instructor. If a student or family member asks, "How did you do on that test?" Just say, "I passed." Case closed. **!**

Rebellion against Authority

Rebelling against a professor only hurts you.

The third cause of procrastination is the desire to rebel against authority. Some students believe that by handing in their homework late or by missing the test they can "get back" at the instructor (whom they may not personally like and whom they may hold responsible for their poor math performance).

These external students usually lack self-esteem and would rather blame the instructor for their poor grades than take responsibility for completing their homework on time. Rebelling against the instructor gives them a false sense of control over their lives.

However, rebellious students are fulfilling the exact expectations placed on them by their instructors: Becoming academic failures. These students discover, often too late, that they are hurting only themselves.

Perfectionism

Another group of students that are prone to procrastination are the perfectionists. This is an unusual group because they usually set goals higher than they can realistic meet. If they cannot meet the high goal of making A's on all their math tests, they want to quit.

Another example of perfectionism occurs when students attend college after working or being out of school for several years. These students feel they have to make up for lost time by making perfect grades and by graduating faster than younger students. These students look at "B's" as a failure, since their goal is to make 100's on all their tests. For the older perfectionist, making a "B" on their math test means they are a failure and they want to quit college. Sometimes these goals are so unrealistic — even a genius would fail. Their motto is, "If I can't be perfect, I don't want to try at all."

These students need help to realize that, with their family and/or work responsibilities, making a B is all right. They must also learn that finishing a degree later than planned is better than not finishing at all. Being a perfectionist is not related to how high you set the goal; rather, it is *the unrealistic nature* of the goal itself.

Extreme perfectionists are more fearful of making a "B" than an "F." These students, who are usually returning students, not only want but need to make "A's" on all their math tests to feel worth while. These students usually are making "A's" in the rest of their courses but are making "C's" and "B's" in their math classes. Even though being a perfectionist may cause some educational problems, being a extreme perfectionist causes problems in learning and testing, and can even cause psychological problems in life.

In a learning situation extreme perfectionists want to learn math by doing homework and getting most of the problems correct on the first try. They may attempt a second try but if the problems become more difficult, they may give up in disgust and stop doing their homework all together. In other words they tell themselves that if I cannot get it right the first time why should I try? In most cases they have little tolerance for frustration.

Some of these students study hard (25 hours a week, just for math) and thus expect to benefit from that studying by making all "A's." This process is fine, until the extreme perfectionist student starts calculating during the test how many problems they can miss to make an "A." They have the skills to do this calculation, but during the test when they missed enough questions to drop from an "A" to a "B" sometimes they give up. Then they tell themselves, "If I cannot make an 'A,' then why should I try on the rest of the test?" They get depressed and stop trying. They will finish the test but will not give 100% on the last set of problems because they know they have made a "B" or lower. This may sound funny to students who will do any thing just to make a "C," but it is the truth. The extreme perfectionists need to get help from the counseling department and from their math instructors to be successful in math. Instead of throwing away their college career these students need to learn how to cope with making "B's" and then move on and graduate.

There are four main causes of procrastination. All students use some of these reasons for delaying studying and doing homework. Some students may use more than one reason to procrastinate. Mark below in order from 1 to 4 (one being the most often used and 4 the least often used) which procrastination strategies that you are using. Use N/A if you never use these procrastination strategies.

Fear of failure _____ Fear of success _____ Rebellion _____ Perfectionism _____

Now that you have selected your reason(s) for procrastination, how much does it affect your learning? BE HONEST!

All the time _____ Most of the time _____ Some of the time _____ Not at all _____

Now you know your type(s) of procrastination and how much it affects your learning.

Procrastination is not a simple issue. Students procrastinate for various reasons. Procrastination is mainly a defense mechanism that protects self-esteem. Most students who procrastinate have poor grades. By understanding the reasons for procrastination, you can avoid it and become a better math student. Another way to avoid procrastination is developing and successfully fulfilling your short-term goals. However, if you answered that procrastination affects your grades all the time or most of the time, talk to your instructor, advisor or counselor about additional strategies to reduce procrastination.

How to Improve Your Self-Esteem

Many students experience problems in both their academic and personal lives because they lack self-esteem. Self-esteem is the part of our personality which allows us to feel good about ourselves and enjoy our accomplishments. Having self-esteem means that you respect others and have a sense of peace within yourself. Students who have self-esteem also have a "can do" attitude about accomplishing their goals.

Students with poor self-esteem may not put forth as much effort to accomplish their goals. These students can improve their self-esteem by taking responsibility for their feelings, thoughts, abilities and behaviors. Students with poor self-esteem need to change their negative emotional reactions into positive emotional reactions.

Improving self-esteem can be accomplished by changing the negative emotional statements you are telling yourself and by changing the behaviors that can result in poor self-esteem.

By developing positive short-term goals you can change the behaviors that can be associate with poor self-esteem. You already developed some of these short-term goals. Then you can change the negative emotional self-statement, which is called self-talk, to positive statements. Follow the procedure developed by Butler (1981) and Dembo (2000) to help understand how to change negative self talk to positive self-talk.

Procedures for Improving Self-Talk

Procedures	*Questions*
1. Write down your self-talk statements. You cannot change self-talk unless you understand what you are telling yourself.	What am I telling myself?
2. Review your self-talk statements to see if they are helpful or harmful. How do the statements affect your motivation, locus of control, emotions and behavior? Keep the statements that are helpful and change those that are harmful.	Are statements made to myself helping me succeed in math, or are they hurting my grades?
3. Keep the self-talk statements that are helping you become successful. Replace your negative self-talk with positive self-talk. Allow yourself to try another strategy to be successful in the task relating to the negative self-statement. Identify one of your positive characteristics (e.g. study skills, motivation, homework skill) that will help you with that task, and use that knowledge to replace your negative self-talk.	How can I convince myself to become more positive?
4. Develop a plan: Decide what strategies you need in order to support positive self-talk. Decide which behaviors or attitudes that need to be changed. Explain this new behavior.	What learning, test taking, attitudinal or motivational behaviors do I need to change in order to support positive self-talk?

The Procedures for Improving Self-Talk can be used to change negative self-talk to positive self-talk. A good example of a student analyzing his self-talk is the story of Joe, who was repeating an algebra course, and who had repeated a number of math courses during his educational career. The following are Joe's responses while using the Procedures for Improving Self-Talk.

Joe's Reponses

Question	*Reply*
1. What am I telling myself about mathematics?	I am telling myself that I will never be successful in math. Since elementary school, I have been bad in all my math courses and cannot pass math.
2. Are my statements helping me succeed in math?	No. I have decided not to try in math because I will not be successful. I can never successfully complete my homework.
3. How can I convince myself to become more positive? Am I going to develop more self-efficacy?	I am telling myself that my poor study skills/attitude are causing me to not try. I need to change my attitude and try to find better study skill methods.
4. What learning, test taking, attitudinal or motivational behaviors do I need to change in order to support positive self-talk?	I am going to tell myself that I can succeed in math. I am going to use the Ten Steps to Doing Your Math Homework to finish my assignments. I could also use some tutoring, and should probably talk to my professor more often.

I worked Joe through this process and he reaped immediate benefits. Now identify a negative self-statement you want to change and follow the process given below. Write your responses in the blank reply section.

Negative self-statement: _____

_____

Question	*Reply*
1. What am I telling myself about mathematics?	
2. Are my statements helping me succeed in math?	
3. How can I convince myself to become more positive? Am I going to develop more self-efficacy?	
4. What learning, test taking, attitudinal or motivational behaviors do I need to change in order to support positive self-talk?	

Positive self-talk statement:_____

_____

Using positive self-talk statements can improve self-esteem.

There are other strategies to improve self-esteem. Review the Ten Ways to Improve Self-Esteem and select the ones you can use to improve your self-esteem.

Examples: A positive emotional self-statement is, "I accept who I am, and I have the strength to accomplish my goals." An example of changing your behavior is using the suggestions in this text to improve your math study skills.

❗Remember: Improving your self-esteem will not happen overnight, but you *can* improve it. ❗

10 Ways to Improve Your Self-Esteem

1. When I do well at something, I am going to congratulate myself.
2. I am going to stop procrastinating and blaming others for my problems.
3. When I fail at something, I am not going to blame myself but find out how to be more successful the next time.
4. I will not worry about what others think of me.
5. I will do something I like to do at least one day per week.
6. I will keep a "To Do" list, and I will feel good about myself when marking off each completed item.
7. I will set up short-term and long-term personal/educational goals.
8. I will like myself and have the courage to take risks to change.
9. I will ask for help without feeling guilty.
10. I will put five positive statements about myself on a 3x5 card, and I will read them to myself when I feel bad.

❗Remember: Students who have followed the suggestions in this text have significantly improved their math grades as compared to similar students who did not use these suggestions. ❗

How to Communicate to Your Math Instructor

Communicating with your math instructor can help you gain control over math. However, many students have difficulty communicating with their math instructor in and out of class. Some students fear talking to their math instructor while other students don't see the need to communicate with them at all. Some of the students fear is based on past experiences. Students have indicated that going to the math instructor is like going to the principal's office. If you are one of these students then you need to take control and realize that communicating with your math instructor is different in college than high school. Also, even if you had a poor experience with a college instructor, that does not mean you will have that same experience with your current instructor. Math instructors want to help you succeed and want you to communicate with them. In fact, one of the biggest complaints from math instructors is that students do not come to see them in their office.

The best time to communicate with the math instructor is early in the semester. However, the first week of classes is a busy time for the instructors, so delay that communication until the second or third week of classes. Make sure you've communicated with your instructor before the first major test. This is to ensure that you understand what material is needed to be learned for the first test. Remember the importance of the first major math test.

With today's new technology there are several ways you can communicate with your instructor. The ways are:

1. Call the math office and make an appointment.

2. Visit the instructor during his/her office hours. Usually the office hours are posted on their door.

3. Call the instructor and talk to him/her on the phone.

4. Email the instructor to his/her personal college email address.

5. If the instructor has a chat room or some type of web-based classroom management program, send your email to that address.

Some students may not want to talk to an instructor by themselves. In that case make an appointment in groups of two or three. You may not procrastinate as much if you agreed to go in as a group to see the instructor. If you visit the instructor during office hours you may only have a limited amount of time. Talking to the instructor on the phone is safe for some students and takes less commitment and planning. Many students find it very safe to email the instructor for help, but don't expect an immediate response. Sending messages to web-sites is very easy and the instructor or other students may be able to help you. Some students start off emailing their instructors and then feel safe enough to visit them.

Now that you have decided to communicate with your instructor, what do you want to discuss? Don't feel that you have to wait until you're having major problems to communicate with your instructor. In fact, it is best to communicate that you have some minor concern or that you just want some more information about the course. Here are some suggested topics for discussion:

1. The course syllabus and grade requirement (it is better to know now than later).

2. Your math background. Don't be afraid to tell him/her you had math problems in the past.

3. How to solve some math problems. You may select some problems you already know how to solve with some you have problems solving.

4. Ask for additional math resources such as tutoring and CDs.

5. Ask how to inform the instructor when you will miss class.

To make it easier you may want to write the questions ahead of time and read them to the instructor. Don't ask or tell the instructor:

1. How many classes can I miss without being withdrawn?

2. Is there extra credit for the course?

3. Is this an easy course?

4. Are you an easy instructor?

5. When will I ever use this math?

6. How much teaching experience do you have?

7. How many students passed your course last semester?

8. Why do I have to do this online homework?

9. You don't teach like my last math instructor. I made a B in that class.

10. I looked you up on rateyourinstructor.com.

These types of questions may give a bad impression and put the instructor on the defensive. Make sure you have appropriate questions for the instructor that you are comfortable asking.

Communicating with the instructor has many benefits. These benefits can improve your learning and help you take control of math. Some of the benefits are:

1. The instructor will know who you are among many of his/her students.

2. The instructor will know you are interested in learning math.

3. In class the instructor may answer your questions quicker than the other students.

4. It will make it easier to meet the instructor with more difficult questions.

5. If you need to miss classes, or get sick, the instructor may give you a break on the attendance policy.

6. Sometimes students learn more working one on one with an instructor and their grades go up.

7. The instructor can locate your problem areas faster which can save you hours of homework time.

8. The instructor may be able to teach to your preferred learning style.

9. If you meet with the instructor several times working on problems then the instructor may realize you know more than your test scores indicated.

10. If you have a borderline grade the instructor may have a reason to give you a C instead of a D or a B instead of a C.

Communicating with the instructor can improve your math learning and even your math grades. DON'T BE AFRAID! Use your internal locus of control and self-efficacy to communicate with your instructor during the second or third week of classes. Then continue meeting with the instructor as needed. If you have an adjunct or part time instructor ask the math department chair who you can see for help. **Your instructor wants you to succeed just as much as you do.**

Summary

- Taking control over math means becoming more internal, avoiding learned helplessness and decreasing procrastination.

- You can start internalizing your locus of control by taking the responsibility for practicing the learning suggestions in this text, while setting and accomplishing realistic short-term academic goals.

- You can reduce your fear of failure by telling yourself that previous math failures were due to poor study skills, not your lack of ability.

- You can avoid learned helplessness by not giving up on making a good grade in math and, if needed, getting help from your instructor and counselor.

- If you have high test anxiety, following the suggestions given in this text can start decreasing procrastination which should relieve some of it.

- If you have a math study procrastination problem, you can immediately set up a time management schedule and plan your study time. If you need help setting up this schedule see your counselor.

- Improve your self-esteem by making positive statements to yourself.

- Do not believe other students when they tell you that "you can't do math."

- Communicating with your math instructor can improve your learning and grades.

Chapter 9 Notes

Name: _____ Date: _____

Assignment for Chapter 9

1. Meet with your math instructor at least three times during the semester to get feedback on your course progress and suggestions to improve your learning.

2. Meet with the math lab staff (or an LRC staff member) for your current math course at least once to discuss what you can do to improve your math grades.

3. Define locus of control in your own words. _____

    _____

    _____

    _____

4. Describe five of your short and long-term goals.

    Goal one: _____

    _____

    Goal two: _____

    _____

    Goal three: _____

    _____

    Goal four: _____

    _____

    Goal five: _____

    _____

5. Describe learned helplessness and how you can avoid it. _____

    _____

    _____

    _____

    _____

    _____

Assignment for Chapter 9

6. Explain the concept of fear of failure in your own words. _____

    _____

    _____

    _____

    _____

    _____

7. Explain the concept of fear of success in your own words. _____

    _____

    _____

    _____

    _____

    _____

8. Explain the concept of perfectionism in your own words. _____

    _____

    _____

    _____

    _____

    _____

9. On a separate sheet, write an analysis of your reasons for procrastination in math and decide how you are going to overcome them. Keep these posted in an area where you will frequently see them.

10. Come up with three appealing rewards for which you would gladly study your math assignments without procrastination.

    Reward one: _____

    _____

    Reward two: _____

    _____

    Reward three: _____

    _____

How to Help Students with Disabilities Learn Math   10

In Chapter 10
you will learn these concepts:

- Learning disabilities (LD), along with traumatic brain injuries (TBI) and attention deficit disorder (ADD), are unique as each individual.

  - ✓ Definitions of learning disabilities

  - ✓ Different ways each learning disability interferes with the learning process and subsequently makes learning math difficult

- To discover alternative ways to process information, specifically mathematics, students with LD, TBI or ADD must find study and memory strategies that "bypass" the disability and complete the necessary learning process.

  - ✓ There are different study strategies for each LD, TBI or ADD.

  - ✓ Usually, it takes a combination of several strategies to help students with LD learn math.

  - ✓ Some learning disabilities are more difficult to deal with in learning math.

- Study strategies alone are not enough for some students with LD, TBI or ADD. They must also receive accommodations for learning and testing, and should develop Individual College Learning/Testing Plans.

Introduction

Community colleges and universities are experiencing a large increase in the number of students with disabilities for several reasons. First, improved special education programs have helped students with disabilities graduate from high school. Second, in the past most students with disabilities had special education classes with direct teacher instruction, helping them in the classroom. Most recently with the inclusion model becoming more predominate the students with disabilities were placed in a regular classroom with some to no support from special education teachers. In many cases these students were left in the classroom without the support to succeed in the class. Now, these students are coming to the college or university and are having difficulty learning in the classroom and in many cases do not want to identify themselves due to their bad experiences in high school.

Finally, more than ever before, mature students make up a higher percentage of college students. Many of these mature students had previous learning problems in school but were diagnosed as disabled *after* leaving high school. Other mature students have not yet been diagnosed as disabled.

Students with disabilities need additional math learning skills and accommodations to reach their educational potential because in many situations, students with disabilities will have more difficulty learning math. One reason for this struggle is that most students with disabilities have poor math study skills just like their non-disabled peers.

Also, students with disabilities have processing deficits that impair their learning or testing skills. Cognitive processing skills are the abilities to input, retain and recall information that is taught. Students with learning disabilities by definition have processing deficits and so do students with attention deficit disorder and traumatic brain injury. Good math study skills and appropriate accommodations, such as assigned note-takers and extended testing times, can compensate for some processing deficits.

Definitions of Learning Disability, Traumatic Brain Injury and Attention Deficit Disorder

In most cases, students with learning disabilities (LD), traumatic brain injuries (TBI), and Attention Deficit Disorder (ADD) will have difficulty in college courses, especially in math. Students with LD may have difficulty in language processing that affects math learning. In almost every case, students with TBI will have problems in math due to short-term memory problems. Students with ADD may have difficulty with math due to concentration problems.

These students will need math study skills to make the most of their cognitive processing strengths and help make up for their processing weaknesses. Even though the suggestions in this chapter are for students with disabilities, students who are not disabled may benefit from the study skills suggestions.

Definition of Learning Disabilities

The term "learning disability" (LD) is used to describe a broad range of neurological dysfunctions. Students with LD have average to above-average intelligence. A learning disability is often misunderstood because it is invisible. The National Joint Committee of Learning Disabilities defines LD as follows:

Learning disabilities is a general term that refers to a heterogeneous group of disorders manifested by significant difficulties in the acquisition and use of listening, speaking, reading, writing, reasoning, or mathematical abilities. These disorders are intrinsic to the individual, presumed to be due to central nervous system dysfunction, and may occur concomitantly with other handicapping conditions (for example, sensory impairment, serious emotional disturbance) or with extrinsic influences (such as cultural differences, insufficient or inappropriate instructions). They are not the results of those conditions or influences.

New research has indicated that learning disabilities are neurologically based and cannot be cured. Students with LD may present one or more of these symptoms:

- Difficulty doing the actual calculations
- Reversals of numbers, variables or symbols
- Copying problems incorrectly from line to line or off the board
- Difficulty learning a series of math steps to solve a problem

- Inability to apply math concepts to word problems
- Inability to understand or retain abstract concepts
- Poor organizational skills
- Easily distracted

Dyslexia is a learning disability that also is neurological in origin. Students with dyslexia have difficulties with accurate and fast word or symbol recognition and usually have poor spelling. These learning problems may come from an issue in the language part of the brain where words are broken down in their basic sounds. The results of this problem can be slower reading speed, the misreading of words or symbols, lower reading comprehension and lower vocabulary level which can lead to problems in long-term memory. Dyslexia can also cause problems in writing, listening, speaking and mathematics. Dyslexia is a lifelong condition with no cure, but it can be partially treated with study skills and accommodations.

These problems are consistent throughout the students' lives and do not just happen every once in a while. There are many famous people in the past, however, who would qualify as learning disabled: Leonardo Da Vinci, Woodrow Wilson, General George Patton, Sir Winston Churchill, Albert Einstein, Thomas Edison and Hans Christian Andersen.

More current famous people with LD are Bruce Jenner, Greg Louganis, Nelson Rockefeller, Cher, Danny Glover and Tom Cruise. From reading these two groups of talented, exceptional people, you should now know that learning disabilities are not associated with retardation, slowness, laziness or lack of motivation. For more information on learning disabilities and famous people who have learning disabilities go to www.academicsuccess.com and click on Winning at Math Student Resources. Put in WAM as the User name and Student as the password to access the site. Click on the Disabilities and review the information.

Definition of Traumatic Brain Injuries

There is an increase in the number of students attending college with mild to severe traumatic brain injuries (TBI). These students have graduated from high school with assistance or are attending college after an accident. In other cases, these students had accidents while in college and are now returning.

A traumatic brain injury is any traumatically induced event that causes a loss of consciousness, memory lost, confusion or disorientation, and which results in a neurological deficit. Some TBI causes are accidents involving automobiles, motorcycles, bicycles and in-line skates. TBIs can also occur from sports such as football and boxing. If the effects of a mild TBI last only one day, the person may not seek medical help or may not be informed about potential future problems.

Recovery is different for each student, and some may not have a full recovery. The effects of TBI's can be physical, sensory, cognitive, communicative, academic and social. The physical and sensory problems could result in decreased speed in performing tasks, spatial perception and eye-hand coordination. The most frequent cognitive problem with students is loss of short-term memory and long-term memory. Communication problems could be difficult in word-finding and reading comprehension. The academic effect of TBIs may be a wide range of grades in different subjects. Low grades in math may be due to problems in reading, speed and following directions. Some other effects of TBIs can be deficiencies in attention, concentration, reasoning and time management. However, with proper study skills and accommodations, many students with TBIs can pass math and graduate. For more information on traumatic brain injuries go to www.academicsuccess.com and click on Winning at Math Student Resources. Put in WAM as the User name and Student as the password to access the site. Click on Disabilities and review the information.

Definition of Attention Deficit Disorder

Attention Deficit Disorder (ADD) is a disability characterized by inattention, impassivity and, sometimes, hyperactivity. Until the mid-1980s, ADD was believed to be a childhood disorder because as children mature they learned more socially accepted ways to manage their behavior. However, these children — as adults — continue to experience academic problems associated with ADD.

In fact, two to five million adults are considered to be ADD, and in almost every case children do not "grow out" of ADD. These students are entering colleges and universities, and they must learn behavior strategies and study skills to help them attain their educational goals.

Their main math learning problems are in the areas of computation, word problems, operations and order of operations, mainly due to auditory short-term memory problems. For more information on attention deficit disorder go to www.academicsuccess.com and click on Winning at Math Student Resources. Put in *WAM* as the username and *Student* as the password to access the site. Click on Disabilities and review the information.

The Reasons Disabilities Cause Math-Learning Problems

Students with learning disabilities, who are having difficulty in learning math, may have a math-learning disability or may have problems with different cognitive processes, which affect math learning. Cognitive processes include how students receive and understand information, but they are not *physical* disabilities.

Cognitive Processing Disorders

LD students may have difficulty correctly copying these graphs.

Cognitive processing disorders block a student's ability to obtain valuable information to learn math and/or to demonstrate math knowledge. If students do not know their types of processing disorders, they should contact the office for students with disabilities for this important information.

How students cognitively process information can be explained through the Stages of Memory. The Woodcock-Johnson III's (Woodcock, R. & McGrew, K, 2001) cognitive factors or subtests have been inserted into the Stages of Memory and Cognitive Factors (Figure 27). Using the general names for cognitive processing disorders (ex. visual disorder), students with disabilities can follow their learning process through the Stages of Memory. Based on their processing disorder they can recognize which stage(s) of memory may be "breaking down" and how it affects math learning. This is the first step to developing more effective math study skills and learning accommodations.

Visual Disorders/Dyslexia

Students with learning disabilities who have *visual processing speed disorders* will have difficulty learning math. Visual processing measures how fast a person can read numbers and symbols. Learning problems may include slow visual speed of working with understood math symbols and numbers — in other words, the student is very slow at copying down recognizable numbers, symbols and problem steps. Students with a *visual processing speed deficit* will concentrate so much on copying down the notes that they do not understand the lecture. These students cannot read as fast as the other students and may run out of time when taking a test. The test will measure their reading speed instead of their math knowledge. Their learning breaks down at the sensory register. See Figure 27 (Stages of Memory and Cognitive Factors), on the next page.

Visual memory deficiency is the inability to recognize and remember complex math symbols and numbers in sequence. Mistakes can occur in miscopying notes, misreading the textbook or misreading questions. For these students, learning breaks down in the sensory register or short-term memory. Instead of just being slow at processing information visually, those students have trouble processing visually at all.

Example: The ability to recognize and remember this polynomial: $4x^2 + 2x + 1$. If you have a visual processing deficiency, you may have difficulty telling the difference between 2, as a factor or an exponent, and between "+" (as a plus sign) and "x" (as a variable).

Auditory Disorders

Students with auditory processing difficulties have problems telling the difference between certain sounds of words. This is not a hearing impairment but the inability for the brain to process certain sounds. "Tone deafness," the inability to tell the difference between certain musical notes, is an example of an auditory processing deficit. These students, especially in a large lecture hall, will "miss" some words in a lecture or replace some words with incorrect ones. Students will have difficulty understanding the instructor while taking notes. Missing one or two words means learning breaks down in the sensory register.

Auditory disorders affect your brain, not your ears.

Example: After math class, the student tells the tutor that he is having difficulty understanding how to solve for vegetables. The tutor says, "Vegetables are what you eat. Don't you mean variables?" Another student tells his instructor that he is having difficulty solving literary equations. The instructor says, "You mean equations with words." "No." says the student, "The equations with letters." "Oh you mean literal equations that contain several letters, which may represent variables or constants (numbers)."

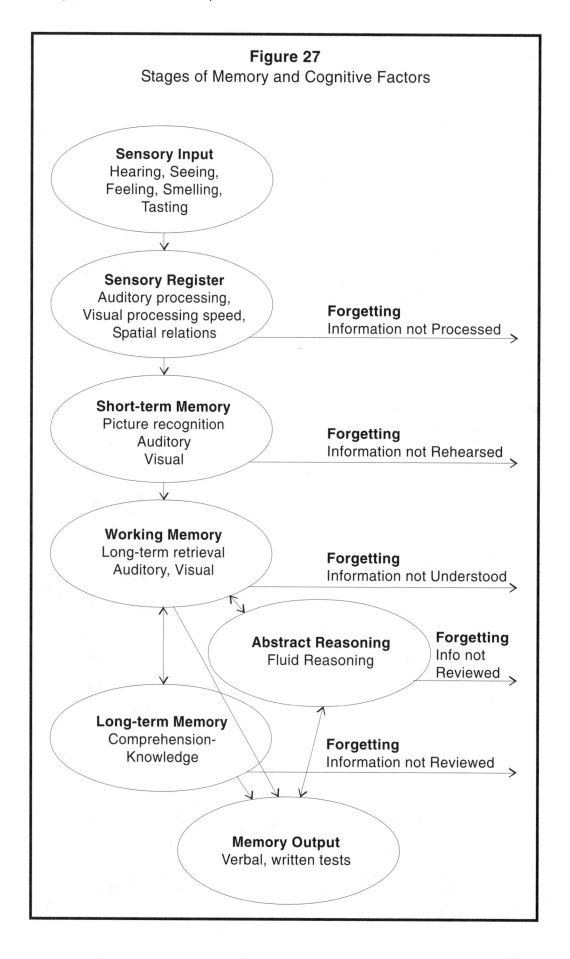

Figure 27
Stages of Memory and Cognitive Factors

Short-term memory Problems

Students with short-term-memory problems may have difficulty learning math. Short-term memory problems can be visual or auditory. Short-term memory difficulties cause problems for students when they must remember numbers, symbols or words in correct order. This problem becomes apparent when a math instructor explains the steps while working a problem. A student forgets the steps of the problem or writes down the steps in the wrong order. Either mistake will cause difficulty in understanding the math concepts, recording notes, doing homework and taking tests.

Short-term memory problems especially affect solving word problems and putting concepts together. Students with short-term memory problems have to read the math word problems several times before understanding the question. By this time many of the other students are already solving the problem. Students who cannot remember several steps in a row will have extreme difficulty understanding the overall concept.

> **Example:** We are teaching a math student how to use the distributive property. I tell the student that a (b + c) is the same as (a) (b) + (a) (c). However, by the time I say (a)(b) + (a)(c) they already forgot a(b + c) or they forgot the entire sentence. They may have the ability to understand the concept, but they cannot hold it in short-term memory to do so. With repetition the student can hold it longer in short-term memory.

Working-Memory Problems

Working memory/long-term retrieval is a two way street to and from long-term memory and abstract reasoning. It can send information to long-term memory and/or into abstract reasoning or send information to memory output. Working memory can also receive information from long-term memory or abstract reasoning to be used to work on math problems. Working memory is like RAM in a computer. Just like RAM in your computer, it can be limited and cause learning problems.

Students with working-memory/ long-term retrieval problems will eventually have difficulty in learning math.

Students with working-memory/long-term *retrieval problems* will eventually have difficulty in learning math. They can't hold new information long enough to remember it later on in the lecture when an instructor refers back to it. They may listen to a math lecture and understand each step as it is explained. However, when the instructor goes back to a previous step discussed several minutes before and asks a question, the student cannot explain the reasons for the steps.

In addition, when interruptions occur in the class or during individual study time, these students have difficulty remembering a series of steps long enough to understand the concept. (In contrast, students with short-term memory problems forget the steps as soon as the instructor explains them.) This aspect of students with working-memory/long-term retrieval problems involves the length of time students are able to hold information in their brains. Students with working memory deficits also have problems putting information into long-term memory and applying concepts to work math problems.

Another aspect of problems with working memory involves the ability to process several pieces of information at one time. Since the working memory is limited, these students have difficulty recalling a math concept from long-term memory into working memory and, at the same time, use the arithmetic to solve the problem. Working memory limits the amount of strategy information that can be used to work the math problems.

Cognitive psychologists in recent research have discovered that test anxiety affects working memory. This research has shown that test anxiety reduces the amount of usable working memory by decreasing its effectiveness. In other words, high test anxiety can reduce 128 Megs of RAM to 64 Megs of RAM, leaving less working memory to solve the math problems. So students with the combination of this processing deficit and test anxiety will have their working memory dramatically reduced. These students need accommodations to compensate for their working memory and techniques to reduce their test anxiety.

Long-term Memory Problems

Some students with LD have difficulty with long-term memory. Long-term memory is the stored-up facts and formulas related to math. These students may be inconsistent when learning new facts or concepts. They may be able to learn how to work fractions one day and a week later have difficulty recalling how to work them. They may have poor achievement in math calculations but have average or above-average math reasoning ability. These students' major problem is putting information into long-term memory.

Students with long-term memory problems benefit from using tools that act like their long term memory while studying. These might include: tape recorded instructions, process cards describing the task to practice, memory devices such as mnemonics, and formula or vocabulary cards. It is also helpful to know what modality the student prefers in deciding which tool might work best. Another strategy is accepting the fact that they may need to practice many more times before the information remains in long-term memory.

> **Example:** A student has practiced factoring problems in the homework assignments over the past two weeks, enough to remember how to factor the problems using the FOIL memory cue. However, during the test the student forgets what FOIL means and missess most of the problems.

Abstract Reasoning Disorders

Another type of learning disability is in abstract/fluid reasoning or thinking. This problem usually occurs when abstract reasoning is required to apply some type of math concept from its law or principle to its application.

> **Example:** You may have difficulty applying a formula to a new homework problem. You may remember the concept but not know how to generalize it to other problems. In general, you will have difficulty applying abstract math concepts to homework and test problems.

> **Example:** Simplify (-11y + 3y) - (-7y - 5y - 4). Students look at the total problem, become confused and do not know where to start. To solve this problem, take a piece of cardboard and cut a small rectangle in the center. Remove the small rectangle which leaves a rectangular hole in the cardboard. Lay the piece of cardboard over the first part of the problem. This allows the student to isolate different factors or signs and concentrate on one part of the problem at a time. This eliminates most of the visual confusion caused by a learning disability.

If you are a student with a disability, reviewing Figure 27 (Stages of Memory and Cognitive Factors) may have given you an idea of where your learning may be "breaking down." If you don't have a disability then you may have a better understanding of your learning process. Students with disabilities need to talk to their counselor about their cognitive processing deficits and how the deficits affect their learning. Students who do not have disabilities may want to use the discussed information to determine your cognitive learning strengths and weaknesses. Then, using the general cognitive processing areas, rate your effectiveness by putting a x in the appropriate area:

Cognitive Learning Area	Strength	Average	Weakness
Sensory Input			
Sensory Register			
Short-term Memory			
Working Memory			
Long-term Memory			
Abstract Reasoning			

Based on the x's, describe your learning strengths and weaknesses: _____

_____

_____

_____

Use this information to help you in the next sections on study skills and accommodations to develop a learning plan to improve your success.

Special Study Skills for Students with Disabilities

Study skills for students with LD may be the same as for other students, but the skills are absolutely essential to their learning. Students with LD usually have organizational problems, including time management because in many cases they are easily distracted. While some non-disabled students may have an "internal" time-management clock, most students with LD do not.

Students Helping Themselves

Students with LD must develop a study schedule and complete a weekly study plan. The weekly study plan must be completed each week so you know when to study for what subjects/tests. Students who have difficulty developing a study schedule or weekly study plan can see the counselor for disabled students for assistance.

Distractions can occur in the classroom, during tutorial sessions, while doing homework and when taking tests. These distractions interfere with understanding the instructor's lectures and with studying. To combat the distraction, students should sit in "The Golden Triangle of Success" and as close to the front of the classroom as is comfortable. Being in the center front of the room decreases most awareness of distractions and provides the best place to record lectures.

! **Remember:** Sitting in the right place will improve your learning. !

How to Get Help from Others

Tutorial sessions help students with disabilities because there is more opportunity for participatory learning. The sessions need to be at a routine time and in a quiet environment. It is best to set up tutorial sessions at the same time each day. The private tutorial sessions may have to be in the late afternoon when the math lab is not crowded.

It is important that the tutor explains "how" and "why" a math process works instead of doing the problem for the student. Ask the tutor what changes and what does not change if a part of the process is different. Be able to explain the basic fundamentals of the process. *Now learning can happen!*

How to Handle Homework

Homework sessions need to be set up on a weekly basis and at the same time each day. Do not skip any homework sessions. Make sure your college study area for doing homework is in an isolated location. At home, study during a quiet time of the day or night and put up a "do not disturb" sign on the door. Make sure the study place is free of distractions.

Here are some tips when doing homework:

- Put simple numbers into the problems to see what process is at work. Aim to understand the concepts and formulas.

- Make up questions for your instructor and tutor.

- If it helps, write out class notes and text samples.

- Check each homework problem for which you do not have the answer.

- For visual learners, close your eyes and say each of the steps to yourself.

- For auditory learners, say each problem step out loud until you know them.

- Finish your homework by doing problems you can do, even if you have to rework a few problems you already know how to work.

Selection of study skills adaptations are based on a student's processing deficit or strength. Some students with visual processing/visual discrimination problems have difficulty doing their homework. Their homework looks like "chicken scratch." They mix up their problem steps in solving math equations with the calculations used to solve the equations. The following technique keeps the problem steps separate from the calculations, reducing the frustration of mixing up the problem steps and calculations for homework and tests.

> **Example:** After working three-fourths of a math problem, they cannot find the equations steps. The calculations are so mixed up with equation steps that they cannot find where they left off working the equation. The problem steps and calculations are scattered all over the page. These students bring in their homework problems to the tutors, but the tutors cannot read the problems. To solve this problem, draw a line down the center of the homework page. On the left side of the page write the problem steps, and on the right side of the page do the math calculations.

Students with visual processing problems benefit from using study aids that simplify the process of discrimination. For example, students misread math notations and signs in their text and while doing homework. Use a 4x6 index card — with no lines on it — as a reading aid. Move the card line by line down the page text or homework page. For those with severe line jumping problems cut a rectangular hole in a 3x5 card. Move the card down the page with only a few numbers or variables showing at one time.

Sometimes it helps to write out problems with larger numbers and more space. A felt-tip pen makes the math numbers and symbols larger, which makes them easier to read. Work each problem step with the felt-tip pen until the problem is finished. If this is still too difficult, turn your note book sideways and use a column (lines in the notebook) for each number or variable. Using enlarged graphing paper to do your homework can also solve this problem.

Another study-skills technique to help discriminate between math numbers and symbols is to use a ballpoint pen that has four colors, or different color pencils: red, green, blue and black.

Using colors, cards, and larger numbers can help you learn math

When doing math homework, use different colors for variables, numbers, exponents, negative signs or positive signs. Highlighting these numbers in different colors is another way to color code the symbols and numbers.

Another way to use color is to distinguish the math you already know from new concepts in the problems. You can use blue for the parts of the math problem you already know how to work and use the other pen colors for the new parts of the math problem. Or, you can follow each math operation by pen color until the problem is completed. Even though it takes you longer to work the problems this way, it decreases visual processing errors and makes it easier to work the problems.

Some students' mental processing speeds get ahead of their writing speeds, which causes them mentally to lose track when solving problems. There are two ways to solve this problem. One way to reduce mental speed errors is to write each math problem step in a different color pen. This will reduce the mental problem-solving speed, allowing each problem step to be accurately written.

Another solution is to write, in English, the reasons for doing each math step. This process not only slows down a student's mental processing speed but also helps him/her learn the reasons for each problem step. This is helpful because some students have difficulty understanding math until they write down the basic processes and concepts. Writing down the reasons for each step during tutorial sessions, homework or studying can help you understand math. The written information can be checked by a tutor and can be used as a future study guide.

For difficult problems, make up multicolored note cards. These note cards will demonstrate a problem representing a difficult concept worked out step by step. Number the reasons for each step on the bottom of the card. If the problem had four steps, there will be four reasons. Highlight the most difficult step so it will stay in your memory. See Figure 28 (Note card Check System) on the next page. Cover up the bottom of the card and recall the reasons for each problem step. Review these cards as often as needed.

> **!** **Remember:** Research has shown that writing can help students go beyond **!**
> the rote learning of math and improve understanding.

Use a Tape recorder

Students with short-term memory problems must use a tape recorder with a tape counter during tutorial sessions. When working on a difficult problem, record the tutor's explanation. Then record yourself rephrasing the reasons for the steps while the tutor listens. After making sure all corrections are made, write down the tape counter number next to the problem. Listen to the tape before doing similar homework problems and use the tape as a future study reference. The same procedure works when going over a test with the instructor.

Appropriate Accommodations for Students with Disabilities

Under Section 504 of the Rehabilitation Act and the Americans with Disabilities Act, students with disabilities are entitled to certain accommodations based on their disabilities. Accommodations for students with disabilities are provided to allow the same access to course material as non-disabled students.

Testing accommodations are provided to make the students with disabilities equivalent to other students. In this way, the disabled students' knowledge rather than their disabilities is tested.

Learning and testing accommodations are based on the students' processing disorders. The following accommodations are commonly suggested for students with learning disabilities, but additional accommodations may also be needed. Some common testing accommodations are extended test time and testing in a private room.

Accommodations: Visual Memory and/or
Visual Speed Disorders and/or Visual-Spatial Thinking

Students with visual processing and/or visual speed disorders visually process materials five to ten times slower than non-disabled students. These students have major note-taking and test-taking problems. Three lecture accommodations include note-takers, tape recorders and large-print handouts. These students may need one or all of these learning accommodations. Testing accommodations for these students would include extended test time, enlarged test print and/or color-coded tests.

Students with visual processing disorders may have difficulty reading the math book and doing their homework problems. Their reading might improve if they put different types of colored plastic sheets that are used as report covers. Also using a colored index card to put under the sentence while reading may help. Students, when adding, subtracting, or multiplying numbers and algebraic terms (polynomials) can highlight the column before doing the required task. Student can also use graph paper to put a number in each box to keep the numbers in the correct column. I have also suggested to students that they turn their note-

---

Figure 28
Note Card Check System

Solve for *x*:

Problem: $4x + 16 = 12x$

1. $4x + 16 + (-4x) = 12x + (-4x)$
2. $4x + (-4x) + 16 = 12x + (-4x)$
3. $16 = 12x - 4x$
4. $16 = (12 - 4)x$
5. $16 = 8x$
6. $16 (1/8) = 8 (1/8 \ x)$
7. $2 = x$

1. Adding -4*x* to both sides of the equation.
2. Commutative property
3. Additive inverse
4. Distributive property
5. Simplifying
6. Multiplicative inverse
7. Simplifying

Now, put your answer back into the original equation to see if the right side equals the left side.

---

book side ways and use the columns to keep their numbers straight and in the same line. Students can also take a 4 x 6 card and line it up on the last column to the right. Then move it one column to the left at a time to keep the columns straight. Tutors and instructors should use different colored pens or magic markers to indicate a variable or numeral so that the student can differentiate between numbers, symbols and variables.

Accommodations: Auditory Processing and/or Short-term Memory Disorders

Students with auditory processing disorders, including short-term memory and auditory processing, have difficulty understanding a math lecture. They may not remember the math steps in correct order or may forget certain problem steps. They may also get words mixed up with other words. Learning accommodations include note-takers, tape recorders, close physical proximity to the instructor and videotapes. Students will also need extended test time because they have to read the problems several times to understand them.

Students who have difficulty remembering or understanding the lecture long enough to write down the information can use a note-taker. They can also take notes from videos that teach the same concept. Almost all the publishers have videotapes that accompany their textbooks.

Accommodations: Working Memory and Long-Term Memory/Reasoning Problems

In most cases, students with working memory and long-term memory/reasoning problems will have extreme difficulty learning math. These students usually have poor organizational skills, poor problem-solving skills and difficulty understanding causal relationships. The difficulties that cause the most of these problems are poor abstract reasoning and difficulty generalizing from one experience/idea to new situations.

Note-takers allow students to understand more from the lecture.

These students may have a 3.5 GPA but are failing math. Learning accommodations for LD students with thinking/reasoning problems can be extensive. Most of these students will need a combination of note-takers, tape recorders, handouts, math videotapes, tutors and calculators. Testing accommodations may include calculators, extended test time, enlarged tests, alternate test forms and, in some cases, formula/fact sheets.

Students can develop their learning accommodations. For example, you can develop note cards to help you learn math concepts. Many students still have problems understanding the relationship between fractions, decimals and percents. To help learn this information look at the card in Figure 29 (Transition Note-Card). This card shows the relationships between several fractions. To remember how to add and subtract integers you can color code the number line. The right side is positive and will use black numbers and the left side will have red negative numbers. Another way is to use your body as a number line. With both arms are stretched out, the left arm can represent negative integers and the right arm can be the positive ones. The body is zero. To add a negative 6 to a positive five the student must pass through the body (0) to a negative 1. For hands on learners doing several problem samples like this helps internalize the motion of crossing the body (0) to correctly solve the problem.

Figure 29 — Transition Note-Card		
Given Fraction	**Decimal Form**	**Percent Equivalent**
1/5	.20	20%
1/4	.25	25%
1/3	.333	33%
1/2	.50	50%
The pattern is that as the denominator of the fraction gets smaller and the numerator stays the same (1) the decimal and percent gets larger at the same rate.		

*Note-takers,
tape recorders,
handouts,
math videotapes,
tutors and
calculators
can all be used
to help you learn*

Kinesthetic learning (hands on learning) using manipulatives especially helps students with long-term memory and abstract reasoning concerns. Developing your own hands on learning strategies and manipulatives may take some imagination, but it will be worth it. If you have difficulty developing kinesthetic learning materials search the Internet for virtual kinesthetic websites. For more information on manipulatives and kinesthetic websites go to www.academicsuccess.com and click on Winning at Math Student Resources. Put in *WAM* as the username and *Student* as the password to access the site. Click on Disabilities and review the information.

Since scientific and graphing calculators are becoming very complicated to use, students may need calculator note cards to help them remember certain keystrokes. Calculator note cards are individual 3x5 cards, which have examples of the key strokes needed for doing certain calculator functions.

Tutors and instructors should increase the discussion time during tutoring sessions to make sure the students understand the material. If the information is difficult, the students must repeat back the information to make sure that they understand it. They also need to have regular meetings with their instructors to make sure they are learning the abstract mathematical concepts.

Students should also discuss with their tutors and instructors that they learn best by being taught from concrete to a representative to abstract sequence of instruction. This means from hands on experiences by using manipulatives to pictures and drawings to abstract symbols. Visit your math lab/ learning resource center or talk to your instructor to see if they have manipulatives and can teach you this way.

To enhance their learning, these students must develop an "Individual College Learning/Testing Plan." This plan needs to be developed with their counselors or learning specialists for students with disabilities. The plan includes their academic strengths, weaknesses, services, learning accommodations, testing accommodations and semester goals. This plan can be part of their confidential student files. Figure 30 (Individual College Learning/Testing Plan) is a sample of a completed college plan for a fall semester. Go to the Winning at Math Student Resource website and click on Disabilities for your blank form to complete.

Accommodations: Traumatic Brain Injury

Since each student with a TBI is different, a cognitive and achievement assessment is needed. If you were assessed after the TBI, talk to your counselor for students with disabilities about your strengths and weaknesses. If you were not assessed after your TBI, ask your counselor for students with disabilities for a cognitive and math achievement assessment. Without knowing your processing strengths and weaknesses, it is very difficult to suggest effective study skills and appropriate accommodations. The study skills you used in the past may no longer be effective. For example, if your TBI affected your visual memory, you may no longer be a visual learner. Use the results from your processing tests to find out how you now learn best. The following suggestions should be the first steps taken in improving academic performance:

1. Focus on improving your self-monitoring, organization and structure skills. Some examples of self-monitoring are thinking before you talk and making a "to do" list every day. Your "to do" list can include attending classes, doing homework, attending tutorial sessions, counselor appointments and personal needs. Review your "to do" list several times a day and cross off the items as you complete them. Add items to your "to do" list as they come up.

2. Keep an appointment book with important dates such as the times for your final exams.

Improving organization can include getting your materials ready for each class and setting up a good study environment.

3. Establish a routine that includes tutorial sessions, doing homework, going to the library and eating lunch at the same time each day. These suggestions can reduce some of the effects of memory problems.

4. Design a system of the study skills that helps you work through the learning process. Review the study skills mentioned in the LD section and consult your counselor for students with disabilities.

Inform your tutors of your learning style.

5. The learning and testing accommodations you will need are based on your processing deficits. You will have processing deficits similar to those of students with LD. Most likely you will have a short-term memory processing deficit. This means you will need a note-taker for your class and a tape recorder to record the important aspects of the tutorial sessions. Other processing deficits may be found in working memory, long-term memory and fluid reasoning. Use the accommodation suggestions for students with LD as a guide for your accommodations. Make sure you talk to your counselor for students with disabilities about appropriate accommodation and make up an Individual College Learning/Testing Plan.

Attention Deficit Disorder

Students with ADD need to be more careful than other students when scheduling their classes. These students should carry a reduced course load, usually twelve or fewer credit hours. There needs to be time in between classes to allow for review and extra time for test taking. Students with ADD should schedule math classes during the time when they are most alert and if they are on medication, when it is most effective. They should also try to have instructors who use multi-sensory teaching techniques. Once you find an instructor with whom you are successful, you must, at any cost, continue with that instructor in your next math classes.

Students need to make sure they are in the correct level of math course. This level should be one in which the students feel challenged but also can experience success in math. Make sure to take the placement or diagnostic test at your college or university. Being at the correct level is a must for students with ADD. In fact, if there is a question about where you should be placed, always take the lower class. It is better to make an "A" in the lower-level math class than a "D" or an "F" in the higher-level course.

Another skill essential for students with ADD is time management. Students should learn to use weekly, monthly and yearly calendars to plan the term. Make sure to complete all the time management suggestions in Chapter 4, "How to Create a Positive Study Environment and Manage Your Time." Keep a pocket calendar for the semester schedule and appointments. Check this calendar daily. It might be wise to have someone else know what your schedule is just to make sure you stay on track.

Figure 30
Completed Individual College Learning/Testing Plan

Semester: Fall 2008

A. Student Information:

   Name: Joe College
   Disability: Learning disability

B. Services:

   Tutoring three times a week in math
   Word processing lessons twice a week

C. Courses:

   Elementary Algebra, History, English, Psychology, Math Study Skills

D. Learning Accommodations:

   Note-taker
   Tape recorder

E. Testing Accommodations:

   Double test time
   Enlarged tests
   Calculator

F. Disability Information:

   Strengths: language skills, short-term and long-term memory, reasoning skill, excellent motivation.

   Weaknesses: visual processing skills, visual memory skills, reading speed, math study skills, math, time management.

G. Semester Goals:

   1. Joe will obtain a 3.0 GPA.
   2. Joe will make a "B" in elementary algebra.
   3. Joe will improve his math study skills weakness by working on the suggestions from the computerized Math Study Skills Evaluation.
   4. Joe will set up a study schedule and each week will complete a study-goals sheet.
   5. Joe will attend his tutorial sessions.
   6. Joe will use his learning and testing accommodations.
   7. Joe will see his math instructor every two weeks and after each major test.

Schedule short periods of time to study math each day rather than studying math for longer periods every other day. Large assignments should be divided into smaller, more manageable chunks. Review previously learned material before each new study session.

Students with ADD need to develop ways to make every minute of class time beneficial. First of all, they need to sit in the front part of "The Golden Triangle of Success" and away from the windows and doors. This area will have the fewest distractions. Second, they need to understand the reason for each step in a procedure instead of just following the instructor. If it becomes too difficult to understand the instructor and take notes at the same time, they should ask their counselors for a note-taker and use a tape recorder. They should ask questions in class as soon as they get confused. If all the questions cannot be answered, they should schedule an appointment with the instructor or review the videotapes for that concept.

Students with ADD should use color and action as much as possible during study time. Colored pencils may be used to highlight key concepts or to distinguish grouping symbols, operations and like terms. When working word problems, ADD students should draw pictures or diagrams to aid in organizing the information. Key words should be colored. Students should then follow the suggestions in this text for solving word problems.

Students with ADD should take tests in a distraction-free environment and be given extended test time. Most students with ADD need extended test time because of their uncontrollable internal and external distractions. These distractions cause short-term memory problems. It takes students with short-term memory problems longer to read the test and work each problem step. The extra test time is given to test the students' math knowledge instead of their disabilities. Review the learning and testing accommodations in the LD section for students with short-term memory. These students will be taking the test in a separate area and should get any special instructions that will be told to the class. They need to talk to a counselor for students with disabilities for any additional accommodations that might be needed and develop an Individual College Learning/Testing Plan.

A final strategy for students with ADD is self-monitoring. They should keep a record of their own progress, recording each grade received and determining the grade average after each test. They should also schedule regular appointments with the instructor to discuss strengths, weaknesses and grades. Self-monitoring can also be applied to homework, test-taking and progress toward educational and personal goals. Use the additional self-monitoring techniques suggested in the TBI section.

ADD is one of the least understood disabilities and is challenged more often by instructors and administrators. Talk to the counselor for students with disabilities about ways to discuss your disability with math instructors.

Students with ADD can be successful in math, but certain personal and study skills, which may not be essential to other students, become essential to the student with ADD. Remember these skills are time management, self-monitoring, math study skills and test-taking skills. By knowing how to study, you can learn more in less time. Once success is achieved, it becomes its own motivator.

How to Make an "Individual College Learning/Testing Plan"

Some students with disabilities may have difficulty developing an "Individual College Learning/Testing Plan" (ICLTP). The purpose of the plan is to set semester goals and to obtain the appropriate accommodations for each class.

Defining the ICLTP

For students with disabilities the ICLTP is similar to the Individual Education Plan (IEP) that they may have had in middle or high school. In most cases, the IEP was conducted through a meeting with parents, teachers and the special education instructor. The IEP detailed the amount and type of help to be received from teachers and special education instructor. The student had little input on the IEP.

Colleges' and universities' accommodations are based on different laws than the IEP. College and university accommodations are based on federal laws, such as Section 504 and the Americans with Disabilities Act. *You need to be prepared to give the Section 504 coordinator or the disability support services office your personal documentation of your disability.* In-

With practice you can learn to focus on a test.

cluded in that documentation should be information on your processing problems and suggested accommodations. You also should be able to explain your disability learning problems to the disability support services office personnel. Unlike the IEP meeting, you will be the one who will have the input on the ICLTP.

The counselor cannot contact your previous teacher or even your parents without your permission. In fact the counselor cannot tell your instructor that you are disabled without your permission.

What You Should Do to Get Help

Several weeks before classes begin, meet with your counselor for students with disabilities to discuss your needs. If you are currently enrolled as a disabled student and do not have accommodations, contact the counselor for disabled students as soon as possible. Use Figure 30 (Individual College Learning/Testing Plan) as a basic plan to obtain services from that office.

Discuss your learning problems and the accommodations with your former middle or high school counselor in order to understand your disability. If your disability was documented after high school, discuss the psycho-educational report results with your counselor. The psycho-educational report should contain information on your learning weaknesses and suggestions for accommodations. If your report does not have these two areas, request the report to be rewritten to include these items.

How to Help Yourself

Ask about the different types of services offered to students with disabilities. You can request tutoring services even though it is not required under Section 504 or the ADA. However, most colleges do offer tutoring through the disability support service office. Also ask for services related to computer training or priority registration. Use all the services that will improve your learning skills.

List all the courses that you will take or are taking. Indicate the courses in which you will need accommodation(s). In most cases, you will not need accommodations in all your classes. The learning accommodations may be the same for each course (such a note-taker), except lab courses. Next, list the testing accommodations you are requesting. In most cases, students can receive double time and testing in a private room. Ask for additional testing accommodations that are based on your previous IEP or documentation.

Completing Your ICTLP

These students used the suggestions in this book to pass math and graduate.

Section F of the ICTLP is for disability information. List your learning strengths and learning weaknesses based on your information and input from your counselor. This will help the counselor remember the best ways to help and work with you in the future.

Section G concerns developing semester goals. You may need a second meeting with your counselor to establish these goals. These goals should relate to your expected grades, study skills improvement, study schedule and using the services offered by the disability support service office.

Developing an Individual College Learning/Testing Plan is in your best interest. The information is confidential and is kept in a separate file, usually in the disability support service office. Information about your disability cannot be placed in your regular college file or in any way be indicated on your transcripts. Only the instructors from which you request accommodations will know that you are disabled, but they cannot obtain any other information about your disability without your permission.

I would suggest that you meet with these instructors and discuss how your disability affects learning. Even with the confidentiality guarantees, some students, based on previous bad experiences, do not want anyone to know about their disabilities. These students put off requesting their accommodations until they are failing the course, which is too late.

Do not wait! Request your accommodations now, so you will have the best chance to pass math and your other subjects.

<u>Summary</u>

- Colleges and universities have more students with disabilities attending math classes.

- Students with disabilities need to know their processing deficits and strengths to become successful in math.

- Math study skills and appropriate learning and testing accommodations can compensate for part of their disabilities.

- Student accommodations must be matched to their processing deficits and must be made on an individual basis.

- Additional study skills techniques, such as color coding and the Note-Card Check System will improve learning.

- Students with disabilities must understand how their disabilities affect their learning and work closely with their instructors and counselors.

- Students must understand how their cognitive process deficits affect their stages of memory and learning.

- Students with LD may have difficulty in visual processing speed and visual discrimination that affects math learning.

- Students with TBI will, in most cases, have problems in math due to short-term memory problems and abstract reasoning.

- Students with a learning disability that involves cognitive problems in long-term memory or abstract reason, and students with TBIs, need to use hands on learning and manipulatives to improve their math learning.

- Students with ADD may have difficulty with math due to concentration and organizational problems.

- For more information on disabilities go to www.academicsuccess.com and click on Winning at Math Student Resources and review the Disabilities section.

- For these students to improve their math learning, they will need to develop an Individual College Learning/Testing Plan (including procedures to improve their math study skills and the appropriate learning and testing accommodations). This plan needs to be developed before class begins each semester or at least during the first week of classes.

- Students with disabilities must educate themselves about their disabilities and become self-advocates.

- Even though these suggestions are for students with disabilities, students who are not disabled may benefit from many of these study-skills suggestions.

 Remember: Students with disabilities must understand their math-learning weaknesses and consult their counselors for appropriate learning and testing accommodations.

Chapter 10 Notes

Name: _____ Date: _____

Assignment for Chapter 10

1. In your own words, what is the definition of a learning disability?

_____

_____

_____

_____

2. Who are some famous people with learning disabilities?

_____

_____

_____

3. Explain two reasons why a learning disability causes math-learning problems.

Reason one: _____

_____

Reason two: _____

_____

4. Review the stages of memory and locate which stage your disability is causing a breakdown in learning. Then list three ways you can solve the breakdown in learning.

Way one: _____

_____

Way two: _____

_____

Way three: _____

_____

5. Describe two special study skills for students with LD.

Skill one: _____

_____

Skill two: _____

_____

6. How are accommodations determined for students with LD, TBI and ADD?

LD: _____

_____

TBI: _____

_____

ADD: _____

_____

7. What are some problems students with TBI will have learning math, and how can they be accommodated?

_____

_____

_____

_____

8. What are some problems students with ADD will have learning math, and how can they be accommodated?

_____

_____

_____

_____

9. For students with disabilities, describe your Individual College Learning/Testing Plan.

_____

_____

_____

_____

10. For students without disabilities, what are two new study-skills suggestions you could use to improve your math learning?

_____

_____

_____

_____

APPENDIX

Scoring the Test Attitude Inventory

Test Attitude Inventory Total Score (T)

To score the Test Attitude Inventory, add the circled items 2 to 20. The maximum score will be 86, and the minimum score will be 19. On question one reverse the values: i.e. , "almost never" is a 4 instead of a 1, "sometimes" is 3 instead of 2, "often" is 2 instead of 3, and "always" is 1 instead of 4. NOTE THAT ONLY THE VALUES OF RESPONSES TO ITEM 1 ARE REVERSED. Add both scores for the total raw score.

Score for items 2–20 _____

Score for item 1　　　 _____

Total Raw Score　　 _____

Now that you have your score we need to find the percentile norm. Look at the chart below and select university/college or community college student. Find your raw score on the left side. Go over to the F (female) or M (male) column and circle that score. That is the percentile score to be put on your graph.

<table>
<tr><td colspan="3"><u>**University/College**</u></td><td></td><td colspan="3"><u>**Community College**</u></td></tr>
<tr><td>**Raw score**</td><td>**M**</td><td>**F**</td><td></td><td>**Raw score**</td><td>**M**</td><td>**F**</td></tr>
<tr><td>80</td><td>100</td><td>100</td><td></td><td>80</td><td>100</td><td>100</td></tr>
<tr><td>79</td><td>100</td><td>100</td><td></td><td>79</td><td>100</td><td>100</td></tr>
<tr><td>78</td><td>100</td><td>100</td><td></td><td>78</td><td>100</td><td>100</td></tr>
<tr><td>77</td><td>100</td><td>99</td><td></td><td>77</td><td>100</td><td>100</td></tr>
<tr><td>76</td><td>100</td><td>99</td><td></td><td>76</td><td>100</td><td>100</td></tr>
<tr><td>75</td><td>100</td><td>98</td><td></td><td>75</td><td>100</td><td>99</td></tr>
<tr><td>74</td><td>99</td><td>98</td><td></td><td>74</td><td>100</td><td>98</td></tr>
<tr><td>73</td><td>99</td><td>97</td><td></td><td>73</td><td>100</td><td>98</td></tr>
<tr><td>72</td><td>99</td><td>97</td><td></td><td>72</td><td>100</td><td>97</td></tr>
<tr><td>71</td><td>98</td><td>96</td><td></td><td>71</td><td>99</td><td>97</td></tr>
<tr><td>70</td><td>98</td><td>96</td><td></td><td>70</td><td>99</td><td>96</td></tr>
<tr><td>69</td><td>97</td><td>96</td><td></td><td>69</td><td>99</td><td>96</td></tr>
<tr><td>68</td><td>97</td><td>95</td><td></td><td>68</td><td>99</td><td>95</td></tr>
</table>

Raw score	M	F
67	96	94
66	96	94
65	96	93
64	96	92
63	95	92
62	95	91
61	94	90
60	94	88
59	93	87
58	92	85
7	92	84
56	91	83
55	89	81
54	89	79
53	87	77
52	86	75
51	85	72
50	84	70
49	82	68
48	79	67
47	78	65
46	75	63
45	73	61
44	71	58
43	68	57
42	65	54
41	63	52
40	60	50
39	57	47
38	55	44
37	53	42
36	51	40
35	48	38
34	44	34
33	42	31
32	39	27
31	38	25
30	32	21
29	29	19
28	26	16
27	23	13
26	17	10
25	15	9
24	12	6
23	10	5
22	7	4
21	4	2
20	2	1

Raw score	M	F
67	98	95
66	98	94
65	96	92
64	96	92
63	93	91
62	93	89
61	93	88
60	93	87
59	93	87
58	93	87
57	92	86
56	91	86
55	90	84
54	89	82
53	88	79
52	88	76
51	85	75
50	84	73
49	82	70
48	81	67
47	80	66
46	78	62
45	77	59
44	72	57
43	71	54
42	69	52
41	68	52
40	65	48
39	51	44
38	54	41
37	50	39
36	46	34
35	40	33
34	40	28
33	38	27
32	35	22
31	33	20
30	31	17
29	26	15
28	22	13
27	19	11
26	16	9
25	11	8
24	6	5
23	4	3
22	2	1
21	1	1
20	1	1

Test Attitude Inventory Worry Subscale (W)

To score The Test Attitude Inventory Worry Subscale (W) add the circled values (1, 2, 3, 4) marked for items # 3, 4, 5, 6, 7, 14, 17, and 20. Enter the sum on the following line _____. This is your raw score. The maximum score is 32 and the minimum score is 8.

Now that you have your raw score we need to find the percentile norm. Look at the chart below and select university/college or community college student. Find your raw score on the left side. Go over to the F (female) or M (male) column and circle that score. That is the percentile score for the Worry Subscale (W).

University/College			Community College		
Raw score	**M**	**F**	**Raw score**	**M**	**F**
32	100	100	32	100	100
31	100	100	31	100	100
30	100	100	30	100	100
29	99	98	29	97	100
28	99	97	28	96	98
27	98	96	27	96	96
26	97	95	26	96	96
25	96	94	25	95	95
24	95	93	24	94	94
23	94	91	23	94	94
22	93	90	22	91	91
21	92	87	21	91	91
20	90	85	20	85	85
19	88	81	19	83	83
18	85	76	18	81	81
17	80	71	17	78	78
16	76	66	16	74	74
15	70	61	15	65	65
14	65	56	14	57	57
13	57	50	13	53	53
12	51	43	12	44	44
11	43	33	11	35	35
10	35	24	10	28	28
9	25	16	9	19	19
8	14	9	8	10	10

Test Attitude Inventory Emotionality Subscale (E)

To score The Test Attitude Inventory Emotionality Subscale (E) add the circled values (1, 2, 3, 4) marked for items # 2, 8, 9, 10, 11, 15, 16, and 18. Enter the sum on the following line _____. This is your raw score. The maximum score is 32 and the minimum score is 8.

Now that you have your raw score we need to find the percentile norm. Look at the chart below and select university/college or community college student. Find your raw score on the left side. Go over to the F (female) or M (male) column and circle that score. That is the percentile score for the Emotionality Subscale (E).

University/College				Community College		
Raw score	M	F		Raw score	M	F
32	100	100		32	100	100
31	99	99		31	100	100
30	98	95		30	100	100
29	97	93		29	99	97
28	96	91		28	97	94
27	94	98		27	97	89
26	93	86		26	96	88
25	91	82		25	94	85
24	89	77		24	93	82
23	87	73		23	90	79
22	84	69		22	88	75
21	78	64		21	87	70
20	74	61		20	84	65
19	70	56		19	79	60
18	65	51		18	72	53
17	59	47		17	62	47
16	52	42		16	55	39
15	46	36		15	44	32
14	38	29		14	39	26
13	32	24		13	30	20
12	25	18		12	26	17
11	20	13		11	19	12
10	14	8		10	10	9
9	8	4		9	4	5
8	4	2		8	2	3

Study Skills and Strategies
Student Instructions for Getting Started

3S is a comprehensive online program that will enable you to assess and improve your use of the study skills and strategies most important for success in school.

Follow the steps below to begin using 3S:

1. Go to the following Internet address: http://3s.studyskillsplus.com/

2. Bookmark this address for future access.

3. On the screen that appears, in the space for Student ID, enter your personal 3S user code. Your code is provided in the box below:

NOTE: 1 = number; I = letter; 0 = number; O = letter

4. On the screen that then appears, enter your first and last name, and your email address. Please note that the name you enter will appear on all assessments and work you complete throughout your use of 3S.

5. A welcome screen then appears showing program menu options. This screen also shows the date and time your access to 3S expires. (Your access will expire exactly six months from the time you first login to 3S.) Click on "User's Guide" to learn how to use all components of 3S. Print this guide for future reference.

APPENDIX

Learning Modality Inventory for Math Students

The following survey can help you discover how you best learn math. Answer the questions based on what you are like. There are no right or wrong answers. The more you answer truthfully, the more you will be able to use the results to improve studying math. "1" means the statement is hardly like you. "4" means the statement is really like you. Then if you think the statement is somewhere in between, decide if it is a "2" or a "3."

Questions	Least like me		Most like me	
1. Reading a math problem out loud helps me learn better when I am studying.	1	2	3	4
2. I learn math better if I can talk about it.	1	2	3	4
3. I select certain problems and memorize what they look like so I can use them to help me remember on a math test.	1	2	3	4
4. Making things with my hands helps me learn better.	1	2	3	4
5. Drawing a picture of the word problem helps me understand how to do it on a test.	1	2	3	4
6. Math makes more sense when I see it worked out on the board.	1	2	3	4
7. Moving around while studying helps me concentrate and learn more.	1	2	3	4
8. I understand written instructions better than ones told to me.	1	2	3	4
9. I memorize what a problem looks like so I can remember it better on a test or quiz.	1	2	3	4

Questions, *continued*	Least like me		Most like me	
10. I repeat steps to a problem out loud or to myself in order to remember what I am supposed to do.	1	2	3	4
11. Watching someone complete a math problem helps me understand more than listening to someone tell me how to do it.	1	2	3	4
12. Talking about a math problem while learning in class helps me understand it better.	1	2	3	4
13. I learn math better when I watch someone do it.	1	2	3	4
14. When I take a test, I read the problems to myself softly.	1	2	3	4
15. When I solve a math problem on a test, I picture my notes in my head to help me remember how to solve it.	1	2	3	4
16. I enjoy making things with my hands for a hobby.	1	2	3	4
17. Math makes more sense when someone talks about it while doing it on the board rather than just doing it on the board.	1	2	3	4
18. Explaining a math problem to someone else helps me learn better when I am studying.	1	2	3	4
19. Looking at a picture from my notes or math book helps me understand a math problem.	1	2	3	4
20. Making study aids with my hands helps me learn better.	1	2	3	4
21. I understand instructions better when someone tells me what they are.	1	2	3	4
22. I memorize sentences or words I can say to myself to help me remember how to do problems on a test.	1	2	3	4
23. Pictures and charts help me see how all the parts of a word problem work together.	1	2	3	4
24. I enjoy putting things together.	1	2	3	4
25. When I solve a problem on a math test, I talk my way through it in my head or softly to myself.	1	2	3	4

Scoring Your Results

Step One: Fill in each answer score in the appropriate question number. Add the column totals. Divide Column Totals A and B by 2. Those numbers will be your final column totals. Leave Column C total as is.

Column A	Column B	Column C
1. _____	3. _____	4. _____
2. _____	5. _____	7. _____
10. _____	6. _____	16. _____
12. _____	8. _____	20. _____
14. _____	9. _____	24. _____
17. _____	11. _____	17. _____
18. _____	13. _____	
21. _____	15. _____	
22. _____	19. _____	
25. _____	23. _____	
A Total _____ /2 = _____ Column Total	B Total _____ /2 = _____ Column Total	C Total _____ (Do not divide.)

Step Two: Fill in the number of squares to represent each column total. Any total greater than 12 indicates that modality style as a strength when you learn math. You can be strong in more than one modality. If none of the totals equal 12 squares, your highest score is your strongest modality. If you have a tie, pick the first one that comes to mind as your strongest.

	Least Like Me				Most Like Me
Modality	1	5	10	15	20
A = Auditory					
B = Visual					
C = Kinesthetic					

The Learning Modality Inventory developed by Kimberly Nolting, © 2007

Math Autobiography

The purpose of the math autobiography is to combine your thoughts and feelings about your mathematics history. This autobiography will discuss both your math anxiety and your math test anxiety. The autobiography will help you understand how you have felt about math in the past as well as how you feel about math today. The autobiography will end with solutions to improve your negative mathematics experiences or ways to maintain your positive math experiences.

Use the questions and answers, as well as the causes and types of math anxiety in Chapter 3, to brainstorm ideas for your paper.

Since the autobiography will be in chronological order, it will first start with your experiences in elementary school, then middle school, continuing to high school and finally college. Your first paragraphs will discuss your math experiences and feelings in elementary school. The next paragraphs will continue this discussion for middle school and high school. Then the next paragraphs will describe your math experiences in the college or university. You may have had quite a few experiences, or this semester may be your first with a math course. Either way, it is important to record everythign you can. The conclusion paragraphs will sum up your mathematics experiences and also state strategies to maintain your positive math experiences or strategies to improve your poor math experiences. You may have to use extra paper to finish your autobiography.

Glossary

Abstract Reasoning — The stage of memory that involves understanding rules, key concepts and properties.

Accommodations — Academic adjustments that allow students with disabilities the same access to information as non-disabled students. These accommodations may be in the form of note-takers, audiocassette recorders, large-print tests and extended test times. Accommodations are given to measure the students' knowledge instead of their disabilities.

Acronym — A memory technique in which one or more words make up the first letter of each of the words in the information you wish to remember. For example, ROY G BIV is an acronym representing the colors of the rainbow — **r**ed, **o**range, **y**ellow, **g**reen, **b**lue, **i**ndigo and **v**iolet.

Active Listening — A way to communicate with the others, including faculty, that maintains concentration and allows for questioning of unclear points.

Adjunct Math Faculty — Part-time math instructors who are employed to teach one to three courses. They usually do not have office hours and usually cannot meet with students who need extra help.

Affective Characteristics — Characteristics students possess that affect their course grades, excluding cognitive entry skills. Some of these characteristics are anxiety, study habits, study attitudes, self-concept, motivation and test-taking skills.

Americans with Disabilities Act (ADA) — Signed into law in 1990, it is intended to provide equal opportunities for persons with disabilities. The ADA did not replace Section 504, but it expanded the provisions of Section 504 to include private businesses. The ADA protects the same student population against discrimination as in Section 504.

Assessment Instruments — Surveys used to determine your math anxiety, study skills, attitude, locus of control and procrastination. Other assessment instruments can measure your math knowledge or predict success in your math courses.

Association Learning — A memory technique used to relate new information to be learned to old information you already know.

Attention Deficit Disorder (ADD) — A neurological-based disability that effects a student's ability to concentrate. ADD students are usually impulsive, easily distracted and may be hyperactive. Students with ADD have difficulty concentrating for short periods of time and have difficulty understanding sequential material.

Auditory Processing — The ability to understand the difference between the sounds of words. This is not a problem with hearing or listening, but a central auditory processing disorder in which certain words are drowned out by other noises or some words that sound like different words. The student, especially in large lecture halls, has difficulty understanding the lecture due to background noises.

Avoidance — A misbelief that there is benefit in avoiding any tasks or goals that are unpleasant, risky or challenging.

Behavior — Observable acts or activities people engage in or do. For example, things people, do, say, or the responses people give.

C3S General Study Skills Evaluation — a web-based survey developed to assess general study skills weaknesses and to provide treatment in the form of an interactive web-based course.

Collaborative Learning — A teaching technique that requires students to get into groups to work on math problems. Each group usually has four members. The instructor works with one group while members in other groups teach themselves. The groups are sometimes graded on their answers.

Conditioned Response — A habit developed by repeating the same behavior over and over again.

Cue-Controlled Relaxation — A relaxation-response technique by which students can relax themselves by repeating certain cue words to themselves. A good example of this is that, upon hearing certain old songs (cue words), your feelings (emotions) often change.

Deep Breathing Relaxation — A breathing pattern that reduces anxiety by using the lower part of the lungs and diaphragm.

Discussion of Rules — Part of the modified, three-column note-taking system in which students write down their lecture notes and important rules used to solve the problems presented in class.

Distance Learning — The process of providing instruction when students and instructors are not in the same classroom and thus physically separated from each other.

Distributive Learning — A learning system in which you spread your homework on a particular subject over several days, instead of trying to do it all at one time. For example, studying for about an hour and taking a five- to 10-minute break before continuing to study.

Effective Listening — A behavior in which you sit in the least distracting area of the classroom and become actively involved in the lecture.

Emotion — Emotions are happiness, sadness, anger, frustration, and joy. Emotions may be controlled by what one thinks.

External Locus of Control — A misbelief that people are not personally responsible for and in control of their feelings and behaviors. Other people or outside happenings are seen as the cause of problems.

External Student — A student who believes that he/she is not in control of his/her own life and that he/she cannot obtain his/her desired goals, such as making a good grade in math. External students blame their teachers, parents — anyone and anything, except themselves — for their failures.

Fear of Failure — A personal defense mechanism by which a student puts off doing his/her homework so he/she may have an excuse when he/she does poorly in or fails the course. Thus the student's real ability is never measured.

Goal Accomplishment — The successful carrying out of a plan to achieve a specific goal.

Glossary of Terms — A section in the back of a notebook, developed by the student, that contains a list of key words or concepts and their meanings.

Highlighting — Underlining important material in the textbook or in your notes with a felt-tip pen.

Individual College Learning/Testing Plan — Developed with a counselor, it lists the type of learning and testing accommodations for students with disabilities. The plan is based on the student's processing strengths and weaknesses. It also contains the student's goals for the semester.

Internal Student — A student who believes that he/she is in control of his/her own life and can obtain his/her desired goals, such as making a good grade in math.

Kinesthetic Learner — This type of student learns best by using their hands and physically working through different problems or scenarios.

Learned Helplessness — A lack of motivation due to repeated tries to obtain a goal, such as passing math, but failing to obtain that goal. An attitude of "Why try?" develops because of numerous previous failures.

Learning Disability — A neurological condition that blocks learning certain types of information. These students have average- to above-average intelligence. The effects of learning disabilities include problems in processing information into the brain and/or understanding the information once it reaches the brain. Learning disabilities cannot be cured; however, some types of learning disabilities can, to a certain extent, be accommodated.

Learning Modalities — A learning style that focuses on how students prefer to input information. The three ways most students input information is visually, auditorially or kinesthetically. Visual learners prefer to see the information they need to learn. Auditory learners prefer to hear the information they need to learn. Kinesthetic learning prefer to touch and feel the information they need to learn.

Learning Modality Inventory for Math Students — A web-based survey that measures: studying efficiency, memory and learning skills, reading and homework skills, classroom learning, test-taking skills and test anxiety.

Learning Resource Center (LRC) — A location on campus, sometimes in the library, that has educational materials and tutors. These centers could help students in different subjects or could be designed to help students in specific subjects, such as math.

Learning Style — The preferred way a student learns information. Learning styles can focus on how students prefer to input information, which are modalities (visual, auditory, kinesthetic). Learning styles also include how a student processes information, which are cognitive styles. Students may have different learning styles for different subjects.

Locus of Control — The belief that one is in control of his/her own life, or that other people or events are controlling his/her life.

Long-Term Goal — An objective that relates to one's personal values and is attainable only after one obtains a series of short-term goals. For example, getting a certain grade in a course or graduating.

Long-Term Memory — Part of the memory chain that retains unlimited information for long periods of time and is considered to be a person's total knowledge.

Long-Term Retrieval — (See working memory.)

Manipulatives — Hand-held objects that can be used to represent arithmetic and algebra concepts. Students can handle these objects, concretely, to obtain a better understanding how math formulas are used.

Mass Learning — Bunching up all your learning periods at once. For example, trying to complete all your math homework for the last two weeks in one night. This technique is an ineffective way of learning math.

Math Achievement Characteristics — Characteristics that students possess which affect their grades, such as previous math knowledge, level of test anxiety, study habits, motivation and test-taking skills.

Math Anxiety — Math anxiety is an extreme emotional reaction or attitude toward using or learning mathematics. It is a feeling of tensions that occurs when talking about mathematics or doing math homework. There are mainly three types of math anxiety: test anxiety, numerical anxiety and abstraction anxiety.

Math Attitude — How a student feels about math. Some students feel positive about math and like the subject. Other students have a negative attitude toward math and do not like it. Your attitude toward math could influence how you study and who you blame for poor grades.

Math Glossary — The description of math words that you put into your own words. It usually consists of the bold-print words featured in the textbook.

Math Knowledge — The level of arithmetic and algebra a student possesses when first entering a particular math course. Students with good math knowledge have a chance to be successful in their math class, while students with poor math knowledge will likely fail their math course.

Math Learning Profile Sheet — A survey that helps develop a math-learning strength and weakness profile.

Memory — The process of receiving information through your senses, storing the information in your mind and recalling the information for later use.

Memory Output — The ability to recall information in verbal or written form. This information is recalled during tests to answer questions or can be used in working memory to solve problems. Memory output can be blocked by high test anxiety.

Mental Cheat Sheet — A mental cheat sheet is created in your head by memorizing different formulas and equations to help you succeed on a test. You can take this memorized information and write it onto the back of your test in order to free your mind up to work on the problems.

Mental Picture — A memory technique in which you visualize the information you wish to learn by closing your eyes and forming an image of the material in your mind's eye.

Metacognition — The thinking process that occurs when solving math problems. It is about thinking and how students can ask themselves question to solve math problems and then check the answers.

Mnemonic Device — A memory technique in which you develop easy-to-remember words, phrases and rhymes, and relate them to difficult-to-remember concepts.

Modalities – Used to indicate the ways in which information is best processed into students' minds.

Negative Math Attitude — A dislike for math that might have been formed during elementary or middle school. A negative math attitude is closely related to math anxiety. It can lead to students putting off math study, and it is an excuse for failing math.

Negative Self-Talk — One of the causes of test anxiety. It is what you tell yourself during a math test that decreases your confidence. For example, during the test, telling yourself that you are going to fail it and there is nothing you can do about it.

Note Cards — 3x5 index cards; students write important concepts on the front of the card and an explanation of the concepts on the back.

Note-Taking Cues — Signals given by instructors to their classes that indicate the material they are presenting is important enough that the students may be tested on it. Notes should be taken on this material.

Number Sense — The same as common sense but used with numbers. The ability to look at your answer to see if it makes sense. For example, in a rate-and-distance problem, the rate of the car cannot be 2,000 miles per hour. Number sense is also the ability to estimate the answer to a problem without using your "mental blackboard."

Online Homework — Homework that is completed and submitted using a web-based software.

Perfectionist — One who expects to be perfect at everything he/she does, including making an "A" in math when it may be, for him/her, virtually impossible.

Positive Imagery — A mental picture or sensory representation of an image that has a positive effect and relaxes the person.

Positive Self-Talk — A way to decrease test anxiety. It is what you tell yourself during a math test that increases your confidence. For example, telling yourself that you are going to work as hard as you can to pass the test.

Prerequisite — A course that preparatory for the course in which you are trying to enroll. Math prerequisite courses have the math background required to be successful in the next math course.

Problem Log — A list of the problems that the instructor worked out in class. In a separate section of your notebook, keep the list of problems your instructor worked out — without the solutions. Use these problems as a pretest before taking each major test.

Procrastination — A personal defense mechanism in which one puts off doing certain tasks, like homework, in order to protect one's self-esteem.

Proximity — a nearness in place, time, order or relation.

Quality of Instruction — The effectiveness of math instructors when presenting material to students in the classroom and math lab. This effectiveness depends on the course textbook, class atmosphere, teaching style, extra teaching aids (videos, audiotapes) and other assistance.

Reasoning — That section of the brain that is used to understand the abstractness of math. Abstract learning is understanding the logical sequence of math problem-solving. Reasoning can also be called nonverbal learning.

Reworking Notes — The process of reviewing class notes to rewrite illegible words, fill in the gaps and add key words or ideas.

Section 504 — A federal law that prohibits discrimination based on disabilities at all post-secondary educational programs receiving federal funds. Section 504 includes students with LD, TBI and ADD. Section 504 suggests academic adjustments (accommodations) that will assist in compensating for students' disabilities.

Self-Esteem — A person's overall evaluation of himself or herself. The ranges are usually from positive to negative.

Sensory Input — The stage of memory having to do with the taking in of information.

Sensory Register — The first part of the memory chain that receives the information through your senses (seeing, hearing, feeling and touching).

Self-Efficacy — Self-efficacy is a person's personal belief about their abilities to perform or to accomplish specific tasks. For example — A student can have a high level of self-efficacy in an English course, while maintaining a low self-efficacy in mathematics.

Self-Management — Directing a person's affective behavior and thinking in an organized way to obtain a specific goal, such as graduation.

Self-Monitoring — The ability to record your own behavior to evaluate the progress of obtaining a certain goal. For example, recording the amount of hours studied per week and comparing it to your goal.

Self-Talk — A way in which one gives advice by talking to him or herself. Self-talk can range from positive to negative.

Sequential Learning Pattern — A learning pattern in which one concept builds upon the next concept. The ability to learn new math concepts is based on your previous math knowledge. Not knowing underlying math concepts causes gaps in learning, which often results in lower future test scores and even failure.

Short-Term Goals — Objective that can be obtained by activities or behaviors that occur within a limited period of time such as a few days or a week.

Short-Term Memory — The second part of the memory chain that allows you to remember facts for immediate use. These facts are soon forgotten.

Skimming — The first step in reading a textbook. It involves over-viewing the chapter to get a general understanding of the material.

SMART — A mnemonic device geared at helping student's set achievable goals for themselves. It stands for *Specific, Measurable, Action, Realisti* and *Timely.*

Stages of Memory — The stages in which our brain takes in, processes and reproduces information.

Study Buddy — A student who is usually taking the same math course as you, and whom you can call for help when you have difficulty doing your math homework.

Study Skills Plus/C3S — A web-based survey developed to assess general study skills, assess study skills weaknesses and to provide treatment in the form of an interactive web-based course.

StudyStack.com — This website is designed to have students make their own online note-cards on a variety of different subjects.

Syllabus — Information given to the students enrolled in a course to describe the course. The syllabus includes objectives, textbooks, and expectations, grading policies and the instructor's contact information.

Test Anxiety — A learned emotional response or thought pattern that disrupts or delays a student's ability to recall the information needed to solve the problems.

Test Attitude Inventory — A survey to assess college test anxiety that can indicate how much test anxiety you have compared to other college students.

Test Analysis — A process of reviewing previous tests for consistently misread directions, careless errors, application, test-taking and study errors to help prevent their future occurrences.

Time Management — A process of gaining control over time allotment to help you obtain your desired goals. Using a study schedule is an example of gaining control over time.

Tools of Your Trade — Any material you require to begin studying.

Traumatic Brain Injury (TBI) — Caused by a blow to the head, which causes the person to lose consciousness, creates memory loss and confusion, resulting in a neurological deficit. TBI is a disability that usually causes short-term memory problems and, sometimes, problems associated to reasoning.

Values — That which a person considers meaningful or important.

Video Tapes — Tapes on math concepts that are made by the textbook publisher, math instructors or bought commercially. The tapes can be previewed before class or after class to better understand the concept.

Visual Discrimination — The ability to tell the difference between numbers and letters that look similar. It is not a problem with "seeing" the numbers or letters. Students with visual discrimination problems will have difficulty telling the difference between a "b "and a "d" or between an "x" and a "+" sign. Students with major visual discrimination problems are dyslexic.

Visual Processing — The ability to remember visual information and recognize the difference between similar symbols. Students with poor visual processing may have poor visual memory and/or not be able to tell the difference between similar mathematical symbols. This student may copy material incorrectly off the board and miscopy algebra steps.

Visual Processing Speed — How fast a student can visually read information without making mistakes. The information being read can be numbers or symbols. Students with slow visual processing speed cannot quickly write down numbers, and they are poor note-takers.

Visualization — The process of picturing in your mind activities that cause you to relax or that you want to complete.

Weekly Study Goals — The amount of time scheduled for studying each of your subjects over the period of a week.

Winning at Math Student Resources — A section of www.academicsuccess.com that lists useful web-based resources for improving mathematics learning and test-taking skills.

Working Memory — A part of the learning process that is used to understand information long enough to place it into long-term memory. The second part of working memory is the space in the brain that is used to recall information from long-term memory and used to work on problems. Working memory is limited, meaning that only a certain numbers of processes/calculations can be done at the same time. Working memory can be compared to the amount of RAM in a computer.

Bibliography

Bandura, A. (1982). Self-efficacy mechanism in human agency. *America Psychologist*, 37, 122-147.

Bloom, B. (1976). *Human Characteristics and School Learning.* New York: McGraw-Hill Book Company.

Brown, J. & Copper, R. (1978) Learning Styles Inventory. Kirkwood MO: Educational Activities Software.

Butler, P.E. (1981). *Talking to yourself: Learning the language of self-support.* San Francisco: Harper & Row.

Cattell, R. B. (1966). The screen test for the number of factors. Multivariate Behavioral Research, 1 245-276.

Dembo, H. D. (2000). *Motivation and Learning Strategies for College Success.* Mahwah, New Jersey: Lawrence Erlbaum Associates, Inc.

Farr, M. & Shatkin, L. (2006). *Best Jobs for the 21st Century*, Indianapolis, IN: JIST Works.

Mangrum, C. & Strichart, S. (2004). *Study Skills Plus/S3S.* Ft. Lauderdale, Florida: Mangrum-Strichart Learning Resources.

Nolting, K. (2004). *Navigating College: Strategy Manual For A Successful Journey.* Bradenton Florida: Academic Success Press, Inc.

Nolting, Kim. (2008). Learning Modality Inventory for Math Students in the Math Study Skills Workbook. Boston, MA: Houghton Mifflin, Co.

Nolting, P. D. (1987). *How to Reduce Test Anxiety*, an audio cassette tape. Pompano Beach, FL: Academic Success Press.

Nolting, P. D. (1987). *How to Ace Tests*, a CD. Pompano Beach, FL: Academic Success Press.

Nolting, P. D. (1989). *Strategy Cards for Higher Grades.* Pompano Beach, FL: Academic Success Press.

Nolting, P. D. (1991). *The Effects of Counseling and Study Skills Training on Mathematics Academic Achievement.* Bradenton, FL: Academic Success Press.

Nolting, P. D. (1994). *Improving Mathematics Study Skills and Test-Taking Skills.* Boston, MA: D. C. Heath, Inc.

Nolting, P. D. (2000). *Mathematics Learning Disabilities Handbook.* Bradenton, FL, Academic Success Press.

Richardson. F. C., and Suinn, R. M. (1973). "A comparison of traditional systematic desensitization, accelerated mass desensitization, and mathematics anxiety." *Behavior Therapy.* No. 4, pp. 212-218.

Schunk, H. (1991). Goal setting and self-evaluation: A social cognitive perspective on self-regulation. In M. L. Maehr & P. R. Pintrich (Eds.), *Advances in motivation and achievement* (Vol. 7, pp.85 – 113). Greenwich, CT: JAI.

Smith, H. (1994). *The 10 natural laws of successful time and life management. New* York: Warner Books.

Spielberger, C. S. (1980). *Test Attitude Inventory.* Redwood, California: Mind Garden.

Suinn, R. (1970). The mathematics anxiety rating scale: Psychometric data. Journal of Counseling Psychology, 19, 551-554.

Tobias, S. (1978). "Who's afraid of math and why?" *Atlantic Monthly.* September, pp. 63-65.

Wolpe, J. (1958). Psychotherapy by reciprocal inhibition. Stanford, CT: Stanford University Press.

Woodcock, R & McGrew, K. (2001). Woodcock-Johnson III, Boston, MA: Riverside Publishing.

Index

Figures Index

About the Author

Over the past 25 years, Learning Specialist Dr. Paul Nolting has helped thousands of students improve their math learning and earn better grades. Dr. Nolting is a national expert in assessing math learning problems — from study skills to learning disabilities — and developing effective learning strategies and testing accommodations.

Dr. Nolting is also a nationally recognized consultant and trainer of math study skills and of learning and testing accommodations for students with learning disabilities. He has conducted two PBS workshops on math study skills and learning styles.

Dr. Nolting has conducted numerous national conference workshops on math learning for the National Developmental Education Association, the National Council of Educational Opportunity Association, the American Mathematical Association of Two-Year Colleges, and the Association on Higher Education and Disabilities. He was a consultant for the American College Test (ACT) and the Texas Higher Education Coordinating Board. He is also a con-

Dr. Paul and Kimberly Nolting

sultant for Houghton Mifflin Faculty Development Programs, conducting workshops on math study skills for math faculty. His text, *Winning at Math: Your Guide To Learning Mathematics Through Successful Study Skills* is used throughout the United States, Canada and the world as the definitive text for math study skills.

Dr. Nolting has consulted with numerous universities and colleges. Some of the universities with which Dr. Nolting has consulted are the University of Massachusetts, the University of Colorado-Bolder, Texas Tech. University, Black Hills State University, Tennessee Tech. University, Clemson University, Rutgers University, Florida Gulf Coast University, Dakota State University and the University of Connecticut.

Some of the colleges with which he has consulted are San Antonio College, St. Louis Community College, J. Sargeant Reynolds College, Montgomery College, Broward Community College, Miami-Dade College, Northeast State Technical Community College, Landmark College, Denver Community College, Valencia Community College, Brevard Community College, Palm Beach Community College, Suffolk Community College, Gilford Technical Community College, Trident Technical College, Georgia Military College, Raritan Valley Community College, Palo Alto College, Kentucky and Community College System, El Paso Community College, Martin Community College, Bergen Community College, Lake Sumter Community College, South Texas College and Austin Community College. Dr. Nolting has provided consultation to over 100 colleges, universities and high schools over the last 25 years.

Dr. Nolting holds a Ph.D. degree in Education in Curriculum and Instruction from the University of South Florida. His Ph.D. dissertation was "The Effects of Counseling and Study Skills Training on Mathematics Academic Achievement." He is an adjunct instructor for the University of South Florida and Gulf Coast University, teaching Assessment and Appraisal courses at the graduate level.

His book, *Winning at Math: Your Guide to Learning Mathematics Through Successful Study Skills* was selected Book of the Year by the National Association of Independent Publishers. "The strength of the book is the way the writer leads a reluctant student through a course from choosing a teacher to preparing for the final examination," says *Mathematics Teacher*, a publication of the National Council of Teachers of Mathematics.

His two CDs, *How to Reduce Test Anxiety* and *How to Ace Tests* were also winners of awards in the National Association of Independent Publishers' competition. "Dr. Nolting," says *Publisher's Report*, "is an innovative and outstanding educator and learning specialist."

A key speaker at numerous regional and national education conferences and conventions, Dr. Nolting has been widely acclaimed for his ability to communicate with faculty and students on the subject of improving math learning. One of Dr. Nolting's latest projects is conducting Math Summits at different colleges which involves the entire institution in developing a plan to improve the success of mathematic students.

Kimberly Nolting, who is completing her dissertation on a math related topic, has also consulted with numbers of colleges and universities in the area of math study skills, learning styles, improving Learning Resources Centers and freshman experiences courses and with math departments/colleges to improve the overall retention of students, especially in the area of mathematics. She is also the author of the *Winning at Math Teacher's Manual*, "Learning Modality Inventory for Math Students" and *Navigating College: Strategy Manual for a Successful Voyage,* which is used in Freshman Experience courses.